The European Union in International Climate Change Negotiations

T0330718

The EU has been portrayed as a leader in international climate change negotiations. Its role in the development of the climate change regime, as well as the adoption of novel policy instruments such as the EU Emissions Trading Scheme in 2005, are frequently put forward as indicative of a determination to push the international climate agenda forward. However, there are numerous instances where the EU has failed to achieve its climate change objectives (e.g. the 2009 Copenhagen Conference of the Parties). It is therefore important to examine the reasons behind these failures.

This book explores in detail the involvement of the EU in international climate talks from the late 1980s to the present, focusing in particular on the negotiations leading up to Copenhagen. This conference witnessed the demise of the top–down approach in climate change policy and dealt a serious blow to the EU's leadership ambitions. This book explores the extent to which negotiation theory could help with better comprehending the obstacles that prevented the EU from getting more out of the climate negotiation process. It is argued that looking at the role played by problematic strategic planning could prove highly instructive in light of the Paris Agreement.

This broad historical perspective of the EU's negotiations in international climate policy is an important resource to scholars of environmental and European politics, policy, law and governance.

Stavros Afionis is a Teaching Fellow in Environmental Politics at the School of Politics, Philosophy, International Relations & Environment (SPIRE), Keele University, UK. Previously, he was a Postdoctoral Research Fellow at the Sustainability Research Institute (SRI) of the School of Earth & Environment, University of Leeds, UK. His doctoral research examined the role played by the European Union in international climate change negotiations. His research interests focus on environmental politics and, in particular, international climate change negotiations and global biofuel policies. He is an associate editor for *Environmental Policy and Governance* and a member of the UK ESRC Centre for Climate Change Economics and Policy (CCCEP).

Routledge Studies in Environmental Policy

Land and Resource Scarcity
Capitalism, struggle and well-being in a world without fossil fuels
Edited by Andreas Exner, Peter Fleissner, Lukas Kranzl and Werner Zittel

Nuclear Energy Safety and International Cooperation
Closing the world's most dangerous reactors
Spencer Barrett Meredith, III

The Politics of Carbon Markets
Edited by Benjamin Stephan and Richard Lane

The Limits of the Green Economy
Matthias Lievens and Anneleen Kenis

Public Policy and Land Exchange
Choice, law and praxis
Giancarlo Panagia

International Arctic Petroleum Cooperation
Barents Sea scenarios
Edited by Anatoli Bourmistrov, Frode Mellemvik, Alexei Bambulyak, Ove Gudmestad, Indra Overland and Anatoly Zolotukhin

Why REDD will Fail
Jessica L. DeShazo, Chandra Lal Pandey and Zachary A. Smith

The European Union in International Climate Change Negotiations
Stavros Afionis

The European Union in International Climate Change Negotiations

Stavros Afionis

Routledge
Taylor & Francis Group

LONDON AND NEW YORK

First published 2017
by Routledge

2 Park Square, Milton Park, Abingdon, Oxfordshire OX14 4RN
711 Third Avenue, New York, NY 10017

Routledge is an imprint of the Taylor & Francis Group, an informa business

First issued in paperback 2018

British Library Cataloguing in Publication Data
A catalogue record for this book is available from the British Library

Library of Congress Cataloging in Publication Data
Names: Afionis, Stavros, author.
Title: The European Union in international climate change negotiations /
Stavros Afionis.
Description: Milton Park, Abingdon, Oxon ; New York, NY : Routledge,
2016. | Series: Routledge studies in environmental policy | Includes
bibliographical references.
Identifiers: LCCN 2016032769 | ISBN 9781138776067 (hb) | ISBN
9781315773469 (ebook)
Subjects: LCSH: Climatic changes–Government policy–European Union
countries. | Environmental policy–European Union countries. | Climatic
changes–International cooperation. | Environmental policy–International
cooperation.
Classification: LCC QC903.2.E85 A45 2016 | DDC 363.738/
74561094–dc23
LC record available at https://lccn.loc.gov/2016032769

ISBN: 978-1-138-77606-7 (hbk)
ISBN: 978-0-367-03015-5 (pbk)

Typeset in Goudy
by Wearset Ltd, Boldon, Tyne and Wear

To my family

Contents

Tables

Acknowledgements

This book grew out of my PhD thesis, which I wrote at Keele University, UK, during 2006–09 under the supervision of Professor John Vogler. I am extremely grateful to him for his support and guidance. In the years that followed, he would often urge me to turn my PhD into a book. I thought of him when Routledge offered me a contract. Robert McElroy and the late Kieron Legge kindly proofread all my PhD chapters back then and I will always be indebted to them. More recently, a number of colleagues, who read and commented on drafts of various chapters of this present book, also deserve my warmest thanks. I especially thank James Porter for his help and encouragement. James read all the chapters twice and his comments and suggestions were invaluable. After all these years, Professor John Vogler kindly accepted to read and comment on a number of chapters and I cannot thank him (again) enough for his help. Many thanks are also due to Lindsay C. Stringer, Harriet Thew, Ross Gillard and Vivek Mathur for proofreading and commenting on various chapters. Obviously, any mistakes or omissions are the sole responsibility of the author.

I am also thankful to all the policymakers I interviewed for giving their time to help me collect my empirical data. At Routledge, I am particularly obliged to Margaret Farrelly and Annabelle Harris for their patience and their continuous interest in this project. I also wish to acknowledge the financial support of the UK ESRC Centre for Climate Change Economics and Policy (CCCEP). A great thank you is owed to Lindsay C. Stringer for her endless support since I started my academic career. My final thanks are of course for Eleni and my family, who made it all possible. Without their ever-lasting support and warmth there would be no PhD, no book, no academic career...

Abbreviations

AAUs	Assigned Amount Units
AGBM	Ad hoc Group on the Berlin Mandate
AIJ	Activities Implemented Jointly
AOSIS	Alliance of Small Island States
AP6	Asia-Pacific Partnership on Clean Development and Climate
AR4	Fourth Assessment Report (IPCC)
ASEAN	Association of South East Asian Nations
AWG	Ad hoc Working Group on Further Commitments for Annex I Parties
AWG-KP	Ad hoc Working Group on Further Commitments for Annex I Parties under the KP
AWG-LCA	Ad hoc Working Group on Long-term Cooperative Action under the Convention
BAPA	Buenos Aires Plan of Action
BASIC	Brazil, South Africa, India and China
BTU	British Thermal Unit
CDM	Clean Development Mechanism
CERs	Certified Emission Reductions
CFCs	Chlorofluorocarbons
CITES	Convention on International Trade in Endangered Species
Comecon	Council for Mutual Economic Assistance
COP	Conference of the Parties
COP/MOP	Conference of the Parties serving as the Meeting of the Parties
COREPER	Committee of Permanent Representatives
CO_2	Carbon dioxide
DGs	Directorates-General (of the European Commission)
EC	European Community
ECCP	European Climate Change Programme
EEC	European Economic Community
EFTA	European Free Trade Area
EIG	Environmental Integrity Group
EIT	Economy in Transition
ERUs	Emission Reduction Units

EU	European Union
G-77	Group of 77
G-8	Group of Eight (G7 major industrialized countries plus Russia)
GCMs	General Circulation Models
GDP	Gross Domestic Product
GEF	Global Environmental Facility
GMOs	Genetically-modified Organisms
GPOA	Gleneagles Plan of Action
HBFCs	Hydrobromofluorocarbons
HCFCs	Hydrochlorofluorocarbons
HFCs	Hydrofluorocarbons
INC	Intergovernmental Negotiating Committee (FCCC)
INDC	Intended Nationally Determined Contribution
IPCC	Intergovernmental Panel on Climate Change
JI	Joint Implementation
JUSCANZ	Japan, United States, Canada, Australia, and New Zealand
LCDS	Low Carbon Development Strategies and Plans
lCERs	Long-term CERs
LDCF	Least Developed Countries Fund
LDCs	Least Developed Countries
LRTAP	Long Range Transboundary Air Pollution (Convention)
LULUCF	Land Use, Land Use Change and Forestry
MEM	Major Economies Meeting (on Energy and Climate Change)
MRV	Measurement, Reporting and Verification
N_2O	Nitrous Oxide
NAMAs	Nationally Appropriate Mitigation Actions
NAPAs	National Adaptation Programmes of Action
NASA	National Aeronautics and Space Administration
NGO	Non-governmental Organization
NO_2	Nitrogen Dioxide
ODA	Official Development Assistance
ODS	Ozone Depleting Substances
OECD	Organisation for Economic Co-operation and Development
OPEC	Organization of the Petroleum Exporting Countries
PAMs	Policies and Measures
PDD	Project Design Document (for CDM project activities)
PFCs	Perfluorocarbons
PIN	Processes of International Negotiations (program)
QMV	Qualified Majority Voting
RAF	Resource Allocation Framework
RD&D	Research, Development and Demonstration
REIO	Regional Economic Integration Organization
RGGI	Regional Greenhouse Gas Initiative
RMUs	Removal Units
SAR	Second Assessment Report (IPCC)

SBI	Subsidiary Body for Implementation
SBSTA	Subsidiary Body for Scientific and Technological Advice
SCCF	Special Climate Change Fund
SD-PAMs	Sustainable Development Policies and Measures
SEA	Single European Act
SF_6	Sulphur Hexafluoride
SWCC	Second World Climate Conference
TAR	Third Assessment Report (IPCC)
tCERs	Temporary CERs
UK	United Kingdom
UN	United Nations
UNCED	United Nations Conference on Environment and Development
UNEP	United Nations Environment Program
UNFCCC	United Nations Framework Convention on Climate Change
UNICE	Union of Industrial and Employers' Confederations of Europe
US	United States (of America)
USSR	Union of Soviet Socialist Republics
WCC	World Climate Conference
WCCC	World Conference on Climate Change (3rd, Moscow 2003)
WCED	World Commission on Environment and Development
WMO	World Meteorological Organization
WPIEI	Working Party on International Environmental Issues
WSSD	World Summit on Sustainable Development
WTO	World Trade Organization

Introduction

Success! Not a word we normally associate with international climate change policy, but this all changed in Paris in 2015, when 195 countries agreed the first-ever universal climate deal. Failures to get political leaders to commit to, or even abide by, the Kyoto Protocol, as well as the debacle that the 2009 Copenhagen climate negotiations became, were forgotten. Decades of disappointment have been replaced with renewed hope. Indeed, the Paris Agreement seeks to avoid dangerous climate change by keeping global temperature rises well below 2°C. Anything above this could have 'severe, pervasive, and irreversible' effects for natural and human systems (IPCC 2014, p. 8). New efforts will be made to reduce emissions globally (mitigation) and international support will be provided to help developing countries prepare for the impacts to come (adaptation). But how did we get to this point? Or more tellingly, why didn't we get here sooner? This book explains why international climate negotiations have historically failed and what we might learn from these experiences.

Before we go any further, it's worth explaining why climate change is so concerning for all of us. Try and imagine the hottest day you have ever experienced, where you couldn't get comfortable or find any respite from the zapping heat. Now imagine that day again but this time it is 4°C warmer, and this is not happening once in a while but happening over and over again. Imagine the effect this would have on those least able to adapt, on the availability of water, and on the growing of crops. By contrast, too much water, in the wrong place, at the wrong time, is equally concerning. Without serious efforts to reduce greenhouse gas emissions, the Intergovernmental Panel on Climate Change (IPCC) warns that global temperature increases could exceed 4°C by the end of the century. The longer we wait to act, the harder it'll be to avoid dangerous climate change.

The greenhouse effect is not in itself a bad thing. In fact, it is a vital natural phenomenon that keeps the planet warm and habitable whereby certain gases create a natural, greenhouse or blanket effect, without which the planet's surface temperature would be about 35°C lower than at present (Maslin 2004, p. 4). Carbon dioxide (CO_2), water vapour, ozone, methane and nitrous oxide (N_2O) are all naturally occurring greenhouse gases, with the former two being largely responsible for the natural greenhouse effect. Since the onset of the Industrial Revolution, however, anthropogenic emissions of CO_2 have been increasing exponentially, raising atmospheric concentrations to levels that in all probability will threaten the very stability of life on Earth. From 280 ppm during the pre-industrial period, the figure has now surpassed 400 ppm, and keeps on rising each year.

Even though climate change had been discussed in academic and other circles for decades, it only hit the political radar as late as 1988 (see Chapter 1). It was a year characterized by severe weather events that shook communities across the world, bringing increasing credibility to scientists' claims of global warming. Alarmed by the risks posed, the international community quickly accepted the need to take urgent action to minimize, or avoid, the worst effects. From the onset, it was recognized that an effective response to this highly complex and long-term challenge would necessitate international cooperation at an unprecedented scale. Unilateral action by state actors was simply inadequate, given the cross-border and cross-sectoral nature of the task at hand. What followed was a flurry of international activity, which culminated in a February 1991 decision to initiate formal negotiations towards the adoption of an international treaty. Out of this, two cornerstones of the international climate change regime were born: the 1992 United Nations Framework Convention on Climate Change (UNFCCC) and the 1997 Kyoto Protocol.

Aside from states and institutions of global governance, including the United Nations (UN) and the World Trade Organization (WTO), climate change governance has broadened to include a wide array of societal actors, ranging from non-governmental organizations (NGOs) to business and industry lobbyists. Climate change is now a persistent topic in decision-making fora at the apex of global political power, such as the Group of Eight (G-8) and the UN General Assembly. Yet, recognizing that climate change is one of the biggest challenges ever to face humanity and placing it firmly on the political agenda was the easy part. What has proved exceptionally difficult since 1992 has been mobilizing the political will (and associated resources) to implement mitigation and adaptation policies to address climate change and avoid irreversible and dangerous effects.

This slow progress is not overly surprising, however. Despite the constant flow of new technical and scientific input on the gravity of the problem, international negotiations have repeatedly slowed, stalled, or even become deadlocked (Dessai *et al.* 2013). Regrettably, climate change belongs to the particular category of problems that have been characterized as 'wicked', due to the fact that they challenge established institutional frameworks, social values, norms and practices that are predicated on high levels of fossil fuel consumption and the depletion of natural and environmental resources (Vogler 2016). Studies showing growing public indifference towards climate change (Scruggs and Benegal 2012), coupled with the pressing, highly complex and multi-causal nature of climate change, mean emissions have inevitably gone in one direction: up (Collins and Ison 2009).

During the greatest part of this period of UNFCCC negotiations, the international community relied on a centralized top–down international agreement approach, whereby states jointly agreed, within the UN framework, on how to effectively tackle this ultimate global commons problem. This approach met its demise at the 2009 Copenhagen summit, as the hurdles to successfully negotiate a top–down, legally binding agreement to succeed the Kyoto Protocol proved exceptionally difficult to overcome. In practice, Copenhagen symbolized the inability of the international community to collaborate to tackle the problem. Post-Copenhagen a more bottom–up climate policy regime has progressively emerged whereby countries unilaterally nominate their own voluntary climate measures and actions based upon domestic political feasibility. Target-setting processes were effectively cast 'outside' of the UNFCCC framework as a result. The dawn of a new era for international climate change policy had broken.

But why did the top–down approach fail? Why, instead of a legally binding agreement with robust mitigation goals, did we end up with a voluntary bottom–up process? And what might this mean for tackling climate change? This book follows Faure and Zartman (2012) when it comes to the manner in which it employs the term 'failure'. As they note (p. 4), 'failure' refers to 'a discrete negotiation round' which instead of achieving an agreed outcome, degenerates into continued disagreement. Parties may well resume negotiations at a later stage and even conclude an agreement that eluded them in the first round. Not achieving the objective(s) for which the first round was convened is what makes it a failure (Faure and Zartman 2012). Copenhagen marks a turning point here. While the Kyoto negotiations dragged on following the Copenhagen debacle, the focus of the climate regime had irreversibly shifted to giving shape to the parallel bottom–up framework that had just emerged, and for which the 2015 Paris Agreement serves as the latest milestone.

Largely surpassing expectations, Paris concluded with an agreement that provided a much-needed reinvigoration to the climate change regime. Even though parties submitted voluntary (i.e. non-binding) targets, the request on them to 'communicate or update' these contributions on a five-yearly basis signals a shared understanding among them that each successive review should lead to further strengthening of target ambition (UNFCCC 2015, p. 4). This conclusion is further corroborated by the surprising inclusion of the aspirational objective to cap temperature rises at 1.5°C above pre-industrial levels. Yet, while the Paris agreement is an ambitious one, it will require serious political commitment to deliver. In the run-up to Paris, a multitude of studies highlighted that even if implemented in full, the national pledges submitted by parties would be grossly inadequate in keeping global warming below 2°C (IEA 2015; Hood *et al.* 2015).

Whether the new negotiating round that commenced post-Copenhagen will succeed in putting countries on track towards limiting global warming to 1.5°C or 2°C remains to be seen. What can be said for certain is that a lot will depend on the extent to which parties bear in mind the lessons from past failures when engaging with each other. This study draws upon the literature on why international negotiations fail and identifies some of the most important factors that undermined the effectiveness of the top–down approach in the context of the climate change regime. To do this, two inter-related objectives are pursued. First, the European Union (EU) serves as a useful case study through which to analyse these factors over the last two decades. In particular, this book explores the impact of its negotiating attitudes, positions, policies or interests on the shaping of the climate regime. The focus, therefore, is on the EU as a negotiator in international climate negotiations, not on assessing the EU's leadership credentials or influence. A substantive literature already exists that deals with these topics.

Second, the book provides a detailed historical record of EU involvement in UNFCCC negotiations (1986–2009). To be better able to understand why failure occurred, one first needs to know how we arrived at it. Furthermore, the added value of having such a record is that it can be used by anyone wishing to explore a particular period of EU engagement without having to go through a wide range of sources, both primary and secondary, so as to obtain a good understanding of the multitude of issues deliberated over the years. The literature on EU climate policy is vast and it is often challenging to meaningfully add to it. This book provides a historical analysis which aims to assess longitudinally the strengths and weaknesses of the EU as a negotiator in the context of the UNFCCC. It seeks to not only find out what happened in the past, but also to reveal the reasons why events occurred the way they did.

Why do international negotiations fail?

A rich literature has developed to explain why international agreements can fail to materialize. These may include cultural differences (Brett 2014), communicative considerations (Jonsson and Hall 2005), the absence of win–win options (Metcalfe and Metcalfe 2002), and scientific uncertainties (Sjöstedt 1993), amongst others. While acknowledging the limitations in attempting to make up an exhaustive list of problems that prevent parties from concluding negotiations successfully, Faure (2012) recently summarized three decades of findings from the Processes of International Negotiations (PIN) program,[1] and recommends a framework consisting of 39 factors which contribute to negotiation failures. Some of these factors naturally stand out as being more important than others. The literature is generally in agreement as to the identity of these factors. Faure (2012, p. 380), for instance, views six factors as the main ones 'around which other causes may aggregate, producing a multiplicative effect'. These are demonization;[2] inability to adapt to external changes; improper mediation; absence of trust; lack of a 'zone of agreement'; and poor timing. In their analysis, Odell and Tingley (2016) focus on conflicting preferences, uncertainty, lack of trust and national biases, among others, as representing barriers to agreement. Finally, Underdal (1983; 1991) suggests that there are a handful of key obstacles that stand out and which deserve our attention: uncertainty, inaccurate information (i.e. zone of agreement), process-generated stakes and politically inadequate solution design models. Underdal (1983, p. 192) is keen to note that while the effect on the negotiation process of each individual obstacle may not necessarily be detrimental, their combined net effect could be that of 'disturbing and impeding the search for mutually advantageous solutions'.[3] Underdal's widely acknowledged academic contributions span more than four decades. During this time he has sought answers to a number of inter-related questions: Why do negotiations fail? What are the conditions for regime success? How can we measure regime effectiveness (see Midgaard 2006)? This book builds on Underdal's work, as he provides a clear analytical framework with which to meaningfully describe, explain and predict the likely effect of his four principal obstacles upon a party's negotiating behaviour. He therefore offers a valuable theoretical lens which can be readily adapted to study failure in climate change negotiations.

The paragraphs below sketch out Underdal's four obstacles to negotiation success and the impact these have upon parties when negotiating in international fora. From the early 1990s to 2009, there have been four main deadlines set by the international community relating to climate change cooperation: Rio (1992), Kyoto (1997), The Hague (2000) and Copenhagen (2009). More details with respect to Underdal's framework will be offered in the chapters that deal with The Hague and Copenhagen Conferences of the Parties (COPs), i.e. the main two instances when climate change negotiations have failed in the past (see Chapters 5, 9 and 10). Of course, interesting insights can be gained from applying the framework to the occasions where negotiation rounds ended positively, i.e. in Rio and Kyoto (see Chapters 2 and 4).

Starting with Underdal's first factor, a *sine qua non* when negotiating is having collected in advance all the information that will enable a party to accurately estimate when the right time to compromise has arrived. Parties may unknowingly push for an agreement that goes beyond the security point of the counterpart, only to blame the inevitable failure on the latter's bad will (Faure 2012). Starkey *et al.* (1999, p. 111) stress the importance of having or trying to create a **zone of agreement**, i.e. an overlapping area of acceptable outcomes for parties. A prerequisite for such a zone to be established is for a party to be competent enough to be able to accurately estimate the preference structure of its opponent(s). Indeed, negotiations occasionally fail when a party (a) overestimates or underestimates this preference structure, or (b) a party believes the opponent to misperceive its preference structure (Underdal 1983). The 20-year-long UNFCCC process abounds with examples of the EU misinterpreting the preferences of its opponents and vice versa (e.g. Copenhagen).

Uncertainty or lack of trust is a perfectly normal feature of international negotiations, especially since in most cases parties 'see the negotiation table as another arena for war' (Faure 2012, p. 381). Of course, the amount of uncertainty and mistrust can vary considerably, with contributing factors including, among others:

> Cultural or ideological differences; a tendency to assume that the opponent understands one's own problems better than he actually does; the fact that [...] states frequently do send ambiguous or inconsistent signals to their

environment; and the fact that [...] concealing one's real preferences or actively misleading the opponent about them is a much-used bargaining tactic...

(Underdal 1983, p. 186)

Underdal (1983) notes that trust basically pertains to whether you trust your opponents or the motives/rationale behind their tabled solutions. Inability to reduce the doubts of one's negotiating opponents and vice versa results in messages from either side being looked upon with scepticism and disbelief, a quite common occurrence in UNFCCC deliberations. EU ambivalence in the 1990s as to whether forests or flexibility mechanisms should be included in the climate change mitigation arsenal are prime examples. Another offshoot of lack of trust is being overly cautious, which expresses itself in inclination to make moves that are characterized by low specificity and low commitment. Indeed, during the past two decades the EU has been widely criticized for tabling greenhouse gas emissions reduction targets that have failed to pass the specificity and commitment test.

Moving on, a **politically inadequate solution design model** refers to the distance between a scientifically 'appropriate' solution to a problem and a politically 'acceptable' or 'feasible' agreement. As Underdal (1983; 1991) argues, an adequate solution to a collective policy problem must satisfy three main criteria: efficiency, fairness and feasibility. Efficiency primarily refers to a regime that is ecologically sound. However, proposed solutions that have been developed in accordance with scientific standards will most often fall outside the actual settlement range. The reason for this is that parties usually have different interpretations of what should be considered fair and feasible. While the EU has consistently urged that the international response to climate change should be inclusive and underpinned by scientific evidence, other parties have often cited fairness and feasibility concerns in order to justify their differing viewpoints.

Finally, **process-generated stakes** concern the manner in which pressure on a party to live up to its reputation could prevent it from capturing the bigger picture of the negotiation process. While securing substantive outcomes is obviously important, parties are also aware that the fashion in which they conduct their international negotiations will inevitably reflect upon their own image and reputation. Linking this to the EU and climate change policy, a point to be made here is that there is a connection between leadership and negotiating ability. Image concerns, for instance, may cause a party to reject a promising solution it itself might have been willing to propose simply because it originated from a foe rather than from an ally (Underdal 1983). Emissions trading could serve here as a prominent example. Another point to be made is that when it comes to the EU, the situation is inherently more complex. In particular, its structural inflexibility has an effect on both its leadership ambitions and negotiating performance. It is therefore important for EU actors to take into account these special EU characteristics before deciding on both the level of leadership they will exert and the negotiating strategy they will pursue. Insisting on a very progressive proposal, for example, could potentially alienate fellow EU partners, both in the domestic field (e.g. the CO_2/energy/tax) and/or the international arena (e.g. The Hague COP). Apart from potentially alienating fellow EU Member States in the domestic front, leadership ambitions may also lead to undesired outcomes in the international negotiating arena. The 1992 Rio Summit or The Hague and Copenhagen COPs offer pertinent examples in this respect (see Chapters 2, 3 and 5). As a concluding remark, leadership has far too often become an end in itself, thus preventing the EU from critically weighing the pros and cons of its selected negotiating approach.

The EU in the international climate change regime

To date, state actors have proved largely unwilling to lead the world towards adequate and implementable climate change solutions. Arguably, one exception has been the EU and many of its Member States, for whom climate change is a key political concern. The EU has not, of course, escaped criticism for its implementation deficits and the gap between rhetoric and action. Yet it has nevertheless taken from the outset a leadership role in the international negotiations on climate change, pushing hard for a legally binding climate regime that would facilitate substantive cuts in greenhouse gas emissions. Despite its best efforts, the process of promulgating a robust top–down international system ended in failure, with the international community opting instead for the less demanding bottom–up alternative (Falkner *et al.* 2010).

It was not a foregone conclusion that the EU would emerge as a leading force in climate policy. Like climate change, the EU is very complex. Even though it resembles a federal state in various aspects, through for example its common currency or market, the EU, as Vogler (2003) notes, is obviously not a state, having being denied *inter alia* the powers to tax or coerce the citizens of its Member States. The degree of autonomy that the EU possesses in relation to its Member States is also limited. While non-state actors, such as the Commission or the European Parliament, are central to its structure and internal operations, their power is always exercised under the 'ultimate authority of the Council of Ministers' (Vogler 1999, p. 40). Space constraints here do not allow for a detailed review of the decision-making functions and procedures of the EU's various internal bodies. However, the edited volumes by Jordan and Adelle (2013) and by Wurzel and Connelly (2010) provide excellent accounts in this respect. Clearly, with such a constellation of actors, including a growing number of Member States and various large institutions (e.g. EU Commission, Parliament and Court of Justice), the conduct of EU environmental affairs is an inherently complex process. Indeed, the 1987 negotiations on ozone protection in Montreal, where the EU acted as a laggard, clearly exposed its constraints and limitations as an international environmental actor during the early days of global environmentalism.

Yet, the EU has since made significant progress in developing its overall environmental policy. While the United States (US) had made enormous strides in this arena in the 1970s and 1980s by championing an array of global treaties and agreements,[4] the political dynamics of international environmental policy shifted dramatically during the period that led to the 1992 'Earth Summit' in Rio de Janeiro (Kelemen 2010). US reticence encouraged the EU to assume a leadership role in multilateral environmental politics and has ever since been widely celebrated as the actor carrying 'the sustainable development flag on the international scene' (Lightfoot and Burchell 2004, p. 337). In the course of subsequent decades, the EU has ratified every major international environmental agreement. By contrast, the US has refrained from entering into new international environmental regimes altogether (Kelemen and Vogel 2010).

Nowhere else is the EU's adherence to conferring environmental leadership more evident than in the case of the climate change regime. A central prot-agonist in the climate regime saga, the EU has gained significantly in stature and international recognition over time. The rescue of the Kyoto Protocol fol-lowing the US exit in 2001, the EU–Russia deal on Kyoto's ratification in 2004 and the introduction of the EU Emissions Trading Scheme in 2005 are fre-quently put forward as indicative of the EU's determination to push the inter-national climate agenda forward. The EU, as Yamin (2000, p. 47) observes, 'considers itself to be a "leader" in international climate negotiations and has been widely regarded as such by others'. Even more assertively, Gupta and Ringius (2001, p. 294) note that 'undoubtedly, the EU has been quite successful as an international leader'.

While the EU is often portrayed as the spearhead of world efforts for the development of an effective and comprehensive regime on climate change, the truth of the matter is that the climate regime is largely perceived to have failed, or at least locked in deadlock. Ultimately, a regime can be classified as successful if it adequately deals with the environmental problem it was meant to solve (Vogler 2016). The 2015 Paris Agreement undoubtedly brought some fresh air into the climate regime, but such had been the case with all major past milestones, such as the 1997 Kyoto Protocol, the 2001 Marrakech Accords or the 2007 Bali Action Plan. Actual success post-Paris will thus depend on whether countries are prepared to implement (and also augment) their pledges by turning them into actual public policies and programmes. International negotiations fail, drag or reach an impasse for a multitude of reasons, including strategic miscalculations or the nature of the issue(s) or actors involved. Praise aside, the EU is certainly not devoid of its share of responsibility for the failure of the international community to move the climate change regime forward. In a process spanning over two decades, there have been a good number of occasions where the EU slowed down or created a stalemate in negotiations. Some pertinent examples were tentatively out-lined in the previous section. EU officials have customarily pointed to the Union's hard-won record of success and leadership in the climate regime. Former EU Environment Commissioner Stavros Dimas, for instance, flagged up this perspective by noting that:

This is not just leadership for the sake of leadership, or because we think we can fight climate change on our own – we clearly can't. The EU's commitment and success has been an inspiration to our global partners.

(Dimas 2005)

While not dismissing the EU's authentic interest for successfully advocating a norm-driven climate change policy, this book challenges this EU rhetoric by presenting a study in failure, at least up until the Copenhagen COP.

In addition to problematic strategic planning, a considerable amount of literature has explored the repercussions of the EU's complex organizational structure on the coherence of its negotiating strategy, as well as on its interactions with other UNFCCC parties (e.g. Vogler 1999; Elgström and Strömvik 2003; Jordan and Rayner 2010; Afionis 2011). The half-yearly rotating EU Presidency, inefficiencies related to climate policy integration, as well as problematic internal coordinating capacities, have all been flagged as contributing factors to the EU's inability to often get its climate change message across and push the process forward.

Structural complications

As noted, the EU is a rather unique entity, unlike anything the world has ever known.[5] It is thus inevitable that it will face unique problems when negotiating – problems that are not to be found in other parties but that are EU-specific. One such complication is its identity. Depending on the issue being negotiated, the EU may either appear as a single actor, in which case the Commission is in charge, or as a group of sovereign states represented by the Presidency. As a result of the continuous process of treaty reform, the EU (i.e. the Commission) has been entrusted with exclusive competence to negotiate and conclude agreements over certain issues, such as trade or commercial policy.[6] When it comes to climate change, however, competence is shared. This means that both the Commission and the Member States are present around the negotiating table, jointly formulating common positions (Vogler 1999; Delreux 2011). Absence of clearly determined competences, coupled with a congested policy space with multiple players across multiple jurisdictions and departments, has often impeded the EU's performance at international negotiations (Tabau 2013).

A first complication relates to the half-yearly rotating EU Presidency. The tasks of the Member State holding the Presidency include leading the EU decision-making process, coordinating the Member States and presenting the EU common position at environmental international fora (Oberthür and Ott 1999; Delreux and Van den Brande 2013). Up until the reforms of 2004, this arrangement effectively meant that each Presidency had to appoint a team of about 20 negotiators that would need to quickly become familiar with the situation before handing over to the next team six months later. This created a heavy work burden, especially for smaller Member States. The arrangement was thus associated with a number of drawbacks, such as impeding continuity and long-term strategic planning, as well as hampering the preservation of institutional memory (House of Lords 2004). The EU prior to 2004 had 'become increasingly known for its failure to deploy capable and experienced negotiators with institutional memory as well as for its navel gazing and bunker mentality resulting in a lack of outreach activities to others' (Oberthür and Pallemaerts 2010, p. 41).

To augment external policy coordination and representation, the EU's institutional set-up was reformed by the Irish Presidency of 2004.[7] The 2004 Irish Presidency was concerned it lacked the capacity to handle such a complex agenda, and decided to introduce an informal system based on 'lead negotiators' and 'issue leaders'. Both posts were to be open to individuals from any Member State or the Commission, who would be tasked with negotiating on behalf of the EU for longer periods of time on a particular set of issues (Van Schaik and Egenhofer 2005; Schunz 2014). Lead negotiators were to be high-ranking, experienced officials who would represent the EU at international deliberations, assisted in their duties by a group of issue leaders, well-versed in the nitty-gritty details of specific dossiers (Delreux and Van den Brande 2013). So far, the verdict has been rather positive. Apart from enhancing continuity and allowing for the pooling of the expertise and know-how of 29 actors (Commission and Member States), a further advantage of this institutional innovation has been that it allowed different EU Member States the opportunity to specialize in specific issues. This in turn has left 'the Presidency more space to focus on the overall strategy' (Van Schaik and Egenhofer 2005, p. 8; see also Delreux and Van den Brande 2013; Delreux 2014). These reforms have also been positively embraced by EU climate negotiators, facilitating the emergence of an EU identity among their ranks (Oberthür 2013). On the downside, the new system has led to further 'independence and compartmentalization of individual expert groups', thereby making their coordination more demanding (Oberthür and Dupont 2010, p. 80).

Another Presidency-related reform concerns the altered rotating system introduced in 2007. Every 18 months the three Presidencies due to hold office prepare a common agenda in close cooperation with the Commission and work together over this period to accomplish its objectives (Jordan *et al.* 2012). One advantage of this new system is that it enables Member States with a greater interest in this policy area to relieve smaller ones of the burden of conducting negotiations in which they have no active interest (Afionis 2009). According to Wurzel (2013), initial results from this novel procedure have so far been rather positive.

A second complication relates to the predominance of environment ministries and the under-representation of economics and trade ministries in climate change negotiations. While the EU has a strong rhetorical commitment to policy coordination, i.e. integration of environmental concerns into all policy areas, performance has not so far been encouraging. There are two main reasons for this mismatch between rhetoric and practice (Jordan *et al.* 2013). Unlike most sovereign states, the EU lacks a 'core executive' that can ensure effective coordination. The Council of Ministers, which is supposed to perform this function, meets too infrequently to be able to consistently guide and direct EU day-to-day affairs. The Commission is also handicapped in this respect due to the dispersal of decision-making competencies across different sectors and tiers of governance. Its capacity is especially constrained by the fact that it lacks a firm grip on core sectors, such as energy or transport. In these two areas, the requirement for Council unanimity on measures of a fiscal nature (e.g. environmental taxation), plus measures 'significantly affecting a Member State's choice of energy sources and the general structure of its energy supply',[8] effectively gives Member States veto power over core climate protection policy areas (Oberthür and Dupont 2010). Member States themselves fare little better when it comes to mainstreaming climate policy into other policy fields. Only a few – e.g. the United Kingdom (UK) – possess an actively coordinated system of national government whose departments 'sing from the same hymn sheet' (Jordan and Schout 2006, p. 95).

Despite constant efforts to improve coordination capacities, progress has been hampered by a number of obstacles. In the Commission, for example, the Directorate-General (DG) for Environment had found it difficult to follow suit and remained poorly informed about developments in other sectors (Jordan and Schout 2006). Early efforts, such as the creation of a network of environmental correspondents spanning the various DGs, bore few fruits in practice due *inter alia* to the difficulties encountered by these correspondents when it came to promoting environmental policy integration 'in battles between different DGs' (Jordan *et al.* 2013, p. 234). Following the flawed performance of the EU at the COP in The Hague in 2000 (see Chapter 5), a number of EU-wide remedial measures were adopted, including strengthening the role of the Committee of Permanent Representatives (COREPER), plus having economic, trade, and foreign ministries more involved in the climate change decision-making process (Van Schaik and Egenhofer 2003). In the Commission, an inter-service coordination group of officials from various DGs was instituted in preparation for the 2009 Copenhagen COP, while new administrative capacities were created in 2010 following the establishment of a new DG for climate (Barnes 2010). Despite the drive towards better integration, the problem remains open, as the EU has not managed to tackle it in a holistic manner, not least because economic and social imperatives have progressively taken precedence over environmental factors in the sustainability equation (Oberthür and Dupont 2010; Jordan *et al.* 2013).

A third complication for the EU during the course of international climate change negotiations has been the difficulty of reaching an agreement internally on different issues, known as the 'EU bunker'. Both the EU and the Member States participate in international negotiations, as both will (potentially) become a party to the international agreement. Changing positions and agreeing on new proposals by other international actors necessitates internal consultations that can be a 'major source of delay and frustration, with endless co-ordination meetings and the inflexibility of Council Mandates' (Vogler 2003, p. 70). As a rule, coordination meetings take place once a day, but during the course of the negotiations they can often be held twice, thrice or even more frequently if necessary (Delreux 2009). These intra-bloc negotiations, however, often resemble 'a conference within a conference' (Barston 2006, p. 87). Other parties do not sit idle. While the EU coordinates, they negotiate in its absence (Delreux 2009). Other countries used to complain of the fact that EU representatives 'never came to talk to you because they were always talking to each other' (Andersson and Mol 2002, p. 62).

For example, during the final night at Kyoto the EU's ministers were still deliberating internally when Chairman Estrada rubber stamped the critical text on the Clean Development Mechanism (CDM) (Grubb and Yamin 2001). When they informed the Chairman of their opposition to the pre-budget crediting of emission reductions, the decision had already been taken and could not be reopened (Oberthür and Ott 1999). The same situation reoccurred during COP-6 in 2000, when EU ministers were still debating amendments they wished to propose to the Chairman's Pronk compromise paper after amendments from all the other groups, even the much larger and under-resourced Group of 77 and China (G-77/China), had been circulated and the final night's crucial negotiations had begun (Grubb and Yamin 2001). In Copenhagen, as Giddens (2010) notes, due to the 'EU bunker' effect, the EU was unable to 'deliver the very rapid decision-making that had to take place late on in the negotiations to get anything from them at all'.

When it comes to climate negotiations, alleviating the bunker problem is crucial, especially following the post-2004 series of enlargements, which almost doubled the number of Member States. This of course is easier said than done:

> The EU cannot be as flexible as, for instance, the US and we just have to accept this. We can strive for enhanced flexibility but we cannot dominate in the same way as the US because our common positions and compromises need to be negotiated through often very difficult negotiations. This is a weakness of the EU and will always be our weakness.[9]

The increased number of meetings at the expert level have somewhat addressed this complication as far as international deliberations are concerned (Andersson and Mol 2002). Internally, the problem remains largely unchecked, as evidenced by the fact that the majority of new eastern Member States have strongly criticized or delayed the adoption of highly progressive EU climate policy measures; see for example the 2007 negotiations on the climate and energy package, the December 2008 EU Council coinciding with the Poznań COP or the internal talks throughout 2009 on the level of EU financial assistance to developing countries (Afionis 2011).

Methods and structure of the book

Whilst the EU's decision-making structure is far from ideal, any structural deficiencies cannot alone explain why the EU has failed to put up a convincing performance during some climate talks. Organizational problems are, of course, an important factor but only provide part of the answer. If we are to identify the nature of the barriers that have prevented EU negotiators from formulating promising approaches or agreeing mutually satisfactory compromises, we need to unpack the EU's performance at UNFCCC talks. This is not easy, but thankfully the literature offers us clues as to why international negotiations fail.

This book draws on secondary data from government documents, published reports and scientific studies, as well as interviews and personal communications with EU Commission and Member State officials. Primary data were gathered through 15 semi-structured interviews carried out across the EU, whereby a purposive sample and snowballing approach were used to identify respondents. The UNFCCC's list of participants for each COP were also drawn upon. Interviews were conducted during the second half of 2015 and the first half of 2016. The latter set of interviews therefore allowed the author to explore the question of whether EU officials applied any of the lessons learned from past failures to better prepare for the Paris COP. Interviewees from both the Commission and the Member States were predominantly senior-ranking officials with substantial negotiating experience that were directly involved in strategy formulation. Almost all of the Member State interviewees have served or are serving as Heads of Delegation for their respective countries. Officials from seven Member States were interviewed. In a few cases, it was possible to interview two officials from the same Member State, as the official in charge of the climate change dossier at the time would introduce me to their predecessor (or vice versa). An effort was also made to talk to individuals who had engaged in international climate change negotiations for prolonged periods of time, as they would be in a position to offer a more long-term perspective. This proved possible in the great majority of interviews. As a first step, this book investigates the self-perceptions of EU and Member State officials, acknowledging that looking into those of third parties could provide future scope for research. Doing so would add to studies that have already scrutinized perceptions of EU leadership and power in the context of the climate change regime (see e.g. Karlsson *et al.* 2011).

Interview data collection was purposely narrowed down to two sets of negotiations: those surrounding the COPs in The Hague and in Copenhagen. This was done for the following reasons. First, these two meetings represent the two occasions in which international negotiations actually failed. Second, time constraints meant that interviews needed to be focused if usable empirical data were to be collected. Third, access to officials participating in the negotiations during the 1990s proved much harder than access to officials involved in the deliberations during the 2000s onwards. Negotiations have been ongoing for more than 20 years and inevitably people have since changed jobs, retired, and so on. Fourth, it is often easier for senior officials to recall details for landmark events, such as The Hague or the Copenhagen COPs, than it is for them to do so for COPs of lesser importance. Note here that officials participate annually in a constellation of UNFCCC-related meetings, including, among others, the COPs themselves or the meetings of the Subsidiary Bodies and ad hoc working groups.

In term of structure, each chapter deals with a particular time period. Chapter 1 gives an overview of the series of conferences and workshops (e.g. in 1988 in Toronto) that raised awareness with respect to climate change and prompted several industrialized countries – including the (then) European Community (EC) and several of its Member States – to make unilateral commitments to reduce their CO_2 emissions. These developments pushed the international political process towards a convention on climate change. The progressive role of the EC and its Member States during the INC negotiations that ultimately led to Rio is analysed, focusing in particular on their efforts to bring on board a reluctant US. Chapter 2 covers the Commission's unsuccessful proposal to establish an EU-wide carbon/energy tax – a proposal that dominated the internal agenda, generated intense controversy and ultimately compromised the credibility of the EU during the Rio deliberations. Chapter 3 discusses the participation of the EU in the 1995 Berlin and 1996 Geneva COPs, covering also the various preparatory meetings that were held in the run-up to each of those. Chapter 4 focuses on the Kyoto Protocol and the subsequent 1998 Buenos Aires and 1999 Bonn COPs. Following a long period of EU inactivity and lack of leadership in the aftermath of Rio, the EU eventually took the lead and pushed for ambitious emission cuts, with its proposals being also backed by an internal EU burden-sharing agreement. Chapters 5, 6 and 7 detail the EU's ultimately successful efforts to ensure the ratification of the Kyoto Protocol in the aftermath of US withdrawal. Chapter 8 covers the breakthrough in Bali of ensuring a form of US participation in climate negotiations, while Chapter 9 is about the Poznań COP and the debacle in Copenhagen. Chapter 10 employs Underdal's framework in order to bring together all these different threads and evaluate the reasons why the EU proved ultimately unable to push forward with the top–down approach. Finally, the conclusion provides a summary and looks at the role played by the EU during the process that led to the adoption of the 2015 Paris Agreement.

Notes

1 The PIN program, arguably the leading society dedicated to research on this area, involves leading diplomats and scholars from a wide spectrum of countries that have focused since 1988 on improving the understanding and the practice of negotiation.
2 Faure (2012) notes that demonization, or similar conceptual alternatives entering the discursive arena under the guise of synonyms, can play a major role in causing a stalemate in negotiations by quashing attempts by parties to interact in a constructive manner. Making counterparts into a demon effectively delegitimizes their acceptability in the negotiations and allows others to transfer to them the responsibility for the negotiations failure.
3 Afionis (2011) relied on the aforementioned framework to explore the extent to which negotiation theory could help with better comprehending the obstacles that prevented the EU from getting more out of the climate negotiation process.
4 Examples include the 1973 Convention on International Trade in Endangered Species (CITES) or the 1987 Montreal Protocol on Ozone Depleting Substances.
5 Vogler (2003) describes the EU as a *sui generis* political system.
6 Competence is the EU term for 'powers' or, in other words, who has authority to undertake negotiations and initiate policy (the Commission, the Member States or both).

7 The Irish Presidency delegated further authority to the Ad hoc Working Group on Climate Change. This body was established after the first COP in Berlin in 1995 and is nowadays a branch of the Working Party on International Environmental Issues (WPIEI). This latter body is central in the Council's decision-making apparatus, as it is the main preparatory body COREPER and the Environment Council.
8 Article 176 A (Lisbon Treaty).
9 Interview no. 2 (Member State official – Former Head of Delegation).

References

Afionis, Stavros (2009). European Union Coherence in UNFCCC negotiations under the new Treaty of Lisbon (Reform Treaty). *Sustainable Development Law and Policy* 9: 43–7.

Afionis, Stavros (2011). The European Union as a negotiator in the international climate change regime. *International Environmental Agreements: Politics, Law and Economics* 11: 341–60.

Andersson, Magnus and Arthur P.J. Mol (2002). The Netherlands in the UNFCCC Process – Leadership between Ambition and Reality. *International Environmental Agreements: Politics, Law and Economics* 2 (1): 49–68.

Barnes, Pamela M. (2010). The role of the Commission of the European Union: creating external coherence from internal diversity. In Wurzel, Rüdiger K.W. and James Connelly (eds) *The European Union as a Leader in International Climate Change Politics*. London: Routledge, 74–91.

Barston, R.P. (2006). *Modern diplomacy*. Harlow: Pearson Longman.

Brett, Jeanne M. (2014). *Negotiating globally: how to negotiate deals, resolve disputes, and make decisions across cultural boundaries*. San Francisco: Wiley.

Collins, Kevin and Ray Ison (2009). Editorial: living with environmental change: adaptation as social learning. *Environmental Policy and Governance* 19: 351–7.

Delreux, Tom (2009). Cooperation and control in the European Union: the case of the European Union as international environmental negotiator. *Cooperation and Conflict* 44 (2): 189–208.

Delreux, Tom (2011). *The EU as international environmental negotiator*. Farnham: Ashgate.

Delreux, Tom (2014). EU actorness, cohesiveness and effectiveness in environmental affairs. *Journal of European Public Policy* 21 (7): 1017–32.

Delreux, Tom and Karoline Van den Brande (2013). Taking the lead: informal division of labour in the EU's external environmental policy-making. *Journal of European Public Policy* 20 (1): 113–31.

Dessai Suraje, Stavros Afionis and James Van Alstine (2013). Science alone cannot shape sustainability. *Nature* 493: 26.

Dimas, Stavros (2005). Developing the European climate change programme. Speech at the stakeholder conference launching the Second European Climate Change Programme, Brussels, 24 October. Available at: file:///C:/Users/earsaa/Downloads/SPEECH-05-635_EN.pdf.

Elgström, Ole and Maria Strömvik (2003). The EU as an international negotiator. In Elgström, Ole and Christer Jönsson (eds) *European Union negotiations processes, networks and institutions*. London: Routledge, 117–29.

Falkner, Robert, Hannes Stephan and John Vogler (2010). International climate policy after Copenhagen: towards a 'building blocks' approach. *Global Policy* 1 (3): 252–62.

Faure, Guy Olivier (2012). Failures: lessons from theory. In Faure, Guy Olivier (ed.) *Unfinished business: why international negotiations fail.* Athens: The University of Georgia Press, 357–82.

Faure, Guy Olivier and William I. Zartman (2012). Introduction. In Faure, Guy Olivier (ed.) *Unfinished business: why international negotiations fail.* Athens: The University of Georgia Press, 3–16.

Giddens, Anthony (2010). Big players, a positive Accord. Policy Network Opinion. Available at: www.policy-network.net/pno_detail.aspx?ID=3542&title=Big-players-a-positive-Accord.

Grubb, Michael and Farhana Yamin (2001). Climatic collapse at The Hague: what happened, why, and where do we go from here? *International Affairs* 77 (2): 261–76.

Gupta, Joyeeta and Lasse Ringius (2001). The EU's climate leadership: reconciling ambition and reality. *International Environmental Agreements: Politics, Law and Economics* 1 (2): 281–99.

Hood, Christina, Liwayway Adkins and Ellina Levina (2015). *Overview of INDCs Submitted by 31 August 2015.* Paris: OECD/IEA.

House of Lords (2004). *The EU and climate change.* London: The Stationery Office.

IEA (International Energy Agency) (2015). *Energy and climate change: world energy outlook special report.* Paris: IEA.

IPCC (2014). Climate change 2014: synthesis report. Available at: www.ipcc.ch/pdf/assessment-report/ar5/syr/SYR_AR5_FINAL_full_wcover.pdf.

Jonsson, Christer and Martin Hall (2005). *Essence of diplomacy.* Houndmills: Palgrave Macmillan.

Jordan, Andrew and Adriaan Schout (2006). *The coordination of the European Union: exploring the capacities of networked governance.* Oxford: Oxford University Press.

Jordan, Andrew and Camilla Adelle (eds) (2013). *Environmental policy in the EU: actors, institutions and processes.* London: Earthscan.

Jordan, Andrew and Tim Rayner (2010). The evolution of climate policy in the European Union: a historical perspective. In Jordan, Andrew, Dave Huitema, Harro van Asselt, Tim Rayner and Frans Berkhout (eds) *Climate change policy in the European Union: confronting the dilemmas of mitigation and adaptation?* Cambridge: Cambridge University Press, 52–80.

Jordan, Andrew, Adriaan Schout and Martin Unfried (2013). Policy coordination. In Jordan, Andrew and Camilla Adelle (eds) *Environmental policy in the EU: actors, institutions and processes.* London: Earthscan, 227–46.

Jordan, Andrew, Harro van Asselt, Frans Berkhout, Dave Huitema and Tim Rayner (2012). Understanding the paradoxes of multilevel governing: climate change policy in the European Union. *Global Environmental Politics* 12 (2): 43–66.

Karlsson, Christer, Charles Parker, Mattias Hjerpe and Björn-Ola Linnér (2011). Looking for leaders: perceptions of climate change leadership among climate change negotiation participants. *Global Environmental Politics* 11 (1): 89–107.

Kelemen, Daniel R. (2010). Globalizing European Union environmental policy. *Journal of European Public Policy* 17: 335–49.

Kelemen, Daniel R. and David Vogel (2010). Trading places: the role of the United States and the European Union in international environmental politics. *Comparative Political Studies* 43: 427–56.

Lightfoot, Simon and Jon Burchell (2004). Green hope or greenwash? The actions of the European Union at the world summit on sustainable development. *Global Environmental Change* 14: 337–44.

Maslin, Mark (2004). *Global warming: a very short introduction*. Oxford: Oxford University Press.

Metcalfe, Les and David Metcalfe (2002). Tools for good governance: an assessment of multiparty negotiation analysis. *International Review of Administrative Sciences* 68 (2): 267–86.

Midgaard, Knut (2006). The scholarship of Arild Underdal. *Global Environmental Politics* 6 (3): 3–12.

Oberthür, Sebastian (2013). The European Union's performance in the international climate change regime. In Oberthür, Sebastian, Knud Erik Jørgensen and Jamal Shahin (eds) *The performance of the EU in international institutions*. Abingdon: Routledge, 69–84.

Oberthür, Sebastian and Claire Dupont (2010). The Council, the European Council and international climate policy. In Wurzel, Rüdiger K.W. and James Connelly (eds) *The European Union as a leader in international climate change politics*. London: Routledge, 74–91.

Oberthür, Sebastian and Hermann E. Ott (1999). *The Kyoto Protocol: international climate policy for the 21st century*. Berlin: Springer.

Oberthür, Sebastian and Marc Pallemaerts (2010). The EU's internal and external climate policies: an historical overview. In Oberthür, Sebastian and Marc Pallemaerts (eds) *The new climate policies of the European Union: internal legislation and climate diplomacy*. Brussels: VUBPress, 27–63.

Odell, John S. and Dustin Tingley (2016). Negotiating agreements in international relations. In Mansbridge, Jane and Cathie Jo Martin (eds) *Political negotiation: a handbook*. Washington D.C: Brookings Institution Press, 231–85.

Schunz, Simon (2014). *European Union foreign policy and the global climate regime*. Brussels: P.I.E. Peter Lang.

Scruggs, Lyle and Salil Benegal (2012). Declining public concern about climate change: can we blame the great recession? *Global Environmental Change* 22: 505–15.

Sjöstedt, Gunnar (ed.) (1993). *International environmental negotiations*. Newbury Park, CA: Sage.

Starkey, Brigid, Mark A. Boyer and Jonathan Wilkenfeld (1999). *Negotiating a complex world: an introduction to international negotiation*. Lanham: Rowman & Littlefield.

Tabau, Anne-Sophie (2013). Shared accountability of the European Union and its member states in the climate change regime. *Review of European Community and International Environmental Law* 22 (1): 91–102.

Underdal, Arild (1983). Causes of negotiation 'failure'. *European Journal of Political Research* 11 (2): 183–95.

Underdal, Arild (1991). International cooperation and political engineering. In Nagel, Stuart (ed.) *Global policy studies: international interaction toward improving public policy*. Basingstoke: Palgrave Macmillan, 98–120.

UNFCCC (2015). Adoption of the Paris Agreement. FCCC/CP/2015/L.9/Rev.1.

Van Schaik, Louise and Christian Egenhofer (2003). Reform of the EU institutions: implications for the EU's performance in climate negotiations. *CEPS Policy Brief* No. 40, September. Available at: https://www.ceps.eu/publications/reform-eu-institutions-implications-eus-performance-climate-negotiations.

Van Schaik, Louise and Christian Egenhofer (2005). Improving the climate: will the new constitution strengthen the EU's performance in international climate negotiations? *CEPS Policy Brief* No. 63, February. Available at: www.ceps.eu/publications/improving-climate-will-new-constitution-strengthen-eu-performance-international-climate.

Vogler, John (1999). The European Union as an actor in international environmental politics. *Environmental Politics* 8 (3): 24–48.

Vogler, John (2003). The External Environmental Policy of the European Union. In Stokke, Olav Schram and Øystein B. Thommessen (eds.) *Yearbook of International Cooperation on Environment and Development*. London: Earthscan, 65–71.

Vogler, John (2016). *Climate change in world politics*. Basingstoke: Palgrave Macmillan.

Wurzel, Rüdiger K.W. (2013). Member states and the Council. In Jordan, Andrew and Camilla Adelle (eds) *Environmental policy in the EU: actors, institutions and processes*. London: Earthscan, 75–94.

Wurzel, Rüdiger K.W. and James Connelly (eds) (2010). *The European Union as a leader in international climate change politics*. London: Routledge.

Yamin, Farhana (2000). The role of the EU in climate negotiations. In Gupta, Joyeeta and Michael Grubb (eds) *Climate change and European leadership: a sustainable role for Europe?* Dordrecht: Kluwer, 47–66.

1 Climate change

From science to policy

The French scientist Baron Jean Baptiste Joseph Fourier is accredited as the first to describe the 'greenhouse effect' (Edwards 2011). As early as 1827, he suggested that gases, including CO_2 and methane, can act as a blanket trapping the heat of the sun in the atmosphere, like 'glass captures heat in a greenhouse' (Brown 1996, p. 12). By coining the term 'greenhouse effect', Fourier displayed 'a rare knack, for a scientist, of describing a complex process so simply that everyone could understand it' (Brown 1996, p. 12). John Tyndall further developed the theory in the 1860s by measuring the absorption of heat radiation by CO_2 and water vapour (Darwall 2013), while Svante Arrhenius (1896), a Swedish Nobel Prize-winning chemist, calculated at the end of the 19th century that a doubling of CO_2 would increase the temperature of the planet by between 5°C and 6°C. Such hypotheses received little attention from the scientific community for much of the next 60 years, with the exception of Guy Stewart Callendar, an English chemist and amateur meteorologist. In 1938, he presented at a Royal Society meeting arguing that data from 200 meteorological stations around the world demonstrated that average land temperatures had increased between the 1880s and the 1930s (Darwall 2013). Callendar theorized a link between rising temperatures and increased atmospheric CO_2 from the burning of fossil fuels. His views, however, struggled to gain traction as the prevailing scientific discourse of the time was that any extra CO_2 emitted as a result of human industrial activities would be absorbed by the oceans.[1]

Roger Revelle and Hans Suess from the Scripps Institute of Oceanography at La Jolla, California, challenged this assumption in 1957. They posited that nearly half of all emitted CO_2 was not actually absorbed by the oceans, leaving enough excess gas in the atmosphere to gradually warm the planet (Brown 2002). Notably, it was Revelle who encouraged Charles David Keeling, his former graduate student, to establish the first permanent station for measuring global CO_2 levels at Mauna Loa, Hawaii. The resulting Keeling CO_2 curve, which has continued to climb since 1958, has become one of the major contemporary images of climate change. It has proved instrumental in paving the way for scientific opinion to go from tentatively to strongly endorsing the view since the 1970s that average global temperatures are rising as a result of human activities (Maslin 2004).

Apart from climate change, the 1960s and, in particular, the 1970s, also wit-nessed environmental concerns in general entering onto the stage of inter-national high politics for the first time. Modern environmentalism found full expression in 1972 at the UN Conference on the Human Environment in Stockholm. Even though climate change per se was hardly mentioned, the con-ference represented a major shift in the priority given to climate-related prob-lems and acted as a catalyst for a series of UN-sponsored conferences during the 1970s on climatic issues, such as the UN World Food Conference in 1974, the UN Water Conference in 1976 and the UN Desertification Conference in 1977 (Paterson 1996).

Scientific knowledge at the time was extremely facilitated by vast improvements in General Circulation Models (GCMs) which, while still subject to considerable uncertainty, led to increased confidence by scientists in climate change predictions (Edwards 2011). Based on a review of these models, the US National Academy of Sciences came to a stark conclusion in 1979 that 'there is no reason to doubt that climate change will result and no reason to believe that these changes will be negli-gible' (Bodansky 2001, p. 24). As an expression of the increased scientific concern about the atmospheric commons, a number of intergovernmental bodies, including *inter alia* the UN Environment Program (UNEP) and the World Meteorological Organization (WMO), sponsored in 1979 the first World Climate Conference (WCC) in Geneva. Its declaration called upon governments 'to foresee and prevent potential man-made changes in climate that might be adverse to the well-being of humanity' (Børsting and Fermann 1997, p. 55).

The next big step towards a scientific consensus on climate change came with the October 1985 Villach Conference in Austria. Drawing on the most advanced experiments available at the time, scientists urged the international community to adopt a multilateral convention as a means to safeguard against predicted increases in global mean surface temperature of between 1.5°C and 4.5°C (Paterson 1996). Villach therefore marked a 'shift of emphasis away from solely the need for more research, towards including assertions of the need for political action' (Paterson 1992a, p. 176).

In 1987, the World Commission on Environment and Development (WCED) published its seminal report, *Our Common Future*, reproducing recom-mendations of the 1985 Villach Conference and identifying climate change as one of four major environmental threats facing society, alongside urban pollu-tion, acid rain and nuclear accidents (Darwall 2013). Despite this impetus, the international community exhibited considerable inertia towards adopting a con-vention or any sort of political agreement on greenhouse gases, fuelled in part by its concentrated preoccupation with the ozone depletion regime and the associated Montreal Protocol (Paterson 1996).

The year 1988 proved to be a turning point when climate change went from being a scientific priority to a political one too. 'The Changing Atmosphere: Implications for Global Security' conference, held in Toronto, had little impact in terms of its adopted conclusions, but its timing was exquisite. It coincided with one of the hottest years of the 20th century. A record drought had hit the

Midwest, and many other parts of the US, focusing US policymakers' attention on climate change. It set the stage for the events that were to unfold. In one of the drought-related hearings held in Washington at the peak of the hottest summer on record, NASA climate modeller James Hansen testified before the US Senate Energy Committee that he was 'ninety-nine percent confident' that the experienced warming was not a chance event and that the evidence clearly suggested that 'the greenhouse effect is here [and] is changing our climate now' (cited in Brown 1996, p. 18).

Hansen's statement created a media sensation. Climate change stories featuring cracked earth, withering plants and stranded barges headlined media outlets for several weeks. Barely a week after the Hansen testimony, the Canadian government hosted the above-mentioned Toronto Conference, which the sequel of events had consequently turned into 'a media Mecca' (Schneider 1990, p. 194). The Toronto Declaration spoke of an 'uncontrolled globally pervasive experiment' with consequences 'second only to a global nuclear war' (Newell 2000, p. 56) and issued an ambitious 'call for action' to governments to reduce global CO_2 emissions by 20 per cent of 1988 levels by 2005, with an eventual aim to cut emissions by 50 per cent. It further advocated for an international climate change convention and the establishment of a World Atmosphere Fund that would support energy efficiency and CO_2 limitation undertakings while concurrently protecting the development aspirations and increased energy requirements of developing nations (Pallemaerts and Williams 2006; Usher 1989). The fund was to be financed in part by a levy on the fossil fuel consumption of developed countries – the first ever mention of a 'carbon tax' (Brown 1996).

Following Toronto, discussions moved onto an intergovernmental track, with scientists passing the baton to politicians. As nation-states became increasingly aware of the implications of climate change for their energy production and consumption, conference statements became more qualified and consensus harder to reach. Post-Toronto conference declarations 'reflect a retrenchment rather than an advance' (Bodansky 1994, p. 50). Proposals to cut greenhouse gas emissions by 20 per cent gave way to a push to stabilize them instead (Paterson 1996). Later in 1988, the IPCC was established by the WMO and UNEP, for the purpose of developing international consensus on the science, causes, repercussions and response options to climate change. As previous assessments (e.g. in Villach) had been organized by the scientific and environmental communities, the establishment of an intergovernmental panel (i.e. the IPCC) represented to a great extent an attempt by governments to take control over an increasingly politicized debate (Bodansky 1994). Over the years, the IPCC's impact on climate change knowledge, public discourse and policy development has been marked (Hulme and Mahony 2010). Agrawala (1998, p. 611) notes that it is precisely the 'intergovernmental nature of the IPCC that gives its assessments a special *niche*, distinct from the myriad other assessments and vendors'.

In September 1988 the climate change dossier reached the UN General Assembly when Malta requested the inclusion of an agenda item entitled, 'Declaration proclaiming climate as part of the common heritage of mankind'

(Bodansky 1993). Because of widespread objections to Malta's invocation of the 'common *heritage* of mankind' concept, which had previously been applied to deep seabed mineral recourses and the moon, the final resolution merely referred to climate change as a 'common *concern* of mankind' that should be confronted within a global framework (Gupta 2014; Bodansky 1993; Kirgis 1990). A proposal for such a framework was subsequently tabled during The Hague Summit on the Atmosphere in March 1989, where 22 countries, including Italy, France, Japan and Canada, called for negotiations on a climate change treaty that would be endowed with supranational competences (Boehmer-Christiansen 1995). The objective of the organizers (i.e. France and the Netherlands) had been to convene a meeting of environmentally 'progressive' countries so as to build pressure on the rest of the international community (Pallemaerts and Williams 2006, p. 23). The US and USSR[2] were not invited, whereas the UK refused to attend, viewing the summit as a threat to its sovereignty. The UK was also successful in pushing environment ministers to withdraw EC support from the Hague initiative (Boehmer-Christiansen 1995).

Arguably the most significant meeting of 1989 was the Noordwijk Ministerial Conference on Atmospheric Pollution and Climate Change, convened by the Netherlands in November and attended by representatives of 67 countries, 11 international organizations, and the EC Commission. Even though this conference is considered a milestone on the road to international CO_2 emissions targets, it is also where the first basic split among developed countries became apparent (Jordan and Rayner 2010; Andersson and Mol 2002). A proposal by a group of countries, including the Netherlands, Germany, France, Canada, Sweden and Norway, to set a target for developed countries to stabilize their CO_2 emissions by the year 2000 was opposed by the US, along with Japan, the USSR and, to a lesser degree, the UK. In the latter group's opinion, further scientific study was necessary before establishing quantitative limitations (i.e. targets and timetables) on national emission levels of greenhouse gases (Bodansky 2001). Eventually a compromise was hammered out between these two distinct political blocks. The conference's declaration 'recognized' the need for developed countries to stabilize their CO_2 emissions 'as soon as possible', while noting that in the view of 'many' countries, such stabilization should be 'achieved as a first step at the latest by the year 2000' (Hatch 1993, p. 13). Interestingly, as Bodansky (1994, p. 72) notes, 'many' was a compromise between 'most' (supported by the EC) and 'some' (supported by the US).

Due to the participation of developing countries, the Noordwijk Declaration also noted that developed countries should lead by example by initiating action to reduce their own emissions first, while at the same time financially and otherwise assisting developing countries to undertake mitigation initiatives without compromising their need to achieve sustainable development (Gupta 2014). This reference has been interpreted as a first clear sign of the emergence of yet another divide, that between developed and developing nations (Schunz 2014; Pallemaerts and Williams 2006). These developing country demands were to become building blocks of the framework convention. In December 1989, the

UN General Assembly reaffirmed the need for a framework convention and the development of international funding mechanisms. It noted that the UN represented the most appropriate forum for the conduct of negotiations to this effect (UNGA 1989). Compared with the resolution that had followed Malta's proposal in September 1988, the sense of urgency was far more pronounced.

The next notable round of negotiations took place in Bergen, Norway, in May 1990, with the participation of 34 country delegations. Only days before the IPCC had released its interim report. It predicted an increase in temperatures between 1°C by 2025 and 3°C before the end of the 21st century (Brown 1996). As a result of the IPCC's findings, Bergen took on a new significance. The UK, until then supportive of the Americans, reversed its position and accepted the need for targets (Brown 1996). The US, however, reiterated its opposition to targets and timetables, citing scientific uncertainty and the costs involved in reducing emissions as its justification. The US wait-and-see stance provoked a reaction from several countries, including EC members and the then EC Environment Commissioner Ripa di Meana, who attacked the US and called for stronger action (Liberatore 1995). Yet, owing mainly to US opposition, the Bergen Conference adopted a declaration on the lines of the one adopted in Noordwijk. The Bergen Declaration again called for stabilization of greenhouse gas emissions 'as soon as possible', but did not delve into the issue of targets and timetables as it merely recommended that developed countries 'establish national strategies and/or targets and schedules' (Paterson 1996, p. 39). The Declaration, however, did state that in the view of 'most' countries, stabilization of CO_2 emissions 'at the latest by the year 2000 and at present levels must be the first step' (Paterson 1996, p. 39). Note here that 'most' replaced 'many'.

The US found itself increasingly isolated following Bergen. Many developed country actors, including the EC and its Member States, began tabling unilateral commitments in relation to their CO_2 emissions. The status of these commitments at the time the Rio Convention was signed (June 1992) is given in Table 1.1. In August 1990, the First Assessment Report of the IPCC was approved in Sundsvall, Sweden, which predicted that in the absence of mitigation measures global average surface temperature would rise by an average of 0.3°C per decade during the next century – a rate greater than that seen over the past 10,000 years (Rowlands 1995).

The IPCC presented its findings to the Second World Climate Conference (SWCC) in Geneva in November 1990, attended by heads of government and ministers from 137 nation-states and the EC (Andersen and Wettestad 1990). The aforementioned divisions between developed countries persisted, with the EC, joined by the six members of the European Free Trade Area (EFTA), pledging to stabilize emissions of CO_2, or CO_2 and other greenhouse gases not controlled by the Montreal Protocol, by the year 2000 of 1990 levels (Hampson and Hart 1995). Maintaining an EC common front, however, was only made possible following the insertion in the final declaration of text highlighting the need for developed countries with relatively low energy consumption to establish objectives in light of their national economic growth imperatives

Table 1.1 CO_2 emission stabilization and reduction targets from 1990 levels

Country	Stabilization	Reduction
Australia	by 2000	20% by 2005[a]
Austria		20% by 2005
Canada	by 2005	
Denmark		20% by 2005
Finland	by 2000	
France	by 2000[b]	
Germany		25–30% by 2005
Italy	by 2000	20% by 2005
Japan	by 2000[c]	
Luxemburg	by 2000	20% by 2005
Netherlands	by 1995	3–5% by 2000
New Zealand		20% by 2000
Norway	by 2000	
United Kingdom	by 2005	
European Community	**by 2000**	

Source: Paterson (1996, pp. 41–2).

Notes
a Figure for all greenhouse gases.
b This is a *per capita* per year target of less than 2 metric tons of carbon.
c Stabilization of per capita emissions.

(Pallemaerts and Williams 2006). Note here that the EC's position in the nego-tiations had been from the outset that a stabilization target would apply to the Community as a whole. In any case, the EC's position in favour of stabilization by 2000 was shared by Canada, Australia, New Zealand and Japan, while the USSR and the oil-producing states sided with the US in arguing for further sci-entific research. The SWCC Ministerial Declaration therefore simply urged developed countries to establish 'targets and/or national programs or strategies' which would have 'significant effects on limiting [i.e. not stabilizing or reducing] emissions of greenhouse gases' (Paterson 1996, p. 48).

Despite little movement on targets and timetables, the SWCC did establish a number of basic principles, including *inter alia* that of equity and the 'common but differentiated responsibility' of countries at different levels of development, plus the concepts of sustainable development and the precautionary principle (Børsting and Fermann 1997). Finally, the declaration called for the elaboration of a framework treaty on climate change in time for adoption by the 1992 UN Conference on Environment and Development (UNCED). In December 1990, the UN General Assembly followed up on this and established the Intergovern-mental Negotiating Committee (INC) for a Framework Convention on Climate Change with the aim of negotiating a convention for signature at the UNCED in Rio de Janeiro in June 1992 (UNGA 1990). Yet, while climate change was getting onto the political agenda, the scientific case was not universally accepted and countries were firmly divided on how to best deal with it.

The Intergovernmental Negotiating Committee

Negotiations leading up to what would become the UNFCCC took place in five meetings, focusing primarily on the issues of targets and timetables, as well as of transfer of finance and technology to developing countries:

- INC-1: Chantilly, Virginia (4–14 February 1991)
- INC-2: Geneva (19–28 June 1991)
- INC-3: Nairobi, Kenya (9–20 September 1991)
- INC-4: Geneva (9–20 December 1991)
- INC-5: New York (18–28 February and 30 April to 8 May 1992)

Targets and timetables

INC-1 in Chantilly was dedicated to the organization of the negotiations, with two working groups set up, one on substance and the other on legal and institutional matters. EC Member States were quite active during INC-1, arguing in favour of coming up with a draft text as soon as possible. The UK, France, Germany, and the Netherlands followed this up with draft recommendations and principles for the elements of a climate change convention (INC 1991). In particular, some EC Member States, such as the Netherlands, recommended adopting protocols on *inter alia* greenhouse gas emissions, carbon sinks, forestry and adaptation (INC 1991; Hampson and Hart 1995). In their submissions these Member States highlighted the responsibility of developed countries in taking the lead in reducing greenhouse emissions, while also acknowledging the need for developing country access to financial assistance and environmentally sound technologies. Various short-term and long-term targets were tabled, such as stabilization of emissions by 2000 or reduction by 50 per cent by 2030. Member States also held divergent positions as to the greenhouse gases that should be the focus of the regime. While France was calling for special attention to be given to CO_2, Germany argued in favour of including *inter alia* methane and N_2O.

INC-2 in Geneva primarily deliberated on Japan's controversial 'pledge & review' proposal, which involved countries unilaterally pledging targets and concrete measures whose implementation would then be reviewed by international investigative teams (Andresen 2015; Miyaoka 2004). Viewed by Japan as the only possible way of keeping the US in the negotiations, this proposal gained some support from EC members, as both the UK and France circulated 'pledge & review' proposals. In addition, the EC proposed that the stabilization target could potentially be embodied in the agreement as an example of a pledge to which a country could subscribe (Dasgupta 1994). However, objections from other parties, such as the G-77, coupled with environmental NGO criticism (which called the proposal 'hedge & retreat'), caused Japan to drop the idea of unilateral pledges at INC-3 (Dasgupta 1994, p. 65). Keeping the US on board was perceived as imperative by most other countries, given the former's share of global emissions. During the course of the negotiations, however, the US took up clear-cut positions and was not afraid to be isolated (Borione and Ripert 1994; Sands 1992). The US remained in favour of national strategies and programmes, dismissing internationally binding targets and timetables on the grounds of scientific uncertainty and economic cost.

Most developed countries, followed by the great majority of their developing country counterparts, were of the opinion that the scientific basis was robust enough to point towards the direction of adopting a strict quantified target to be included within the convention (Brown 1996). The EC, in particular, in a conscious attempt to claim leadership status, was in the forefront of international pressures to the US to sign up to CO_2 emission targets. The first two INC meetings proved unable to break the deadlock. The US refused to budge and even threatened not to attend the Rio Conference in case the proposed convention bound its signatories to specific obligations (Brown 1996).

Progress during INC-3 (Nairobi) and INC-4 (Geneva) was similarly stalled. A number of issues remained open, including whether the base year would be 1990 or some other formulation that would allow for a three-year average; whether the commitment to a target should be expressed as a national effort or a collective one (the preference of the EC); and whether the agreement should cover CO_2 alone (as the EC preferred on the grounds of a lack of science) or focus on other greenhouse gases as well under a comprehensive approach (Hampson and Hart 1995). Regarding the latter topic, the EC position was that measuring industrial emissions of CO_2 was easier, plus that by focusing on only one gas would allow for targeted action (Gupta 2014). The US argued that a comprehensive approach provided greater flexibility, as emission reductions could be traded among gases, allowing therefore trade-offs of reductions in one gas for increases in others (Morrissette and Plantinga 1991). The US proposal, however, included chlorofluorocarbons (CFCs), which the US was already phasing out under the Montreal Protocol, thereby giving it a huge leeway in that it allowed for US CO_2 emissions to actually increase by 15 per cent by the year 2000 (Paterson 1996). Other countries, though, strongly contested the validity of 'double-counting' credit for reductions that were already being achieved in compliance to other international agreements (Grubb 1993, p. 65).

The heavily bracketed negotiating text that was forwarded to INC-5 (February 1992) caused further stalemate, leading to the decision to hold a resumed session in May. With time running out, efforts concentrated on producing a compromise text that would convince the US to get on board. The UK Secretary of State for the Environment, Michael Howard, is credited with securing that outcome. In late April 1992, he travelled to Washington and worked out a compromise, that provided the foundation for the subsequently-adopted framework convention (Andresen and Agrawala 2002). Since the US administration was opposed to binding emissions targets, a 'voluntary aim' was included in the treaty to return Annex I emissions to 1990 levels by 2000 (Jacoby and Reiner 2001). This compromise now appears more or less unchanged in the cornerstone Article 4.2 of the Framework Convention, where parties are urged to *limit* their emissions, and if possible *try* to stabilize them to 1990 levels by 2000 (UNFCCC 1992).

Financial assistance and technology transfer

Financial assistance and technology transfer offered to developing countries also divided countries. On the one hand, developed countries could not agree over whether 'new and additional' resources should be made available to developing countries, that is, resources over and above the already promulgated 0.7 per cent Official Development Assistance (ODA) target (Gupta 2014).[3] On the other hand, developed countries were also split on whether they should pay the 'full' cost or 'agreed incremental' cost of developing world projects aimed at reducing greenhouse gas emissions (Brown 2002, p. 22). For example, if a developing country proposed installing a power plant that used greenhouse-friendly technologies, should developed countries pay for the full cost of this power plant or just the difference with a conventional one (see Gupta 1995)? The EC and Scandinavian countries, unwilling to commit large funds, generally acknowledged the need to provide developing countries with additional funds, but argued that only 'agreed' rather than 'full' incremental costs should be paid for (Paterson 1992a). The US, Canada and Japan, while sharing the view that only 'agreed' costs should be paid for, were unwilling to discuss 'new and additional' funding to developing countries and argued instead that the international community should aim to make better use of existing multilateral and bilateral funding (Bodansky 1994). The US even called for developing country contributions, depending on the means at their disposal and their capabilities (Schunz 2014). The final compromise fell rather short of what developing countries had pushed for, as under Article 4.3 of the Convention developed countries pledged to provide 'new and additional financial recourses to meet the full costs incurred by developing countries', but only in compiling national inventories of the sources and sinks of greenhouse gases, plus in fulfilling other reporting requirements under Article 12.1 (Nitze 1994). The funds required for developing country compliance with such reporting modalities were relatively minimal, representing only a fraction of the costs that would be incurred by developing countries in implementing the UNFCCC. As to the latter costs, developed nations did not provide additional financial resources and only accepted to cover 'agreed incremental' costs (Pulvenis 1994).

Developed countries, however, did agree to fund the *agreed* full incremental costs of specific projects that were approved by the Global Environmental Facility (GEF), the Convention's financial mechanism. The US was willing to accept this formulation, since it could implement this obligation through its periodic contributions to the GEF (Nash 1993). Developing countries though strongly opposed the GEF serving as the financial mechanism for administering North–South transfers. As a World Bank unit, the GEF's weighted vote structure meant that final decisions about which projects would receive funding rested primarily with major developed countries (Hurrell 1992). Developing countries thus argued that the Bank should provide only development assistance, while a different body should be set up for environmental aspects (Gupta 1995). Developed countries, however, were against the proliferation of multilateral financial instruments and as a result a compromise was eventually reached in the resumed INC-5 according to which the GEF would administer climate transfers on an interim basis (Paterson 1992b). Closing with technology transfer, the Convention does promote it, but developed countries remained unified until the end in their rejection of developing country access demands on preferential, non-commercial terms, as it was deemed incompatible with intellectual property rights protection (Dasgupta 1994).

The Rio Convention

The final Rio Declaration was not as far reaching as most nations would have wanted. The EC and other countries who favoured binding emissions cuts had to concede ground in order to get the US on board, which has been interpreted as the Convention being a victory for the main laggard, that is, the US (Andresen and Agrawala 2002; Nitze 1994). Several European governments, as well as the EC's Environment Commissioner, made little effort to hide their dissatisfaction with the outcome and openly blamed the US (Hampson and Hart 1995). While Article 2 of the Convention contains a strong objective, namely 'stabilization of greenhouse gas concentrations in the atmosphere at a level that would prevent dangerous anthropogenic interference with the climate system', Article 4.2 includes no enforceable targets and timetables for greenhouse gases (Rowlands 1995). Yet, as Paterson (1996) notes, closer observation indicates that the US had moved substantially since INC-1 in February 1991, when it had been opposed to both quantitative targets and timetables, as both were finally included in the agreement (although rather obliquely). In addition, the US had quickly dropped its insistence on including CFCs, eventually accepting the formulation CO_2 'and other greenhouse gases not controlled by the Montreal Protocol' (Paterson 1996, p. 62).

Regarding EC participation in the international negotiations of this period (see also Chapter 2), it should be noted that it swiftly addressed the issue of climate change, overcoming internal divergences to reach a common position on targets and timetables as early as 1990 (Schunz 2014). Gupta (2014) posits that the adoption of mitigation targets by the EC and its members in 1990 actually played a pivotal role in promoting the adoption of the UNFCCC. While it proved unable to convince the US of the political feasibility of committing itself to a binding stabilization target, Haigh (1996, p. 162) argues that the UNFCCC 'would certainly have been much weaker' had it not been for the EC's prior position. It would therefore be fair to say that both the EC and the US had a critical influence on the final outcome, potentially of 'comparable magnitude' (Schunz 2014, p. 62).

As for the actual Climate Convention, very little needs to be said, given that the text had already been finalized in advance. Rio was simply all about 'the fanfare of signing it' (Paterson 1996, p. 64). The UNFCCC was adopted on 9 May 1992 in New York, and opened for signature a month later at the UNCED in Rio de Janeiro, Brazil, where it received 155 signatures; the most significant absentees being Saudi Arabia, Iran and Malaysia. It entered into force on 21 March 1994, after receiving the requisite 50 ratifications, and while it was deemed encouraging by many that it took the international community only 15 months to negotiate and finalize such a complex agreement, others were of the opinion that the pressure of the 1992 deadline had only resulted in parties hurriedly agreeing to a weak and ineffective treaty (Starkey *et al.* 1999). Whatever the case, the fact remains that parties initiated talks of whether Articles 4.2 (a) and (b) of the UNFCCC were adequate to meeting the Convention's objectives even before the UNFCCC's entry into force.

Notes

1 Note here that both Arrhenius and Callendar believed that a warmer climate would actually be beneficial to humankind (see Darwall 2013). Arrhenius believed that the colder regions of the planet in particular would enjoy better and more equable climate, thus bringing forth more abundant crops for the benefit of a 'rapidly propagating mankind' (Arrhenius 1908, p. 63). On his part, Callendar, while sharing Arrhenius's views and optimism with respect to the warming climate's impact on agricultural production, noted that it could also protect Earth against 'the return of the deadly glaciers [of the ice ages]' (see Brown 1996, p. 21).
2 The Union of Soviet Socialist Republics.
3 In 1970, it was agreed at the UN that developed countries would provide 0.7 per cent of their national income as international aid to developing nations.

References

Agrawala, Shardul (1998). Context and early origins of the Intergovernmental Panel on Climate Change. *Climatic Change* 39 (4): 605–620.

Andersson, Magnus and Arthur P.J. Mol (2002). The Netherlands in the UNFCCC process – leadership between ambition and reality. *International Environmental Agreements: Politics, Law and Economics* 2 (1): 49–68.

Andresen, Steinar (2015). International climate negotiations: top–down, bottom–up or a combination of both? *International Spectator: Italian Journal of International Affairs* 50 (1): 15–30.

Andresen, Steinar and Shardul Agrawala (2002). Leaders, pushers and laggards in the making of the climate regime. *Global Environmental Change* 12 (1): 41–51.

Andresen, Steinar and Jørgen Wettestad (1990). Climate failure at the Bergen Conference? *International Challenges* 10 (2): 17–23.

Arrhenius, Svante (1896). On the influence of carbonic acid in the air on the temperature of the ground. *Philosophical Magazine* 41 (251): 236–76.

Arrhenius, Svante (1908). *Worlds in the making: the evaluation of the universe*. New York: Harper.

Bodansky, Daniel (1993). The United Nations Framework Convention on Climate Change: a commentary. *Yale Journal of International Law* 18 (2): 451–558.

Bodansky, Daniel (1994). Prologue to the Climate Change Convention. In Mintzer, Irving M. and Amber J. Leonard (eds) *Negotiating climate change: the inside story of the Rio Convention*. Cambridge: Cambridge University Press, 45–75.

Bodansky, Daniel (2001). The history of climate change science and politics. In Luterbacher, Urs and Sprinz F. Detlef (eds) *International relations and global climate change*. Cambridge, MA: MIT Press, 23–39.

Boehmer-Christiansen, Sonja (1995). Britain and the International Panel on Climate Change: the impacts of scientific advice on global warming part 1: integrated policy analysis and the global dimension. *Environmental Politics* 4 (1): 1–18.

Borione, Delphine and Jean Ripert (1994). Exercising common but differentiated responsibility. In Mintzer, Irving M. and Amber J. Leonard (eds) *Negotiating climate change: the inside story of the Rio Convention*. Cambridge: Cambridge University Press, 77–96.

Børsting, Georg and Gunnar Fermann (1997). Climate change turning political: conference-diplomacy and institution-building to Rio and beyond. In Fermann, Gunnar (ed.) *International politics of climate change: key issues and critical actors*. Oslo: Scandinavian University Press, 53–82.

Brown, Donald A. (2002). *American heat: ethical problems with the United States' response to global warming*. Lanham: Rowman & Littlefield.

Brown, Paul (1996). *Global warming: can civilization survive?* London: Blandford Press.

Darwall, Rupert (2013). *The age of global warming: a history*. London: Quartet.

Dasgupta, Chandrashekhar (1994). The climate change negotiations. In Mintzer, Irving M. and Amber J. Leonard (eds) *Negotiating climate change: the inside story of the Rio Convention*. Cambridge: Cambridge University Press, 129–48.

Edwards, Paul N. (2011). History of climate modeling. *WIREs Climate Change* 2: 128–39.

Grubb, Michael (1993). United Nations Framework Convention on Climate Change. In Grubb, Michael, Francis Sullivan and Kay Thompson (eds) *The Earth Summit agreements: a guide and assessment*. London: Earthscan, 61–73.

Gupta, Joyeeta (1995). The global environment facility in its North–South context. *Environmental Politics* 4 (1): 19–43.

Gupta, Joyeeta (2014). *The history of global climate governance*. Cambridge: Cambridge University Press.

Haigh, Nigel (1996). Climate change policies and politics in the European Community. In O'Riordan, Timothy and Jill Jäger (eds) *Politics of climate change: a European perspective*. London: Routledge, 155–85.

Hampson, Fen Osler and Michael Hart (1995). *Multilateral negotiations: lessons from arms controls, trade, and the environment*. Baltimore: Johns Hopkins University Press.

Hatch, Michael T. (1993). Domestic politics and international negotiations: the politics of global warming in the United States. *Journal of Environment and Development* 2 (2): 1–39.

Hulme, Mike and Martin Mahony (2010). Climate change: what do we know about the IPCC? *Progress in Physical Geography* 34 (5): 705–18.

Hurrell, Andrew (1992). The 1992 Earth Summit: funding mechanisms and environmental institutions. *Environmental Politics* 1 (4): 273–9.

INC (1991). Set of informal papers provided by delegations, related to the preparation of a framework convention on climate change. A/AC.237/Misc.1/Add.1.

Jacoby, Henry D. and David M. Reiner (2001). Getting climate policy on track after The Hague. *International Affairs* 77 (2): 297–312.

Jordan, Andrew and Tim Rayner (2010). The evolution of climate policy in the European Union: a historical perspective. In Jordan, Andrew, Dave Huitema, Harro Van Asselt, Tim Rayner and Frans Berkhout (eds) *Climate change policy in the European Union: confronting the dilemmas of mitigation and adaptation?* Cambridge: Cambridge University Press, 52–80.

Kirgis, Frederick L. (1990). Standing to challenge human endeavors that could change the climate. *American Journal of International Law* 84 (2): 525–30.

Liberatore, Angela (1995). Arguments, assumptions, and the choice of policy instruments: the case of the debate on the CO_2/energy tax in the European Community. In Dente, Bruno (ed.) *Environmental policy in search of new instruments*. Dordrecht: Kluwer, 55–72.

Maslin, Mark (2004). *Global warming: a very short introduction*. Oxford: Oxford University Press.

Miyaoka, Isao (2004). Japan's conciliation with the United States in climate change negotiations. *International Relations of the Asia-Pacific* 4 (1): 73–96.

Morrissette, Peter M. and Andrew J. Plantinga (1991). Global warming: a policy review. *Policy Studies Journal* 19 (2): 163–72.

Nash (Leich), Marian (1993). Contemporary practice of the United States relating to international law. *American Journal of International Law* 87 (1): 103–11.

Newell, Peter (2000). *Climate for change: non-state actors and the global politics of the greenhouse*. Cambridge: Cambridge University Press.

Nitze, William A (1994). A failure of presidential leadership. In Mintzer, Irving M. and Amber J. Leonard (eds) *Negotiating climate change: the inside story of the Rio Convention*. Cambridge: Cambridge University Press, 187–200.

Pallemaerts, Marc and Rhiannon Williams (2006). Climate change: the international and European policy framework. In Peeters, Marjan and Kurt Deketelaere (eds) *EU climate change policy: the challenge of new regulatory initiatives*. Cheltenham: Edward Elgar, 22–50.

Paterson, Matthew (1992a). Global warming. In Caroline, Thomas (ed.) *The environment in international relations*. London: Royal Institute of International Affairs, 155–98.

Paterson, Matthew (1992b). The Convention on Climate Change Agreed at the Rio Conference. *Environmental Politics* 1 (4): 267–73.

Paterson, Matthew (1996). *Global warming and global politics*. London: Routledge.

Pulvenis, Jean-François (1994). The Framework Convention on Climate Change. In Campiglio, Luigi, Laura Pineschi, Domenico Siniscalco and Tullio Treves (eds) *The environment after Rio: international law and economics*. London: Graham and Trotman, 71–110.

Rowlands, Ian H. (1995). *The politics of global atmospheric change*. Manchester: Manchester University Press.

Sands, Philippe (1992). The United Nations Framework Convention on Climate Change. *Review of European Community & International Environmental Law* 1 (3): 270–77.

Schneider, Stephen H. (1990). *Global warming: are we entering the greenhouse century?* San Francisco: Sierra Club Books.

Schunz, Simon (2014). *European Union foreign policy and the global climate regime*. Brussels: P.I.E. Peter Lang.

Starkey, Brigid, Mark A. Boyer and Jonathan Wilkenfeld (1999). *Negotiating a complex world: an introduction to international negotiation*. Lanham: Rowman & Littlefield.

UNFCCC (1992). *Framework Convention on Climate Change*. New York: United Nations.

UNGA (United Nations General Assembly) (1989). Protection of global climate for present and future generations of mankind. Resolution 44/207, 22 December.

UNGA (United Nations General Assembly) (1990). Protection of global climate for present and future generations. Resolution 45/212, 21 December.

Usher, Peter (1989). World Conference on the Changing Atmosphere: implications for global security. *Environment* 31 (1): 25–7.

2 The development of Europe's climate policy (1986–92)

It is often stated that prior to 1973 there was no such thing as an EC environmental policy. For Hildebrand (1992), this assessment is, essentially, correct. Little attention was paid worldwide during the 1950s and 1960s to the wider implications of economic development on the environment. Indeed, the Treaty of Rome did not expressly permit the EC to act in the area of environmental protection, as the main priority for European nations was the harmonization of laws to do away with internal trade barriers (Jordan 1998). Until 1973, EC environmental policy 'was incidental to measures to harmonise laws in order to abolish obstacles to trade between the Member States' (McGrory 1990, p. 304).[1]

The period that followed the 1972 Stockholm Declaration gave rise to the development of a true EC environmental programme. For the first time, the environment was brought onto the political stage. While EC leaders realized the importance of environmental protection, they were also keen to avoid anything that would negatively affect their competitiveness, economically speaking. EC actors were well aware that significant differences in national industrial pollution legislation between the Member States could distort competition and allow laggard or 'dirty states' to profit economically (Lodge 1989, p. 320). With West Germany and the Netherlands at the helm, EC environmental protection gained significantly from the Commission's three Programmes of Environmental Action during 1973–86. The legal ground for environmental expansion, however, was relatively weak. It was not an expressed competence of the EEC Treaty. This allowed various 'laggard' Member States, such as the UK, to obstruct EC common environmental policy. As a result, the legislative process for environmental proposals was turned 'into a very undemocratic operation as a kind of bargaining between Member States' governments and Community bureaucracies' (McGrory 1990, p. 305).

A legal basis for EC action on the environment was only provided when the Single European Act (SEA) was passed in 1987. Apart from seeking to augment the EC's competitiveness and attractiveness to third parties through the creation of a single internal market and trading bloc, SEA also gave the Community competences in fields such as the environment, technological research and development, employment and regional policy (McCormick and Olsen 2014; Pinder 2001). In the realm of environmental policy in particular, the effect of the SEA can be said to have been revolutionary. It put economic and ecological objectives within the EC on a more equal footing. The introduction of qualified majority voting (QMV) for most matters of environmental policy was pivotal in this respect. The only exceptions included provisions of a primarily fiscal nature, policies with limited transnational effects, such as town and country planning, as well as measures that 'affect[ed] a Member State's choice between different energy sources and the general structure of its energy supply' (Hildebrand 1992, p. 37).

Because of SEA, environmental policy undoubtedly gained momentum. It allowed the EC to play a more assertive role in international environmental affairs. Initially, however, the EC, because of intra-European divisions, failed to take a proactive role during the 1987 multilateral negotiations on ozone protection in Montreal. A more progressive EC stance was hindered by the protectionist approach adopted by the French and British governments with respect to their chemical industries (Oberthür and Ott 1999). Lagging behind other parties (mainly the US) in the ozone regime-building process, the EC was now underperforming in yet another field – foreign policy. Germany's unilateral diplomatic recognition of Croatia and Slovenia in direct contravention to the preferences of its fellow EC partners, as well as Member State divisions with respect to the US-led response to Iraq's invasion of Kuwait, brought to the fore the EC's inability to adopt a common line on issues of foreign and security policy (McCormick and Olsen 2014; Bretherton and Vogler 2006; Juncos 2005; Crawford 1996).

The aforementioned setbacks led to widespread scepticism in EC circles. European policymakers therefore sought remedial action to reverse this unpleasant situation. A first step was to take a leadership role at the London revision of the Montreal Protocol in 1990, where the EC supported faster reduction schedules with respect to CFCs and halons than the US and Japan (Oberthür and Ott 1999). At the 1992 Copenhagen meeting, the Community went a step further by supporting expedited action with respect to a number of other ozone depleting substances (ODS), such as methyl bromide, hydrobromofluorocarbons (HBFCs) and hydrochlorofluorocarbons (HCFCs). It was climate change, however, a relatively nascent policy area at the time, which was seen as representing a very suitable candidate for EC leadership. With the US being outright against and Japan not particularly enthusiastic about climate policy, the EU sensed a chance to grab a leadership role (Hovi *et al.* 2003; Bergesen 1991). The EC position was thus not only a reflection of concern for an environmental problem, but also a strategic decision to assert itself as a major player in global governance matters (Andresen and Agrawala 2002). The EC's ability to think strategically was reflected in the conclusions of the June 1990 Dublin European Council:

> The Community and its Member States have a special responsibility to encourage and participate in international action to combat global environmental problems. Their capacity to provide leadership in this field is enormous.
>
> (European Council 1990, p. 22)

First phase (1986–90)

In July 1986, the European Parliament became the first EC institution to address climate change as both a policy and scientific topic (Liberatore 1995). Drawing upon the conclusions of the 1985 Villach Conference, the Parliament recognized climate change as a multifaceted problem, with impacts that could take less direct and more multifarious routes. It called on the Commission and the Member States to integrate mitigation measures into agricultural, forestry, energy and industrial policies. Reference was even made to the need for developed countries – as the main culprits for climate change – to give developing nations 'access to the latest technological know-how' (OJ 1986, p. 273). Despite the call for action, the Commission's 1987 Fourth Action Programme on the Environment simply mentioned the fears of 'certain scientists' as to the impacts of climate change and called for further scientific studies in this context (OJ 1987, p. 12).

The Commission only issued its first communication on the subject in November 1988, mainly as a response to that year's Toronto Conference. That communication summarized greenhouse gas-related scientific developments and the outcome of international scientific conferences, such as the one in Toronto. It also outlined a number of possible response options for the energy, forestry and agricultural sectors, ranging from energy efficiency interventions to the promotion of afforestation. Importantly, the communication concluded that reducing greenhouse gas concentrations did not 'seem at that stage a realistic objective, but could be a very long term goal' (European Commission 1988, p. 44; see also Liberatore 1995; Skjaerseth 1994). Even so, Jordan and Rayner (2010) argue that this communication was notable in at least two respects. First, it marked the formal initiation of EU climate policy, as the Commission autonomously decided to launch a study programme to evaluate the feasibility, costs and impacts of possible mitigation measures. Second, it highlighted that the Commission expected to be involved in internal and external negotiations on climate change in the foreseeable future, especially after having 'fought hard' to secure a role in other multilateral environmental fora such as the one on ozone depletion (Jordan and Rayner 2010, p. 55). In its response, the Council agreed to the Commission's request to be involved at both levels, but only in a role supportive of national policymaking, as stipulated by the informal norm of subsidiarity (Jordan and Rayner 2010).

This 'wait-and-see' approach favoured by Member States shows that climate change was not seen as a priority. The 1988 Rhodes European Council helps to confirm this observation. It concluded that effective action on climate change 'require[d] better scientific research and understanding' (European Council 1988, p. 11; see also Caldwell 1990). Less than two years later, the situation was completely reversed. In June 1989 – a few months after the 1989 Hague Summit – the European Council endorsed an international agreement on climate change and requested the Commission to produce a report outlining potential mitigation measures (OJ 1989). The subsequent Noordwijk conference further pinpointed the need for international action and prompted the EC to take an even more active role, pressing other nations to set firm targets and timetables for stabilizing their greenhouse gas emissions. In March 1990, the Commission – now completely at odds to its November 1988 position – stressed 'the urgent need for a clear commitment by industrial countries to stabilize CO_2 emissions' by the year 2000, as well as achieve 'significant reductions' by 2010 (European Commission 1990, pp. 3–4). Compared with the 1988 Communication, the Community 'had taken the step from a rather vague "problem diagnosis" to specific policy recommendations within less than two years' (Skjaerseth 1994, p. 27).

By that point, the Commission's stabilization proposal was in line with evolving Member State preferences, given that following the May 1990 Bergen conference several of them had commenced with tabling CO_2 stabilization and reduction commitments. In an effort to provide leadership, the June 1990 Dublin European Council urged all countries to immediately adopt targets and strategies to limit their greenhouse gas emissions (European Council 1990). In October 1990, on the cusp of the SWCC, and primarily in order to establish an ambitious Community position for that occasion, a Joint Council of Energy and Environment ministers agreed that CO_2 emissions should be stabilized at 1990 levels within the EC *as a whole* by the year 2000, on the proviso though that other countries made similar commitments (Oberthür and Pallemaerts 2010; Wettestad 2001).

Even so, the political commitment to stabilize CO_2 emissions elevated the status of the Community. As explained in Chapter 1, the 'rich and green' EC countries (Denmark, the Netherlands and Germany) had already adopted more ambitious targets, with Germany, the most committed of the three, seeking to reduce its emissions by 25–30 per cent by 2005. Notably, the shift in position by the UK played a major role in facilitating consensus within the EC. Due primarily to pressure from other EC members, the UK's Prime Minister Margaret Thatcher abandoned the obstructionist tactics of 1989 and declared in May 1990 that the UK would stabilize its emissions at 1990 levels by 2005. Apparently unsatisfied, other EC members continued to criticize the UK – this time for not reducing its emissions quickly enough. Yet, this UK shift enabled the Council to constructively discuss climate change during 1990 and progressively build up its image as the main pusher and leader during the nascent phase of the climate regime (Manners 2000). In order for the EC to maintain its leadership role, it was necessary 'to have some policy flesh to put on the bones of the political decision to stabilise CO_2 emissions' (Haigh 1996, p. 164). The EC needed to be able to clearly demonstrate how it would achieve its stabilization goal. Moving from target-setting to implementation (policies and measures) threw up new challenges for EC policymakers.

Second phase (1991–92)

In October 1990, the Council requested anew the Commission to propose new policies to meet the stabilization goal. The deadline became the UNCED in

Rio, June 1992. Up to that point, policy within the EU had developed 'remarkably rapidly and smoothly' (Skjaerseth 1994, p. 27). The main explanation, according to Jordan and Rayner (2010), was that most Member States were under the impression that harmonization of targets did not necessarily imply harmonization of policies and measures.

Initially, the Commission was overly optimistic about the EU's mitigation potential. A November 1990 draft communication to the Council noted that emissions could be reduced by as much as 15 per cent in a relatively cost-effective fashion (Skjaerseth 1994). Following this, a plethora of draft communications circulated between the Commission's DGs from December 1990 to May 1991, with the Commission appearing to be reaching agreement on the idea of following the acid rain example and allocating different national reduction targets and developing a target-sharing agreement (Manners 2000). This proposal, although, in principle acceptable within the Commission, was rejected by France, Italy and the UK as unfeasible (Wettestad 2000). Other avenues were subsequently explored, and by August 1991, reports indicated that the Community's target could be achieved by energy-saving policies and energy taxes at a relatively low economic cost (Manners 2000). These measures included *inter alia* a carbon tax, various efficiency standards (buildings, water heaters and cookers) and promotion of waste recycling (Collier 1997b).

In late 1991, and with the UNCED deadline looming, the Commission tabled a package of implementation measures, consisting of: (1) a carbon/energy tax; (2) a monitoring mechanism of Community CO_2 and other greenhouse emissions; and (3) measures to improve energy-efficiency and strengthen the development of renewable energy sources, such as the SAVE (on energy efficiency), ALTERNER (on renewable energy), JOULIE (on energy research and development) and THERMIE (on new energy technologies) programmes (Grubb 1995). In the absence of the aforementioned measures, CO_2 emissions were predicted to increase by 12 per cent by 2000 (Grubb 1992). The contribution of each measure to the attainment of the stabilization goal is summarized in Table 2.1.

The proposal for carbon/energy taxes was new and, because of the unanimity-voting rule for fiscal environmental policies, it was clear that it would be contentious (Wettestad 2000). The tax would be implemented in 1993 at a level of

Table 2.1 Projected emission reductions from the EC climate change strategy

Proposed measures for stabilization	Expected CO_2 reduction (%)
Carbon/energy tax	6.5
SAVE	3.0
THERMIE	1.5
ALTENER	1.0
Total	12.0

Source: Collier (1997b, p. 52).

$3 per barrel of oil equivalent and projected to increase to $10 by 2000 (Jaeger *et al.* 1997). From the outset the proposed tax faced opposition from industry, within the Commission and among the Member States. In fact, the Commission had only been able to present its package proposal in October 1991 after the six most involved DGs had agreed on a compromise according to which 'any measures agreed on must be justifiable on grounds other than those based on CO_2 emissions control (e.g. improving energy security), a principle which was termed a "no regrets" strategy' (Manners 2000, p. 44). The Environment Council (12–13 October 1991) accepted 'in principle' the Commission's plan, but the Energy Council (18 October) voiced its opposition to the EU unilaterally adopting an energy tax that would in essence allow its major trading partners (the US and Japan) to gain a competitive advantage. The Commission, in an effort to accommodate the Energy Council's concerns, altered its proposal by inserting substantial exceptions for energy-intensive industries (Manners 2000). Yet, while these adjustments secured the endorsement of the Commission's package by a joint December 1991 Environment and Energy Council, the downside was that the combined effects of the measures were now no longer adequate to stabilize the EC's emissions (Paterson 1996).

Unlike the Energy Council, business interests would prove far more difficult to convince. Indeed, the Commission's proposal found itself subject to the 'most ferocious lobbying ever seen in Brussels' (Hovi *et al.* 2003, p. 9). Carlo Ripa di Meana, then EC Environment Commissioner, described the lobbying as a 'violent assault' and an 'indication of the vigour with which the energy interests pursued their demands' (Newell and Paterson 1998, p. 685). Business interests pushed for the proposal to be withdrawn. They even threatened to move industrial production out of the EC in the event plans for the tax were pushed forward (Collier 1997b). Industry resistance was organized through one of Europe's most powerful business lobby organizations of that period, the Union of Industrial and Employers' Confederations of Europe (UNICE), which dismissed the taxation as running completely counter to the need for concerted international action (Skjaerseth 1994).

By January 1992, it had become apparent that the energy tax would not be a 'no regrets' option (Manners 2000). Consequently, the aforementioned compromise between the six most involved DGs unravelled, as the competiveness concerns of the business sector were now shared by a number of sympathetic DGs, such as DG II for economic analysis, DG III for the Internal Market, and DG XXI for taxation. With respect to energy, these DGs were particularly worried about the competitive advantages the proposed tax implied for US industry, which already enjoyed significantly lower energy taxes and prices.

Unable to withstand the pressure, the forces in favour of the tax (DG XI for environment and DG XVII for energy) yielded. Renewed agreement within the Commission was only secured by making the proposal conditional on comparable action by other OECD[2] countries, as UNICE had also demanded (Haigh 1996). According to Skjaerseth (1994, p. 31), this was a 'clear farewell to the aspiration to leadership by example'. Di Meana, even though firmly opposed to the conditionality principle, decided to accept it in the apparent hope that it represented a temporary hurdle that would be removed before the Rio Summit (Manners 2000). It is worth noting that this conditionality principle was first introduced as it was expected that the US might opt for a harmonized multi-lateral approach and introduce an energy tax at a level that could be said to be comparable (Haigh 1996). Hopes for international coordination never material-ized, though. The proposed legislation for an energy tax on all fuels presented by President Clinton was defeated in Congress in 1993.

The conditionality principle accommodated to a great extent the concerns of the proposal's opponents in industry and within the Commission. Member States, however, failed to bridge their differences, as France, the less developed Member States (Spain, Portugal, Ireland and Greece) and the UK all opposed the tax. France, in particular, relying at the time on nuclear energy for 73 per cent of its electricity (compared with 22.3 per cent in the US, 27.7 per cent in Japan and 33 per cent in Europe as a whole; see Hammond (1996)), opposed the tax for the following reason:

> The proposed tax was to be shared equally between carbon content and energy content on the grounds that a pure carbon tax would have favoured nuclear energy. For this reason alone the joint carbon energy tax was always opposed by France, which favoured a straight carbon tax.
>
> (Haigh 1996, p. 165)

The less developed Member States, for their part, perceived the tax as a threat to their economic progress and argued that it was imperative for their economic growth to increase their emissions so as to catch up with the rest of Europe. Only in the case of additional structural funding were they prepared to accept the tax proposal (Lacasta *et al.* 2002; Ikwue and Skea 1994). Finally, the UK was opposed to the use of fiscal mechanisms at EC level as a matter of principle, invoking the subsidiary principle and also arguing that it could meet its own stabilization target without the need for taxation interventions (Collier 1997a; Haigh 1996). Given the aforementioned requirement for fiscal matters to be decided by unanimity, it felt improbable that the tax proposal would be promul-gated at all, let alone in time for UNCED (Wettestad 2001). In the course of events, and despite several attempts by the Danish, Belgian and German Presid-encies to promote CO_2 taxation, the tax proposal was all but abandoned at the Essen summit of December 1994 (Huber 1997). The UK in particular proved instrumental in ensuring its demise.[3] The summit's final conclusions simply allowed Member States to apply a carbon/energy tax if they so desired (Lacasta *et al.* 2002).

Impact of EU disunity

The internal controversy over the tax proposal dominated the climate policy debate within the EC and effectively prevented it from adopting a more ambitious and proactive stance during the Rio Summit. So intense were the intra-EC disputes in the run-up to Rio that Ripa di Meana, then Environment Commissioner, threatened to boycott it if the Council failed to approve the tax proposal and thus adopt a solid implementation strategy for meeting the EC stabilization target (Zito 2000). The Commissioner did follow through on his threat by declining to attend the June 1992 Rio Summit, resigning from his position soon afterwards (Hovi *et al.* 2003). The inability to adopt the tax proposal meant in practical terms that the EC arrived in Rio without a unified position. Its climate policy consisted simply of a Council-approved political goal of stabilizing CO_2 emissions by the year 2000 at 1990 levels, but an agreement on how to implement this target was sorely lacking. This resulted in finding itself on the defence when insisting on the need for the Convention to include a firm commitment on stabilizing CO_2 emissions. The US seized on the opportunity to dismiss the EC's stabilization target as 'nonsensical', given it was not underpinned by a coherent implementation strategy (Jordan and Rayner 2010, p. 58).

The tax proposal represented a critical test of the EC's resolve to stand forth as a global climate leader. As Underdal (1998, p. 105) notes, by failing to 'adopt strict standards for itself, a government may undermine its credibility as a champion of strict international rules'. By failing to adopt concrete climate mitigation policy instruments, the EC gave political ammunition to its opponents and made itself less than credible in its leadership aspirations. Consequently, this led to uncertainty and mistrust among other parties as to whether the EU was genuinely in a position to bind itself to specific climate policies that displayed commitment and ambition.

Irrespective of its internal divisions, the EC decided to assume a leadership role in the nascent climate regime, which led to the emergence of what Underdal (1998) calls 'process-generated stakes'. As he explains, by entering into negotiations a party enters a game that can have a major impact on its image and reputation. For a leader, therefore, the way in which it is perceived to 'play the game' can be a very important parameter when it comes to international negotiating fora (Underdal 1998, p. 115). Guided by reputational concerns, the EU pushed for a strong Convention that relied on top–down, binding targets and underpinned by scientific evidence.

However, it was proposing what Underdal (1998) points to as a 'politically inadequate solution design model'. This refers to the gap between a scientifically 'appropriate' solution to a problem and a politically 'acceptable' or 'feasible' agreement. As noted in the introductory chapter, for a solution to an environmental problem to qualify as 'good', it needs to meet three main criteria: efficiency, fairness and feasibility. An efficient or 'good' regime is one that is ecologically sound or sustainable. Fairness calls attention to the distribution of costs and benefits, while feasibility refers to political and technical practicability. From the outset, however, the US administration of George H.W. Bush adopted a rather rigid stance, threatening not to attend the Rio Summit and asserting that the 'American lifestyle was not negotiable' (Brown 2002, p. 23).

The EC had thus to confront the US's firm opposition to binding targets, which effectively left it with the following dilemma: push for a strong Convention and take the risk of the US not signing, or strike a compromise which would enable the US to sign while still reflecting the EC's own political commitment (Haigh 1996). A number of Member States were willing to accept a stronger convention without US participation, while others were of the opinion that such a Convention would hardly be worthwhile, since other countries would be given an excuse not to sign. The lack of a unified EC position on the dimensions of a zone of agreement eventually paved the way for the UK Secretary of State for the Environment, Michael Howard, to forge the rather modest agreement with the US that was outlined in Chapter 1. Could this be regarded as an EC contribution to the framing of the Convention? That is a matter of opinion (Haigh 1996). Formally, no Council decisions were taken that gave the UK the mandate to negotiate on targets and timetables, while a number of Member States were not even informed of the UK initiative. Even more, following the conclusion of the agreement the initial reaction of Ripa di Meana and a number of Member States had been to express their disappointment and frustration (Schunz 2014). Yet, Haigh (1996, p. 182) concludes that had it not been 'for the machinery provided by the EC for discussions between ministers' there might not have been a Convention. Schunz (2014, p. 61) argues that given that the UK lacked the clout to unilaterally strike a deal with the US, its actions 'may be regarded – ex post – as a form of implicit task-sharing within the EU'.

Summing up, the EC's announcement of its stabilization target did help move the INC negotiations forward, but its self-declared leadership role was tarnished because of the failure of its Member States to agree on the question of CO_2 taxation. The EC's negotiating performance was not satisfactory either. In formal terms, the Commission was only an observer at the sessions of the INC, meaning it had no voting rights and was not entitled to engage in formal discussions, unless explicitly asked otherwise (Bretherton and Vogler 2006; Bergesen 1991). In this case, the Commission was actually invited to contribute to INC deliberations, but because of its limited competence in the field of climate change it had to rely on the EC presidency as a spokesman for the Community (Bergesen 1991). That said, Commission officials were pivotal in assisting the various Presidencies provide for unity and consistent representation over the course of the negotiations (Schunz 2014). Note at this point that the EC did sign the Rio Convention alongside its Member States, making use of the Regional Economic Integration Organization (REIO) formula. The REIO formulation was invented within the context of the 1979 Long Range Transboundary Air Pollution (LRTAP) Convention as a means of overcoming USSR objections to full EEC participation in the negotiating table. Hoping that a similar status would be accorded to Comecon, the Soviets finally yielded, thus making the EU the first and only (as Soviet hopes never materialized) example so far of an REIO (Vogler 1999). An REIO can be party to a convention without or alongside its Member States, but neither can exercise their voting rights at the same time. In short, the EC and its Member States signed the Convention as a 'mixed agreement', and when ratifying it in 1993 they noted that:

The European Economic Community and its Member States declare that the commitment to limit anthropogenic CO_2 emissions set out in Article 4 (2) of the Convention will be fulfilled in the Community as a whole through action by the Community and its Member States, within the respective competence of each.

(OJ 1993, p. 28)

Because of its political weight, the Community had a significant impact on the international bargaining outcome, but disagreements among its Member States led to problems and inconsistencies. The lack of a unified position allowed the UK to bypass the Community and negotiate a compromise on its own, while the 'rich and green' countries, which had adopted more ambitions emissions reduction targets, played the role of individual pushers (Andresen and Agrawala 2002). An EC official in Rio, commenting on the lack of a coordinated EC policy, noted: 'There is a feeling that it is each country for itself out there' (Sandler 1992, p. 4).

Notes

1 Significant attention was given to product standards because of their potential to develop into a real impediment to the development of a 'common market' for interstate trade. Examples include 'a uniform system of labelling, classification, and packaging for hazardous substances, noise regulation levels, and vehicular exhaust' (McGrory 1990, p. 304).
2 Organisation for Economic Co-operation and Development.
3 Interview No. 1 (Member State official – Former Head of Delegation).

References

Agrawala, Shardul (1998). Context and early origins of the Intergovernmental Panel on Climate Change. *Climatic Change* 39 (4): 605–20.

Andresen, Steinar and Shardul Agrawala (2002). Leaders, pushers and laggards in the making of the climate regime. *Global Environmental Change* 12 (1): 41–51.

Bergesen, Helge Ole (1991). Symbol or substance? The climate policy of the European Community. *International Challenges* 11 (4): 24–9.

Bretherton, Charlotte and John Vogler (2006). *The European Union as a global actor.* London: Routledge.

Brown, Donald A. (2002). *American heat: ethical problems with the United States' response to global warming.* Lanham: Rowman & Littlefield.

Caldwell, Lynton Keith (1990). *International environmental policy: emergence and dimensions.* Durham, NC: Duke University Press.

Collier, Ute (1997a). Sustainability, subsidiarity and deregulation: new directions in EU environmental policy. *Environmental Politics* 6 (2): 1–23.

Collier, Ute (1997b). The EU and climate change policy: the struggle over policy competences. In Collier, Ute and Loefstedt, Ragnar E. (eds) *Cases in climate change policy: political reality in the European Union.* London: Earthscan, 43–64.

Crawford, Beverly (1996). Explaining defection from international cooperation: Germany's unilateral recognition of Croatia. *World Politics* 48 (4): 482–521.

European Commission (1988). 'The greenhouse effect and the Community': Commission work programme concerning the evaluation of policy options to deal with the 'greenhouse effect'. COM(88) 656 final, Brussels, 16 November.

European Commission (1990). Community policy targets on the greenhouse issue. SEC(90) 496 final, Brussels, 15 March.

European Council (1988). Conclusions of the Presidency: European Council, Rhodes, 2 and 3 December 1988. SN 4443/1/88.

European Council (1990). Presidency conclusions – European Council. Doc. SN 60/1/90, Dublin, June.

Grubb, Michael (1992). EC climate policy: where there's a will…. *Energy Policy* 20 (11): 1110–14.

Grubb, Michael (1995). European climate change policy in a global context. In Bergesen, Helge Ole, Georg Parmann and Øystein B. Thommesen (eds) *Green globe yearbook of international co-operation on environment and development*. Oxford: Oxford University Press, 41–50.

Haigh, Nigel (1996). Climate change policies and politics in the European Community. In O'Riordan, Timothy and Jill Jäger (eds) *Politics of climate change: a European perspective*. London: Routledge, 155–85.

Hammond, Geoffrey P. (1996). Nuclear energy in the twenty-first century. *Applied Energy* 54 (4): 327–44.

Hildebrand, Philipp M. (1992). The European Community's environmental policy, 1957 to 1992: from incidental measures to an international regime? *Environmental Politics* 1 (4): 13–44.

Hovi, Jon, Tora Skodvin and Steinar Andersen (2003). The persistence of the Kyoto Protocol: why other Annex I countries move on without the United States. *Global Environmental Politics* 3 (4): 1–23.

Huber, Michael (1997). Leadership in the European climate policy: innovative policy making in policy networks. In Liefferink, Duncan and Mikael Skou Andersen (eds) *The innovation of EU environmental policy*. Oslo: Scandinavian University Press, 133–55.

Ikwue, Tony and Jim Skea (1994). Business and the genesis of the European Community carbon tax proposal. *Business Strategy and the Environment* 3 (2): 1–10.

Jaeger, Carlo C., Terry Barker, Ottmar Edenhofer, Sylvie Faucheux, Jean-Charles Hourcade, Bernd Kasemir, Martin O'Connor, Martin Parry, Irene Peters, Jerry Ravetz and Jan Rotmans (1997). Procedural leadership in climate policy: a European task. *Global Environmental Change* 7 (3): 195–203.

Jordan, Andrew (1998). EU environmental policy at 25: the politics of multinational governance. *Environment* 40 (1): 14–45.

Jordan, Andrew and Tim Rayner (2010). The evolution of climate policy in the European Union: a historical perspective. In Jordan, Andrew, Dave Huitema, Harro Van Asselt, Tim Rayner and Frans Berkhout (eds) *Climate change policy in the European Union: confronting the dilemmas of mitigation and adaptation?* Cambridge: Cambridge University Press, 52–80.

Juncos, Ana E. (2005). The EU's post-conflict intervention in Bosnia and Herzegovina: (re)integrating the Balkans and/or (re)inventing the EU? *Southeast European Politics* 6 (2): 88–108.

Lacasta, Nuno S., Suraje Dessai and Eva Powroslo (2002). Consensus among many voices: articulating the European Union's position on climate change. *Golden Gate University Law Review* 32 (4): 351–414.

Liberatore, Angela (1995). Arguments, assumptions, and the choice of policy instruments: the case of the debate on the CO_2/energy tax in the European Community. In Dente, Bruno (ed.) *Environmental policy in search of new instruments.* Dordrecht: Kluwer, 55–72.

Lodge, Juliet (1989). Environment: towards a clean blue-green EC. In Lodge, Juliet (ed.) *The European Community and the challenge of the future.* London: Pinter.

Manners, Ian (2000). *Substance and symbolism: an anatomy of cooperation in the new Europe.* Aldershot: Ashgate.

McCormick, John and Jonathan Olsen (2014). *The European Union: politics and policies.* Boulder, Colorado: Westview Press.

McGrory, Daniel P (1990). Air pollution legislation in the United States and the European Community. *European Law Review* 15 (4): 198–316.

Newell, Peter and Matthew Paterson (1998). A climate for business: global warming, the state and capital. *Review of International Political Economy* 5 (4): 670–703.

Oberthür, Sebastian and Hermann E. Ott (1999). *The Kyoto Protocol: international climate policy for the 21st century.* Berlin: Springer.

Oberthüur, Sebastian and Marc Pallemaerts (2010). The EU's internal and external climate policies: an historical overview. In Oberthüur, Sebastian and Marc Pallemaerts (eds) *The new climate policies of the European Union: internal legislation and climate diplomacy.* Brussels: VUBPress, 27–63.

OJ (Official Journal of the European Communities) (1986). Resolution on measures to counteract the rising concentration of carbon dioxide in the atmosphere (the 'greenhouse' effect) (Doc. A 2–68/86). C 255, Volume 29, 13 October.

OJ (Official Journal of the European Communities) (1987). Resolution of the Council of the European Communities and of the representatives of the Governments of the Member States, meeting within the Council of 19 October 1987 on the continuation and implementation of a European Community policy and action programme on the environment (1987–1992). C 328, Volume 30, 7 December.

OJ (Official Journal of the European Communities) (1989). Council Resolution of 21 June 1989 on the greenhouse effect and the Community (89/C 183/03). No C 183, 20 July.

OJ (Official Journal of the European Communities) (1993). Council Decision of 15 December 1993 concerning the conclusion of the United Nations Framework Convention on Climate Change (94/69/EC). No L 33, 7 February 1994.

Paterson, Matthew (1996). *Global warming and global politics.* London: Routledge.

Pinder, John (2001). *The European Union: a very short introduction.* Oxford: Oxford University Press.

Sandler, R. (1992). Chaos as 'last chance' summit opens in Rio. *The European*, 4–7 June.

Schunz, Simon (2014). *European Union foreign policy and the global climate regime.* Brussels: P.I.E. Peter Lang.

Skjaerseth, Jon Birger (1994). The climate policy of the EC: too hot to handle? *Journal of Common Market Studies* 32 (1): 25–45.

Underdal, Arild (1998). Leadership in international environmental negotiations: designing feasible solutions. In Underdal, Arild (ed.) *The politics of international environmental management.* Dordrecht: Kluwer, 101–27.

Vogler, John (1999). The European Union as an actor in international environmental politics. *Environmental Politics* 8 (3): 24–48.

Wettestad, Jørgen (2000). The complicated development of EU climate policy: lessons learnt. In Gupta, Joyeeta and Michael Grubb (eds) *Climate change and European leadership: a sustainable role for Europe?* Dordrecht: Kluwer, 25–45.

Wettestad, Jørgen (2001). The ambiguous prospects for EU climate policy – a summary of options. *Energy & Environment* 12 (2–3): 139–65.

Zito, Anthony R. (2000). *Creating environmental policy in the European Union.* Basingstoke: Palgrave Macmillan.

3 Momentum gathers
From Rio to Geneva

According to the UNFCCC's modalities, the treaty would enter into force 90 days after the 50th state had ratified or acceded to it. It was estimated that this would take approximately another two years, sometime in 1994 (Paterson 1993). To make best use of that time the INC agreed to continue meeting during the interim (Gupta 2010). By doing so, nations could prepare for the first COP, as well as debate any possible amendments or protocols to the Convention (Paterson 1996). Six such INC sessions took place during this period, either in Geneva or New York (see Table 3.1).

INC-6 held in Geneva (December 1992), was primarily of an organizational nature. Its most significant outcome was the restructuring of its working groups. Working Group I would now deal with 'commitments and review of information, methodologies, and modalities for the first COP', while Working Group II would deal with 'financing, rules of procedure, and institutional issues' (Paterson 1993, p. 178).

In January 1993, barely a month after INC-6, US President Clinton entered office. Hopes were high that this new administration would lead to a major shift in the US position on climate change. During his election campaign, Clinton had criticized the Bush administration's opposition to the stabilization target. He pledged that once elected he would consider cuts of 20–30 per cent by 2005 (Paterson 1993). Such high hopes seemed justified, initially. In February 1993, President Clinton put forward his economic plan, the cornerstone of which was

Table 3.1 INC sessions in the run-up to Berlin

Session	Date	Venue
INC 6	7–10 December 1992	Geneva
INC 7	15–20 March 1993	New York
INC 8	16–27 August 1993	Geneva
INC 9	7–18 February 1994	Geneva
INC 10	22 August – 2 September 1994	Geneva
INC 11	6–17 February 1995	New York

Source: adapted from Oberthür and Ott (1999, p. 44).

a British Thermal Unit (BTU) tax – based on the heat content of the fuel (Agrawala and Andresen 1999). At the international level, it was assumed that the US would soon join other countries in support of a stronger agreement on climate change in the near term (Royden 2002). Indeed, during INC-7 in New York (March 1993) Madeleine Albright, then Permanent Representative of the US to the UN, criticized the previous administration by stating that 'we are well aware of the disappointment in many quarters that the Convention did not go further' (Paterson 1996, p. 67). Overall, INC-7 was again a largely procedural meeting. The most important decision was the election of Argentine Ambassador Raúl Estrada-Oyuela as the Chairman of the INC, replacing Jean Ripert of France, who had led the negotiations on the Convention.

At INC-7, the EC welcomed the US proposal for the new BTU tax on energy as an important contribution to climate change mitigation. Yet, prospects for effective climate policy in Europe were less rosy. Member States failed to agree on the CO_2/energy tax. Affected by economic recession during the early 1990s, most European countries were increasingly unwilling to support strong action to tackle climate change (Oberthür and Ott 1999). In the US, analysts were arguing that once the coal and oil lobby mobilized itself, Clinton and Gore would find themselves frustrated in their ability to live up to their electoral promise, despite their party controlling both the White House and Congress for the first time in 12 years (see Paterson 1993). The BTU tax only narrowly made it through the House of Representatives in May 1993, before meeting its demise in the Senate Finance Committee a month later. When the Republican Party won a landslide victory in the Senate and House of Representatives in November 1994, all hope of support for stringent climate policy in the US legislative branch was lost (Oberthür and Ott 1999). With taxes off the table, the US saw no other alternative than to push for a market-based approach involving emissions trading (Downie 2014). Consequently, with both the US and the EC reluctant to support tighter climate change policies, the process building up to COP-1 went largely without strong leadership (Oberthür and Ott 1999).

With highly developed countries unwilling to accept new commitments, the pace of discussions progressed slowly. The EC's submission to INC-8 (August 1993) focused primarily on technical questions relating to greenhouse gas inventories (see INC 1993c), as well as on the criteria that should underpin the Joint Implementation (JI) mechanism. The latter proved tricky. The rationale behind JI is that if a global perspective is taken, it is irrelevant where greenhouse gas emissions reductions take place. Mitigation action should be taken wherever it's cheapest. Under the UNFCCC, developed countries had the option of implementing their commitments either individually or jointly. If emission reductions were thus achieved as a result of an investment by state A in state B, these would then count towards the fulfilment of the former's mitigation obligations (Oberthür and Ott 1995). Intense North–South disagreements arose, however. A number of developed countries, including Norway, argued that JI's geographical scope needed to be widened to include developing countries (Paterson 1996). Developing countries, however, were vehemently sceptical of JI. They feared it would lead to a shift of responsibility away from developed countries. As Paterson (1996, p. 66) explains, developing countries suspected that JI could develop into 'a new way of entrenching an "eco-colonial" division of the world's resources, with high consumption in the North compensated by investments in the South in forests, energy efficiency projects, and so on'. Consequently, the vast majority of developing countries in INC-8 argued that JI should only be applied to developed countries (Oberthür 1994). The EC supported the position of developing countries. It argued that although the cost-effectiveness of mitigation action should be taken into account, Article 4.2 of the Convention clearly stated that developed countries, and them alone, were the ones required to take the lead in stabilizing their emissions (INC 1993a; see also INC 1993b). If this principle was not adhered to, the stabilization commitment taken by developed countries 'could have a very limited effect in these countries' (INC 1993a, p. 2). The EC further argued that JI between developed countries should be first tested during a pilot period. This meant JI would not be used to fulfil the stabilization commitment, but would only come into the fore for emissions reductions achieved post-2000. The EC did leave a window open for developing countries to be included in JI activities, noting that those that decided to take part could do so by notifying the COP of their intention to be bound by UNFCCC Article 4.2 (a and b).

During INC-8 there were also the first tentative, albeit informal, discussions around the adequacy of commitments contained in Articles 4.2 (a) and (b) of the UNFCCC. A number of delegations suggested that these articles were too weak and inadequate for the purposes of the Convention (Paterson 1996). In December 1993, a landmark event took place. The EU ratified the UNFCCC. Back in March 1993, the Environment Council had decided that both the EU and its Member States would deposit instruments of ratification simultaneously by 31 December 1993 at the latest. This never materialized, as Germany and five other of the greener Member States attempted to link the ratification of the UNFCCC by the EU to an approval by the rest of the carbon/energy tax (Jordan and Rayner 2010; Goldman and Hajost 1994). The UK avoided being pinned down and broke EU ranks by unilaterally deciding to ratify the Convention on 8 December, with Germany, the Netherlands, Spain, Portugal and the EU itself following suit soon afterwards. Despite the ratification, the EU still lacked a coherent implementation strategy – a paradoxical situation described as both 'fluid and ambiguous' (Macrory and Hession 1996, p. 114).

INC-9 took place in Geneva (February 1994). Long discussions focused on the modalities of the financial mechanism and whether the institutions of the Convention itself should be directly involved in GEF policies or, as the North preferred, whether the GEF should maintain its institutional integrity (Kjellén 2008). The real issue at stake was about control (Gupta 1995). Whereas developing countries wanted the COP to control the GEF, developed country donors preferred the GEF to be in charge so as to have a degree of control over contentious issues. Finally, INC-9 discussed again whether Articles 4.2 (a) and (b) of the UNFCCC were adequate to meeting the Convention's objectives. Most delegations repeated their scepticism. But no developed countries were prepared to propose reductions in emissions. This issue was not up for negotiation (Paterson 1996). The UK, for example, avoided any reference to reductions at INC-9 and emphasized instead its commitment to implement the Rio stabilization target (Prynn 1994). France argued it had already reduced its emissions substantially during the 1970s and 1980s, while Spain and Ireland highlighted the need to increase their emissions if they were to catch up with the rest of Europe (Arts and Rüdig 1995).

The adequacy of commitments was formally discussed for the first time during INC-10 in Geneva (August/September 1994). The US argued that there was widespread agreement on the fact that current efforts would not be adequate (Pearce 1994). The EU also noted that current commitments were clearly inadequate to make sufficient progress towards the Convention's ultimate objective. It proposed a number of options that could be considered by parties instead, such as amending Article 4.2 or adopting a decision to strengthen the Convention's target beyond the year 2000 (INC 1994a). Hoping to avoid the first COP to be hosted in Berlin to be remembered in history as a failure, the German EU Presidency broke the stalemate by tabling a formal proposal for a protocol on CO_2 emissions that should be adopted preferably during COP-1 (INC 1994a). There was the expectation in the run-up to INC-10 that Germany was intending to put forward a proposal for a protocol that would contain significant reduction targets for greenhouse gas emissions (Oberthür 1994). Most environmental NGOs, anticipating a proposal with a CO_2 reduction target of 20 per cent by 2005, were very disappointed by the final text. It simply said: 'At COP-1 ... the Annex I Parties [developed countries] should commit themselves to reducing their CO_2 emissions by the year (x) individually or jointly by (y) percent' (Paterson 1996, p. 68).

Despite all major developed countries agreeing that the commitments under UNFCCC Article 2 (a) and (b) were inadequate, most were not yet ready for a protocol or immediate new commitments. In the EU, only Denmark and the Netherlands backed the German proposal, with the Commission and several Member States, such as the UK and the less developed ones, being instead of the opinion that adopting a protocol during COP-1 was rather premature (Schreurs 2002; Williams 1994). The German proposal also mentioned the possible inclusion of commitments by developing countries, a statement also supported by the US but which put many developing countries on the defensive since it was vague as to which developing countries should participate (Morgan 1995). Closing with JI, during INC-10 a split occurred within the G-77. Irrespective of scepticism from Brazil, India and China, some Latin American states and a number of the 'small tigers' of South-East Asia expressed a more favourable attitude towards JI (Oberthür 1994). Eventually, an agreement in principle was reached to experiment with JI by way of a pilot phase, a proposal which the EU supported (INC 1994b; see also Oberthür and Ott 1995). Developed countries remained divided on the issue of credit. The EU, unlike the US, felt that parties should not be credited for reductions achieved by projects during this pilot period (INC 1994b; see also Morgan 1996).

The EU took a greater lead at the December 1994 Environment Council in Brussels. Besides acknowledging the inadequacy of the commitments, the EU now expressed that it was in favour of 'progressive limitations and reductions of CO_2 and other greenhouse gases by 2005 and 2010' (Environment Council 1994). Adopting a protocol at COP-1 was still not an option. This was because the EU believed that COP-1 should instead initiate negotiations, which would be concluded by COP-3, 'on the further development of the commitments under the Convention in a protocol' (Environment Council 1994). Finally, instead of volunteering (as Rio stipulates), the EU called upon other Annex I parties to bindingly commit at COP-1 to stabilizing their CO_2 emissions at 1990 levels by 2000. Yet, it was becoming increasingly obvious at the time that most developed countries would not be in a position to meet their UNFCCC stabilization target. Of the top ten emitters, only Germany, the UK and Russia (the latter because of its economic collapse) were expected to meet their stabilization targets (Pearce 1995). The US, Japan, Canada, Italy and France were projected to increase their emissions (Pearce 1995). China and India had no commitments under the Convention. For the EU as a whole, it was estimated that its collective target would be missed by about 3 per cent (Victor and Salt 1994).

Disappointed that the German proposal did not go far enough, Trinidad and Tobago, acting on behalf of the Alliance of Small Island States (AOSIS), had formally submitted a proposal during INC-10 for a draft protocol which instead of x's and y's called for a 20 per cent reduction of CO_2 emissions of developed countries by 2005 (Werksman 1994). While both the AOSIS and German proposals were discussed during INC-11 (February 1995), negotiations came to a stalemate when the so-called JUSCANZ group (Japan, the US, Canada, Australia, and New Zealand) argued that in the case of new commitments some of the more advanced developing countries, such as China, India or Brazil, should also take on obligations to limit their greenhouse gas emissions (Oberthür and Ott 1995). Submissions by the EU[1] echoed similar language, as they called for 'limitation of emission growth for certain more advanced developing countries' (INC 1995a, p. 14). The response by G-77/China was to block all discussions on further international measures, making it impossible for the INC to reach a decision on the issue of adequacy of commitments. Consequently, the INC simply decided to 'transmit [to the COP] for consideration and appropriate action' the proposed protocols from the AOSIS and Germany (Paterson 1996, p. 69).

Parties were only able to agree that the commitments under the UNFCCC were a 'first step' (Oberthür and Ott 1995). The US avoided speaking of a protocol, simply referring to the need to consider 'new aims' for the post-2000 period (ENB 1995c, p. 9). The EU repeated its preference for a protocol and noted that it should include not only targets and timetables but also specific policies and corresponding measures on a wide range of areas, including energy efficiency, renewable energy, land use and agriculture (INC 1995a). Regarding

JI, the EU further refined its position through the submission of a detailed position paper (see INC 1995c). Another submission (INC 1995b) outlined the EU's approach on the issues of adaptation, mitigation, finance, capacity-building and technology transfer. On adaptation, for instance, the EU noted that it would provide financial support, particularly to vulnerable countries, but noted that mitigation should receive highest priority. This was because if the Convention's ultimate objective were to be met adaptation would not be needed.

To bring to a close the INC process, the Environment Council conclusions in March 1995, just a few weeks before COP-1, repeated the position the EU had adopted and was going to push for in Berlin:

> A protocol on policies and measures as well as targets and timetables in order to limit and progressively reduce greenhouse gas emissions would need to have been adopted in 1997 in order to enter into force by 2000.
>
> (Environment Council 1995, para 4)

Because of the lack of preparatory work and the slow pace of the INC process, adopting a protocol was no longer on the agenda for COP-1. Its agenda merely included a decision on a mandate for negotiating such a protocol (Oberthür and Ott 1995; Oberthür 1994).

COP-1: the Berlin Mandate

Upon arrival to COP-1, held in Berlin (28 March–7 April 1995), the positions of states fell into three main groups. On one end there were the JUSCANZ countries. They were prepared to accept that existing commitments were inadequate, but were opposed to them being strengthened, particularly in the form of targets and timetables (Paterson 1996). The US and Australia were particularly opposed to the mention of 'reductions' in any agreed text from Berlin. They also insisted on the more advanced developing countries taking on commitments to limit their emissions on the grounds that the global nature of the problem at hand required 'broad international participation' (UNFCCC 1995c, p. 76). As a result of the JUSCANZ stance, the G-77 remained adamant in its opposition to any further international measures and argued that focusing on the implementation of the Convention's current commitments should be the regime's chief objective (ENB 1995a). It further argued that responsibility should remain with Annex I parties and not shift to Non-Annex I parties. OPEC[2] members, supported by Russia, even questioned whether existing commitments under the Convention should be dismissed as inadequate (Oberthür and Ott 1995).

At the other end were the EU and the AOSIS countries that supported strengthening existing commitments. The latter favoured a Toronto-style CO_2 reduction target for developed countries of 20 per cent reduction by 2005. The EU was also supportive of reductions in greenhouse gas emissions beyond 2000, with a number of Member States even tabling concrete numbers. For instance, the UK called for a 5–10 per cent reduction from 1990 levels by 2010

(Pomerance 1995), whilst Denmark sided with AOSIS calling for a 20 per cent cut by 2005 (ENB 1995b). Overall, the EU repeated its position for a comprehensive protocol that included targets and timetables, as well as policies and measures (PAMs) (UNFCCC 1995d).

Key actors' positions differed in major respects. No basis for a workable protocol was obvious (Arts and Rüdig 1995). The only way out of the impasse would be 'to break up the anti-protocol position of G-77' by excluding developing nations from any commitments (Arts and Rüdig 1995, p. 485). The EU, led by the host country, Germany, did exactly that. It assured developing countries that they would not be asked to undertake any commitments to limit their emissions (Oberthür and Ott 1999). Germany had contemplated during the INC process the possible inclusion of commitments for affluent developing countries, but moved away from that position so as to allay the fears of G-77 and secure its support. India responded by welcoming the altered EU stance and took the lead within the G-77 by preparing a draft decision on the adequacy of commitments, which called on developed countries to reduce their CO_2 emissions by 20 per cent by 2000. After this Indian-led G-77 text was blocked by OPEC, India convened a meeting of like-minded developing states – known as the 'Green Group' – which tabled the proposal for a second time (the 'Green Paper' as it came to be known). This draft called for developed countries to adopt Toronto-style targets. It explicitly stressed that consultations were not to 'introduce any new commitments whatsoever for developing country Parties' (UNFCCC 1995g, p. 1). This time, the EU and the AOSIS countries immediately lent their support to the draft. This left the JUSCANZ and OPEC countries completely isolated.[3] In the meantime, environmental NGOs used the media to ensure the public was kept well informed of who was responsible for the impasse (Oberthür and Ott 1999).

The US delegation was headed by individuals with extremely pro-environmental inclinations. For instance, Rafe Pomerance, one of the founding fathers of the 1988 Toronto target and, more importantly, Timothy E. Wirth, then Under-Secretary of Global Affairs and a former Democrat Congressman with a strong environmental profile, were involved (Arts and Rüdig 1995). Even so, and despite the support of a sympathetic White House, hostility from Congress towards commitments exerted significant influence over the agenda. As Arts and Rüdig (1995, p. 486) note, the fossil fuel lobby present at the COP 'smelled blood and lobbied hard, certain of the support of Republican Congressmen back home'. Yet, in the face of isolation and mounting pressure from civil society, the US eventually agreed to a compromise that was much closer to the initial position of the EU and its allies. Unable to count on the support of their most prominent ally, Canada, Australia and most OPEC members followed suit shortly afterwards, with only Saudi Arabia, Kuwait and Venezuela voicing reservations (Oberthür and Ott 1999).

The Berlin Mandate, as this compromise was termed, stated that parties agreed to elaborate by COP-3 on PAMs and negotiate a 'protocol or other legal instrument' that would 'set quantified limitation and reduction objectives' for the Annex I countries 'within specified time-frames, such as 2005, 2010, and 2020' (UNFCCC 1995f, p. 5). In addition, the Berlin Mandate explicitly precluded any new commitments by developing countries to go alongside the targets to be adopted by developed countries.

When explaining the rationale behind the US's decision to endorse this compromise, Pomerance noted that the US's main objective was to 'keep the EU from pinning us [the US] down on a target and to save JI' (cited in Royden 2002, p. 425). US delegates fought hard to finalize the agreement on JI – the 'signature piece of the Berlin Mandate as far as we're concerned', according to Timothy Wirth (cited in Atkinson 1995, p. A24). It was eventually agreed to initiate a pilot phase lasting until 2000, which would be open to any country that expressed an interest, but under the proviso that no credits 'accrue[d] to any Party' as a result of greenhouse gas emissions reduced or sequestered during the pilot phase (ENB 1995d, p. 10). The formulation did allow the 'crediting of reductions achieved after this period by projects initiated during the pilot phase' (Oberthür and Ott 1995, p. 147). Finally, instead of JI, a name change was agreed: 'activities implemented jointly' (AIJ). The new name implied that there was still 'no acceptance on the criteria' for JI (Børsting and Fermann 1997, p. 75; see also Gupta 2014).

Overall, it should be noted that unlike the Bush administration in Rio, for which a settlement was not crucial, the Clinton administration actually wished for an agreement to be concluded. Even though isolated towards the end, JUSCANZ countries had been able to achieve a number of concessions. First, as Schunz (2014) notes, pressure from the US delegation led to certain slight modifications in the text that in its opinion allowed for the issue of developing country participation to be readdressed. Instead of 'no commitments whatsoever', the final text read as follows:

> Not introduce any new commitments for Parties not included in Annex I, but reaffirm existing commitments in Article 4.1 and continue to advance the implementation of these commitments in order to achieve sustainable development.
>
> (UNFCCC 1995f, p. 5)

Second, parties had only agreed to initiate a 'process' that could lead to the adoption of a 'protocol or other legal instrument' (Oberthür and Ott 1995, p. 145). Third, rather than 'targets and timetables' the text referred to 'quantified limitation and reduction objectives within specified time-frames, such as 2005, 2010, and 2020'. The latter phrasing allowed for greater flexibility. When a US delegate was asked about the prospects of the agreement making it through Congress, the response was that the US would have 'to delay the process as much as possible and go for the 2020 deadline' (Arts and Rüdig 1995, p. 487). Finally, there was no mention in the text of 1990 serving as the base year for future obligations, thereby leaving the option of going for a higher baseline on the table (Oberthür and Ott 1999).[4]

Summing up COP-1, most participants agreed that it had at the very least 'achieved something' (Arts and Rüdig 1995, p. 487). The EU lived up to its leadership ambitions and played a pivotal role along with India in brokering the final compromise. Germany not only escaped the embarrassment of a failed conference but was also able to secure a decision to locate the UNFCCC secretariat in Bonn, with Montevideo, Toronto and Geneva being the defeated candidates. In terms of future work, COP-1 established an ad hoc committee: the Ad hoc Group on the Berlin Mandate (AGBM). This new committee's task was to negotiate a protocol or other legal instrument to include targets and timetables for emissions limitations and reductions of developed countries. The deadline for the AGBM was set for COP-3 in 1997 in Kyoto, Japan.

The AGBM process

Between COP-1 in Berlin and COP-3 in Kyoto, eight meetings of the AGBM were held. COP-2 in July 1996 in Geneva was held in conjunction with AGBM-4, dividing the process in half (see Table 3.2). From AGBM-6, negotiators met in Bonn, the new location of the Secretariat (Oberthür and Ott 1999).

The main function of the AGBM was to produce a draft protocol in time for COP-3 in Kyoto. As Schreurs (2002) explains, there were a number of questions left outstanding:

- Should there be differentiated targets or just a flat emissions reduction target?
- Which greenhouse gases should be included in the final agreement?
- Should sinks be counted?
- To what extent should flexibility mechanisms be used to meet targets?
- What would be the role of developing countries?

Little progress was achieved during the first two sessions of the AGBM. A lack of funding meant only a small number of parties could participate in deliberations (UNFCCC 1995e). According to the Berlin Mandate, the negotiating

Table 3.2 AGBM sessions

Session	Dates	Venue
AGBM-1	21–25 August 1995	Geneva
AGBM-2	30 October – 3 November 1995	Geneva
AGBM-3	5–8 March 1996	Geneva
AGBM-4 & COP-2	8–19 July 1996	Geneva
AGBM-5	9–13 December 1996	Geneva
AGBM-6	3–7 March 1997	Bonn
AGBM-7	31 July – 7 August 1997	Bonn
AGBM-8	22–31 October 1997 & 30 November 1997	Bonn & Kyoto

Source: adapted from Oberthür and Ott (1999, p. 50).

process should include in its early stages an analysis and assessment, aimed at identifying possible PAMs for Annex I parties, which could contribute to limiting and reducing their emissions (UNFCCC 1995e). The EU in its submission for AGBM-1 (August 1995) even provided a tentative list of potential PAMs covering CO_2 and other gases (UNFCCC 1995a). In what has been described as a 'largely diversionary discussion', the US and other laggard states (mainly OPEC) insisted at AGBM-1 that an in-depth analysis and assessment of PAMs was needed before initiating negotiations on any targets and time-tables (Lanchbery 1997, p. 8). The EU took the bait as a number of Member States were under the impression that the US was more willing to discuss PAMs than targets and timetables (Oberthür and Ott 1999).

In AGBM-2 (October/November 1995), Spain, on behalf of the EU, submitted a proposal for a protocol structure, which elaborated further the group's stance on targets and timetables, as well as PAMs (see UNFCCC 1995b). No specific proposals were made regarding the former, apart from that targets should be set within specified timeframes, such as 2005, 2010 and 2020. More detail was provided with respect to the latter. The EU believed the protocol should adopt three annexes: mandatory, highly recommended and voluntary PAMs (UNFCCC 1995b). The EU's experience with internal harmonization and a single market was helpful in this respect. It provided a long list of examples (19 pages in total), including options such 'as minimum fuel excise taxes, broader environmental taxes, improvements in energy efficiency, and fuel switching' (Schreurs 2002, p. 181).

The EU, throughout the AGBM process, devoted considerable time and energy to pursuing binding common and coordinated PAMs. Apart from virtually no other party sharing its enthusiasm, Grubb et al. (1999, p. 67) suggest the PAMs proposal lacked precision:

> Measures that could plausibly benefit from international coordination were included, along with many for which no such case existed; the innocuous were listed alongside those which some Parties found inflammatory; the general ("measures to improve energy efficiency") alongside the specific ("adopt energy efficiency standards for domestic appliances").

Eventually, the US, followed by the G-77 and several of the parties with economies in transition, flatly rejected the EU proposal and refused to even submit proposals on PAMs, arguing that each party should be allowed to identify PAMs that suited its own circumstances (Yamin 2000). The US administration, 'anti-interventionist by inclination [and] sensitive to their citizens' and industries' attachment to cheap fuel', pushed instead the idea of flexibility in meeting national commitments (Grubb et al. 1999, p. 65). Only Japan, Switzerland, and a few Eastern European countries aspiring to join the EU membership showed some limited support, but ultimately the EU proved unable to secure a strong role for PAMs in the final text of the Kyoto Protocol, which merely lists in Article 2 a number of PAMs on which parties could draw (Gupta and Ringius 2001).

Little progress was achieved during the first two sessions of the AGBM, a situation that changed dramatically following the release shortly after AGBM-2 of the IPCC's Second Assessment Report (SAR) in December 1995. For the first time anthropogenic emissions were held at least partly responsible for climate change. The IPCC concluded that the evidence suggested there was a 'discernible human influence on global climate' (IPCC 1995, p. 5). The release of the SAR had a great impact on the US administration and greatly benefited progress during AGBM-3 (March 1996), where the US, in a significant change of position, called for speeding up the negotiations and putting an end to the phase of analysis and assessment of PAMs – up to then so insistently called for by a number of laggard states aiming at hindering the negotiation process (Downie 2014; Oberthür 1996). The IPCC report had a great impact on the US administration, as illustrated by numerous studies (see e.g. Downie 2014). The US went even further by announcing that it would be in a position to table its proposal on targets at COP-2 in Geneva. Notably, the term 'negotiations' had not been included in the Berlin Mandate less than one year ago because of US objections (Oberthür and Ott 1999).

While the US shift was welcomed by the EU, it nevertheless caught it by 'surprise' and unable to react (Gupta and van der Grijp 2000, p. 78). Until then its main focus had been on PAMs, with targets being somewhat left behind (Schunz 2014). The Italian Presidency of the EU simply noted that following the IPCC projections, a level of 550 ppm should 'guide limitation and reduction efforts' (ENB 1996a, p. 5). Even so, Germany made an effort to increase the momentum by calling for CO_2 emissions to be reduced by 10 per cent of 1990 levels by 2005 and by 15–20 per cent by 2010 (ENB 1996a). The above targets were a German initiative, with only the dates 2005 and 2010 having been agreed in advance with the rest of the Member States (Oberthür and Ott 1999). During AGBM-3 the majority of OECD members had unequivocally supported the findings of the IPCC SAR. Yet, various countries, such as Australia, Russia and OPEC members, continued to put forward the argument that scientific uncertainties still remained. This resulted in the Subsidiary Body for Scientific and Technological Advice (SBSTA), whose functions include the transmission of IPCC scientific findings to the negotiating bodies (e.g. AGBM, COP), being unable to agree on the need to consider additional action based on the key SAR findings (Oberthür 1996; see also UNFCCC 1996b).[5] Thus, the forthcoming COP-2 had two major items on its agenda: (1) evaluate the conclusions of the SAR, and (2) give guidance to the AGBM process.

COP-2 (Geneva)

COP-2 in Geneva (8–19 July 1996) was held in conjunction with AGBM-4. Unlike in Berlin, where the EU had dominated, the upper hand in Geneva was held by the US. Environmentalists in the administration had by that time 'gained in strength', and President Clinton, aided by the improved US economic situation, aimed to augment his environmental profile in view of the approaching US presidential elections (Kjellén 2008, p. 92; Oberthür 1996). In the Ministerial Segment of COP-2, Under-Secretary Timothy Wirth, following his announcement made at AGBM-3, called for intensified international negotiations on 'realistic, verifiable and binding medium-term commitments [...] met through maximum flexibility in the selection of implementation measures, including the use of reliable activities implemented jointly, and trading mechanisms around the world' (Schreurs 2002, p. 181). Regarding the IPCC SAR, Wirth underscored its integrity and even dismissed its critics as 'naysayers and special interests bent on belittling, attacking and obfuscating climate change science' (cited in Masood 1996, p. 287). Later on he stated: 'Let me make clear the US view: the science calls upon us to take urgent action; the IPCC report is the best science we have and we should use it' (cited in Stuart 1996, p. 15). A closer reading of the US position, however, would have been enough to cause scepticism. No numbers or base years were indicated, flexibility mechanisms such as emissions trading were still at the time highly controversial, while the renewed call for developing countries to limit their emissions was bound to meet with resistance from most G-77 nations (Oberthür 1996; Masood 1996).

Turning to the EU, it largely failed to make its presence felt at COP-2, mainly because it was preoccupied with its own deliberations on the form of its internal burden-sharing agreement (Andresen and Agrawala 2002). As an EU interviewee argued, 'at the time the discussion was still ongoing and there was no timeline for the EU to come up with a target by COP-2'.[6] While the EU had just endorsed the 2°C target and had pledged to commit to emissions reductions after 2000, the question of how these were going to be allocated among Member States was yet to be answered. The EU position, although progressive, remained largely unchanged from AGBM-2, where it had proposed a framework protocol which contained no targets. According to the conclusions of the June 1996 Environment Council, it could be 'feasible for the Community as a whole to reach a reduction of CO_2 emissions by 2010 compared to 1990 levels' (Environment Council 1996). Again, no targets were offered. Instead, the Council stated again that 'global average temperatures should not exceed 2°C above pre-industrial level and that therefore concentration levels lower than 550 ppm CO_2 should guide global limitation and reduction efforts'. It was noted that meeting the aforementioned goal could necessitate reductions in emissions of greenhouse gases other than CO_2, in particular methane and nitrogen dioxide (NO_2). Finally, the EU supported the AIJ concept as a means to maximize the cooperative effort between all parties, and continued – in the face of complete isolation – to argue in favour of PAMs.

Returning to COP-2, the US shift facilitated agreement on the Geneva Ministerial Declaration which endorsed the SAR as currently 'the most comprehensive and authoritative [scientific] assessment' on climate change and urged parties to 'accelerate negotiations on the text of a legally binding protocol or another legal instrument' (UNFCCC 1996a, p. 9 and p. 73 respectively). It had been the first time that it was made clear that the forthcoming agreement was going to be binding. Reference to 1990 as a base year, as well as mention of maximum concentration levels of greenhouse gases in the atmosphere that should not be exceeded, was not made in the Declaration as a result of opposition from JUSCANZ members, which were against the inclusion of figures, such as the 550 ppm limit proposed by the EU (Oberthür 1996).

To conclude with, the procedure followed for adopting the Geneva Declaration 'proved to be as important as its content' (Oberthür and Ott 1999, p. 54). One of the major shortcomings of COP-2 was its failure to agree on the Rules of Procedure. In the absence of such rules, decisions had to be made by consensus, thus giving OPEC and its allies an actual veto over decisions. As one NGO put it, unless resolved, this issue would continue to 'dangle like the sword of Damocles over these negotiations' (ENB 1996b, p. 13). At COP-1, Germany had secured an agreement early in the process with OPEC not to block proceedings by insisting that all decisions be taken by consensus. However, a similar agreement at COP-2 was not to be forthcoming as laggards were determined to make best use of this bargaining chip. Unwilling to allow this small obstructionist minority to stalemate the process, instead of formally adopting the Geneva Declaration, the majority of parties simply 'took note' of it by 'consensus minus x'. Attempts to object to the procedure 'were swept away by the sustained applause of the great majority of delegations' supporting the procedure proposed by the Chair, Chen Chimutengwende of Zimbabwe (Oberthür and Ott 1999, p. 54). Opponents were left with the options of placing reservations (Australia), making qualifications (New Zealand) or refusing to sign the declaration altogether (OPEC and Russia).

Undoubtedly, COP-2 took the process one small step further. It made clear that the goal of future negotiations would be to promulgate a legally binding instrument, which would contain legally binding targets. The US emerged as the leading force, even though years later a US delegate would admit that 'the implications [of taking on a binding target] were not fully clear at the time'. 'We needed,' as he added, 'a target in order to make emissions trading work' (Royden 2002, p. 428).

Notes

1 In January 1995, Austria, Finland and Sweden joined the EU.
2 Organization of the Petroleum Exporting Countries.
3 Interview No. 3 (Member State official – Former Head of Delegation).
4 On its part, the EU was in favour of 1990 as a base year primarily because it would be able to benefit from emission reductions that had taken place in subsequent years as a result of the collapse of the East German economy and the switch from coal to natural gas in the UK – reductions that were of such magnitude that they almost offset increases in emissions in the remaining EU countries.
5 SBSTA is one of two permanent subsidiary bodies to the Convention. The other is the Subsidiary Body for Implementation (SBI). SBI's tasks include the assessment and review of the effective implementation of the UNFCCC and its Kyoto Protocol.
6 Interview No. 1 (Member State official – Former Head of Delegation).

References

Agrawala, Shardul and Steinar Andresen (1999). Indispensability and indefensibility? The United States in the climate treaty negotiations. *Global Governance* 5 (4): 457–82.

Andresen, Steinar and Shardul Agrawala (2002). Leaders, pushers and laggards in the making of the climate regime. *Global Environmental Change* 12 (1): 41–51.

Arts, Bas and Wolfgang Rüdig (1995). Negotiating the Berlin Mandate: reflections on the first "Conference of the Parties" to the UN Framework Convention on Climate Change. *Environmental Politics* 4 (3): 481–7.

Atkinson, Rick (1995). Greenhouse gas cutback goals left up in air. *Washington Post*, 8 April.

Børsting, Georg and Gunnar Fermann (1997). Climate change turning political: conference-diplomacy and institution-building to Rio and beyond. In Fermann, Gunnar (ed.) *International politics of climate change: key issues and critical factors*. Oslo: Scandinavian University Press, 53–82.

Downie, Christian (2014). *The politics of climate change negotiations: strategies and variables in prolonged international negotiations*. Cheltenham: Edward Elgar.

ENB (1995a). Climate Change Convention COP-1 Highlights: Wednesday, 29 March 1995. *Earth Negotiations Bulletin* 12 (14): 1–2.

ENB (1995b). Climate Change Convention COP-1 Highlights: Wednesday, 5 April 1995. *Earth Negotiations Bulletin* 12 (19): 1–2.

ENB (1995c). Summary of the Eleventh Session of the INC for a Framework Convention on Climate Change: 6–17 February 1995. *Earth Negotiations Bulletin* 12 (11): 1–10.

ENB (1995d). Summary of the First Conference of the Parties for the Framework Convention on Climate Change: 28 March – 7 April 1995. *Earth Negotiations Bulletin* 12 (21): 1–11.

ENB (1996a). Report of the Third Session of the Ad hoc Group on the Berlin Mandate: 5–8 March 1996. *Earth Negotiations Bulletin* 12 (27): 1–9.

ENB (1996b). Summary of the Second Conference of the Parties to the Framework Convention on Climate Change: 8–19 July 1996. *Earth Negotiations Bulletin* 12 (38): 1–14.

Environment Council (1994). *Environment Council press release*, 273 No. 11870/94, Brussels, 15–16 December.

Environment Council (1995). *Environment Council press release*, 70 No. 5424/95, Brussels, 9 March.

Environment Council (1996). *Environment Council press release*, 188 No. 8518/96, Luxembourg, 25 June.

Goldman, Todd and Scott A. Hajost (1994). Global climate. In Handl, Günther (ed.) *Yearbook of international environmental law* 4 (1993). Oxford: Oxford University Press, 142–7.

Grubb, Michael, Christiaan Vrolijk and Duncan Brack (1999). *The Kyoto Protocol: a guide and assessment*. London: Royal Institute of International Affairs.

Gupta, Joyeeta (1995). The global environment facility in its North–South context. *Environmental Politics* 4 (1): 19–43.

Gupta, Joyeeta (2010). A history of international climate change policy. *WIREs Climate Change* 1: 636–53.

Gupta, Joyeeta (2014). *The history of global climate governance*. Cambridge: Cambridge University Press.

Gupta, Joyeeta and Nicolien van der Grijp (2000). Perceptions of the EU's role: is the EU a leader? In Gupta, Joyeeta and Michael Grubb (eds) *Climate change and European leadership: a sustainable role for Europe?* Dordrecht: Kluwer, 67–82.

Gupta, Joyeeta and Lasse Ringius (2001). The EU's climate leadership: reconciling ambition and reality. *International Environmental Agreements: Politics, Law and Economics* 1 (2): 281–99.

INC (1993a). Matters relating to commitments: criteria for joint implementation, A/AC.237/Misc.30.

INC (1993b). Matters relating to commitments: criteria for joint implementation, A/AC.237/Misc.33.

INC (1993c). Matters relating to commitments: methodological issues, A/AC.237/Misc.32.

INC (1994a). Matters relating to commitments, A/AC.237/Misc.36.

INC (1994b). Matters relating to commitments: criteria for joint implementation, A/AC.237/Misc.37.

INC (1995a). Matters relating to commitments, A/AC.237/Misc.43.

INC (1995b). Matters relating to arrangements for the financial mechanism, A/AC.237/Misc.41.

INC (1995c). Matters relating to commitments: criteria for joint implementation, A/AC.237/Misc.44.

IPCC (1995). IPCC second assessment: climate change 1995. Available at: www.ipcc.ch/pdf/climate-changes-1995/ipcc-2nd-assessment/2nd-assessment-en.pdf.

Jordan, Andrew and Tim Rayner (2010). The evolution of climate policy in the European Union: a historical perspective. In Jordan, Andrew, Dave Huitema, Harro Van Asselt, Tim Rayner and Frans Berkhout (eds) *Climate change policy in the European Union: confronting the dilemmas of mitigation and adaptation?* Cambridge: Cambridge University Press, 52–80.

Kjellén, Bo (2008). *A new diplomacy for sustainable development: the challenge of global change.* New York: Routledge.

Lanchbery, John (1997). What to expect from Kyoto. *Environment* 39 (9): 4–11.

Macrory, Richard and Martin Hession (1996). The European Community and climate change: the role of law and legal competence. In O'Riordan, Timothy and Jill Jäger (eds) *Politics of climate change: a European perspective.* London: Routledge, 106–54.

Masood, Ehsan (1996). United States backs climate panel findings. *Nature* 382 (6589): 287.

Morgan, Jennifer L. (1995). Global climate. In Handl, Günther (ed.) *Yearbook of international environmental law* 5 (1994). Oxford: Oxford University Press, 164–70.

Morgan, Jennifer L. (1996). Global climate. In Handl, Günther (ed.) *Yearbook of international environmental law* 6 (1995). Oxford: Oxford University Press, 1996, 223–33.

Oberthür, Sebastian (1994). Preparations for the First Conference of the Parties. *Environmental Policy and Law* 24 (6): 299–303.

Oberthür, Sebastian (1996). The Second Conference of the Parties. *Environmental Policy and Law* 26 (5): 195–201.

Oberthür, Sebastian and Hermann E. Ott (1995). UN Convention on Climate Change: The First Conference of the Parties. *Environmental Policy and Law* 25 (4–5): 144–56.

Oberthür, Sebastian and Hermann E. Ott (1999). *The Kyoto Protocol: international climate policy for the 21st century.* Berlin: Springer.

Paterson, Matthew (1993). The politics of climate change after UNCED. *Environmental Politics* 2 (4): 174–90.

Paterson, Matthew (1996). *Global warming and global politics.* London: Routledge.

Pearce, Fred (1994). Greenhouse targets beyond 2000. *New Scientist* 143 (1941): 7.

Pearce, Fred (1995). Climate treaty heads for trouble. *New Scientist* 145 (1969): 4.

Pomerance, Rafe (1995). The Framework Convention on Climate Change: expectations for Berlin. *U.S. Department of State Dispatch* 6 (16): 346–8.

Prynn, Jonathan (1994). Out-of-town shopping falls from favour. *The Times,* 8 February.

Royden, Amy (2002). U.S. climate change policy under President Clinton: a look back. *Golden Gate University Law Review* 32 (4): 415–78.

Schreurs, Miranda A (2002). *Environmental politics in Japan, Germany, and the United States.* Cambridge: Cambridge University Press.

Schunz, Simon (2014). *European Union foreign policy and the global climate regime.* Brussels: P.I.E. Peter Lang.

Stuart, John (1996). United Nations. *Greener Management International* 16: 13–17.

UNFCCC (1995a). Implementation of the Berlin Mandate, FCCC/AGBM/1995/Misc.1.

UNFCCC (1995b). Implementation of the Berlin Mandate, FCCC/AGBM/1995/Misc.1/Add.3.

UNFCCC (1995c). Matters relating to commitments, FCCC/CP/1995/Misc.1.

UNFCCC (1995d). Matters relating to commitments, FCCC/CP/1995/Misc.1/Add.1.

UNFCCC (1995e). Report of the Ad hoc Group on the Berlin Mandate on the Work of its first session held at Geneva, FCCC/AGBM/1995/2.

UNFCCC (1995f). Report of the Conference of the Parties on its first session, held at Berlin from 28 March to 7 April 1995, FCCC/CP/1995/7/Add.1.

UNFCCC (1995g). Review of the adequacy of Article 4, Paragraph 2 (A) and (B), FCCC/CP/1995/CRP.1.

UNFCCC (1996a). Report of the Conference of the Parties on its second session, held at Geneva from 8 to 19 July 1996, FCCC/CP/1996/15/Add.1.

UNFCCC (1996b). Report of the Subsidiary Body for Scientific and Technological Advice on the work of its second session, held at Geneva from 27 February to 4 March 1996, FCCC/SBSTA/1996/8.

Victor, David G. and Julian E. Salt (1994). From Rio to Berlin … managing climate change. *Environment* 36 (10): 6–32.

Werksman, Jacob (1994). Institutions for global environmental change. *Global Environmental Change* 4 (4): 339–40.

Williams, Frances (1994). Climate talks end without accord. *Financial Times,* 2 September.

Yamin, Farhana (2000). The role of the EU in climate negotiations. In Gupta, Joyeeta and Michael Grubb (eds) *Climate change and European leadership: a sustainable role for Europe?* Dordrecht: Kluwer, 47–66.

4 The Kyoto Protocol and beyond

COP-2 undoubtedly advanced the negotiations. But the issue of targets and time-tables was left unresolved. This continued to be the case during AGBM-5 (December 1996). Neither the US nor the EU tabled any concrete proposals on the level and timing of targets. The EU's submission to AGBM-5 contained a draft protocol structure calling for an Annex X, which would involve both 'developed country Parties and other Parties' (UNFCCC 1996a, p. 19). Each of the Annex X parties would need to achieve significant emission reductions in the post-2000 period of 1990 levels, relying upon a wide range of mandatory, highly recommended and voluntary PAMs that would be set out in three different Annexes (A, B and C). The EU's proposal generated confusion and came under criticism, especially because it initially lacked clarity as to the countries that would be listed in this new Annex X (Schunz 2014). What should be noted here in relation to AGBM-5 is the submission by the US (UNFCCC 1996b; see also Oberthür and Ott 1999), according to which the final deal should include:

a   multi-year targets, thereby allowing parties flexibility in determining the pace at which to meet their mitigation objectives;
b   banking (i.e. carrying over unused emissions from one phase to the other) and borrowing (i.e. against targets for the next period in order to emit more in a current period);
c   a comprehensive approach for six gases;
d   emissions trading and JI.

As Oberthür and Ott (1999) note, 'borrowing' is the only element that was not included in the final text of the Kyoto Protocol. AGBM-5 concluded with its chairman being requested to prepare a compilation of all existing proposals on the elements of a protocol or another legal instrument.

This compilation was presented during AGBM-6 (March 1997). It included various informal proposals tabled by EU Member States on the scale of ambition for targets and timetables during the AGBM process (see Table 4.1). In the run-up to AGBM-6 the EU had clarified its Annex X proposal (see UNFCCC 1997a), by noting that 'other parties' meant new OECD members and countries with economies in transition (see also Schunz 2014). Although only Mexico and

Table 4.1 Informal proposals by EU Member States during the AGBM negotiations

UK	Reduce overall greenhouse gas emissions by 5–10 per cent below 1990 levels by 2010.
Belgium	Reduce CO_2 emissions to 10–20 per cent below 1990 levels by 2010.
Germany and Austria	Reduce CO_2 emissions to 10 per cent below 1990 levels by 2005 and 15–20 per cent by 2010.
Denmark	Reduce CO_2 emissions by 20 per cent of 1990 levels by 2005 and by 50 per cent by 2030.
Netherlands	Annex I parties together reduce total greenhouse gas emissions by an average of 1–2 per cent per year.
France and Spain	Adopt greenhouse gas emissions paths converging eventually to similar levels of emissions per capita or per unit of Gross Domestic Product (GDP), leading to an overall emissions reduction within specified timeframes.

Source: UNFCCC (1996a; 1997a).

South Korea fell in the former category, developing countries perceived it as an effort to break their ranks and retained their opposition to the EU's proposal.

Yet, AGBM-6 is notable in that the Dutch Presidency of the EU formally tabled the group's position on targets and timetables, according to which all Annex X countries should cut the combined emissions ('basket') of CO_2, methane and N_2O by 15 per cent by 2010 compared with 1990 emission levels (Environment Council 1997a). The proposal was also backed by an internal EU burden-sharing agreement. The 15 per cent target would be divided between Member States as shown in Table 4.2. Targets ranged from increases of 40 per cent (Portugal) to decreases of 25 per cent (Germany, Denmark and Austria). The combined commitments only added up to a total reduction of 9.2 per cent, with additional PAMs expected to cover the difference in the event the final agreement in Kyoto went beyond a 10

Table 4.2 The EU burden-sharing agreement (March 1997) (%)

Member State	Commitment	Member State	Commitment
Austria	−25	Italy	−7
Belgium	−10	Luxembourg	−30
Denmark	−25	Netherlands	−10
Finland	0	Portugal	+40
France	0	Spain	+17
Germany	−25	Sweden	+5
Greece	+30	UK	−10
Ireland	+15		

Source: Environment Council (1997a).

per cent reduction (Environment Council 1997a, para.16).[1] This has been viewed as representing a clear sign to the EU's negotiating partners of its willingness to engage in bargaining over the final numbers (Schunz 2014). Unexpectedly for the Dutch, the EU proposal came under heavy fire. JUSCANZ dismissed it as hypocritical on the grounds that it allowed the EU the advantage of differentiated targets internally whilst calling for a flat target for the rest of the developed countries (Yamin 2000). Why should France or Finland, they argued, two of the most developed countries in the world, be allowed to merely stabilize their emissions? The EU's justification was based on its status as a supranational institution with its own parliament and regulatory rules (Schreurs 2002). The fact that the Kyoto Protocol offers the possibility of 'bubbling' to any group of countries suggests that the EU argument that it should be 'entitled to unique treatment' failed to be convincing (Grubb et al. 1999, p. 123). It's interesting to note at this point that France's decision to hold out for a stabilization target has been widely criticized. Indeed, Szarka (2011, p. 114) argued it was a 'fatal error' and a 'wasted opportunity' for France, and in turn the EU, to demonstrate climate leadership.

The AGBM meetings resumed in July–August 1997 (AGBM-7) in the shadow of the US Senate's Byrd–Hagel Resolution. Wary that the Clinton administration would succumb to international pressure for major cuts in emissions, this July 1997 resolution stated that the Senate would not ratify any treaty that did not require meaningful commitments to action by developing countries, especially economically competitive ones, such as China and India. While it expressed its concern for this negative turn of events, the EU in AGBM-7 repeated its proposal for a 15 per cent reduction. Plus it called for an interim target for Annex X parties to individually or jointly reduce emissions levels for CO_2, methane and N_2O together by 2005 by at least 7.5 per cent below 1990 levels (Environment Council 1997b). The EU also took a stand over emissions trading, noting that such mechanisms should be supplementary to domestic action. However, both the US and EU signalled their readiness to compromise. The EU indicated it would be receptive to the trading concept if the targets agreed upon were adequate, while the US signalled its partial openness to the EU 'bubble' (ENB 1997b).

With only one AGBM session left, time was running out. In the US, President Clinton came to the conclusion that furthering the negotiation process while at the same time winning over the Senate would require an agreement that would allow for maximum use of flexibility mechanisms, as well as include firm commitments on the part of the most affluent developing countries (Schreurs 2002). In the run-up to AGBM-8 (October 1997), all remaining major actors (except Russia) came forward with a formal proposal on targets and timetables. The G-77/China, effectively allying with the EU, called for Annex I gas-by-gas reduction targets relating to CO_2, methane and N_2O with reductions of 7.5 per cent by 2005, 15 per cent by 2010 and 35 per cent 2020. Japan called for developed countries to reduce emissions of the same gases by up to 5 per cent until 2010 (ENB 1997a). Finally, the US proposed returning emissions of a basket of the aforementioned three gases plus hydrofluorocarbons (HFCs), perfluorocarbons (PFCs) and sulphur hexafluoride (SF_6) (six gases in total) to 1990 levels by 2008–12, and to reduce them afterwards. The EU was critical of the US's proposal. It felt it was less ambitious than Japan's and failed to meet 'the outcome the world needs' (ENB 1997a, p. 4). The task for delegates at COP-3 would be to synthesize these disparate results into an international agreement. During AGBM-8, sinks were also discussed in great detail for the first time. Various parties, including the US, Norway and Iceland, supported the inclusion of these activities. The EU had given conflicting signs during the AGBM process. It had previously argued that sinks should not be included in the first commitment period because of lack of research data. But it reversed that position during AGBM-8 and supported their inclusion on the proviso that modalities be defined at the first meeting of the parties to the Protocol (Höhne *et al.* 2007).

Up until COP-2, the EU's impact on the AGBM process had been rather limited. Since Berlin its position had remained practically stagnant. According to Oberthür and Ott (1999, p. 67) this had been largely due to the 1996 EU Presidency being held by Italy and Ireland, two countries known for their lack of a 'progressive stance on climate change'. Indeed, scrutiny of the December 1995 and April 1996 Environment Council meetings reveals that climate change was very low on the agenda or absent altogether. The situation was completely reversed when the Netherlands took over the Presidency in early 1997. Under the Dutch, the EU not only exerted substantial leadership by committing to significant emission cuts, but also concluded an internal burden-sharing agreement that enhanced its credibility. For all its 'posturing on the need for legally binding targets', the truth was that by 1996 the EU lacked a common position on how, by when or to what extent greenhouse emissions should be reduced (Yamin 2000, p. 54). The Dutch Presidency allowed the EU to play a major role in the run-up to Kyoto and put significant pressure on the US and other parties to contribute to significant mitigation commitments.

COP-3: the Kyoto Protocol

The EU and the US entered the fray holding opposite positions. The EU called for emission reductions of 15 per cent below 1990 levels, with an interim target of 7.5 per cent by 2005. The US argued in favour of stabilizing CO_2 emissions by 2012, basically allowing itself another 12 years to meet its 1992 Rio target (Newell 1998). But the US target was conditional upon commitments from developing countries. When the negotiations were over, the Kyoto Protocol had established national emissions reduction targets for parties listed in Annex B, relative to 1990 baseline emissions, during a 2008–12 commitment period (see Table 4.3). Furthermore, it had provided an outline of various mechanisms, such as JI, Emissions Trading (ET), the CDM and sinks. Finally, the rules for entry into force of the Kyoto Protocol required 55 parties to the Convention to ratify it, including Annex I parties accounting for 55 per cent of that group's CO_2 emissions in 1990.

Table 4.3 The differentiated quantitative obligations of Annex B parties (%)

Target	Party
–8	EU-15, Bulgaria, Czech Republic, Estonia, Latvia, Liechtenstein, Lithuania, Monaco, Romania, Slovakia, Slovenia, Switzerland
–7	USA
–6	Canada, Hungary, Japan, Poland
–5	Croatia
Stabilization	New Zealand, Russia, Ukraine
+1	Norway
+8	Australia
+10	Iceland

One could look at the Kyoto Protocol as a genuine compromise. '[T]he EU got their numbers, the US got their institutions, Japan got prestige as a host, the [JUSCANZ] countries got their differentiation and the developing countries avoided commitments' (Andresen and Agrawala 2002, p. 47). Even so, it is generally agreed that it was the US who had the greatest influence over the final text. As Grubb et al. (1999, p. 112) note, 'within that panoply, US dominance is striking'. They then go on to add that 'to discover the source of most ideas in the Protocol, one needs only to read the US proposal of January 1997'. Indeed, the US had managed to secure several concessions from other parties. The EU was willing to sign an agreement that fell outside its initial negotiating position, mainly because its leaders were not prepared to leave Kyoto without one (Downie 2014).

First, the agreement supported the use of flexibility mechanisms. Instead of taking domestic action, the US could achieve the majority of its greenhouse reduction target via investments in mitigation projects in third countries or through credits obtained for carbon sequestered in its forests (Brown 2002). An EU interviewee recalled a meeting a month prior to Kyoto where Stuart E. Eizenstat, the US chief climate negotiator, bluntly stated: 'do not imagine that the US is in any way going to meet its proposed stabilization target through domestic action.'[2] US policymakers estimated that by including flexibility mechanisms, sinks and the three additional gases, the US target of –7 per cent was in reality equivalent to only a 3 per cent reduction (Gupta 2014). This is also why the Russian target was 'so important for the Americans'.[3] The EU argued against heavy reliance on such mechanisms on the grounds that they should be 'supplemental' to domestic action. The EU was especially critical of the CDM but, overall, the compromise on flexibility mechanisms was seen as a necessity by EU policymakers if they wanted to get fixed and quantified reduction targets in the Kyoto Protocol. As an interviewee noted:

> I remember the mood in the meeting when we had to take a decision on the CDM and certainly the feeling was that this was almost blackmailing; that we were put with our backs against the wall and told that either you take this or there won't be an agreement.[4]

Second, the EU's position that all Annex I parties agree a flat-rate cut never made it into the text. During the negotiations, the EU watered down its stance and accepted that only Japan and the US would be held to a common target (Newell 1998). Struggling to hold that ground, the EU compromised further. It agreed that the US and Japan 'as main competitors could have different targets as long as the burden was comparable to that of the EU' (Newell 1998, p. 156). Given that the US and Japan would not sign up to a 15 per cent reduction target, the EU was forced to accept an 8 per cent reduction in order to get them on board. Schunz (2014) gives an interesting account of how an initially-proposed cascade of 8 per cent for the EU, 5 per cent for the US and 4.5 per cent for Japan was eventually crystalized in the final 8–7–6 cascade that is to be found in the final text of the Kyoto Protocol. Giving in on targets and abandoning the –15 per cent objective because of pressure from Japan and the US was not well received by a number of Member States, including Germany, which argued that the troika (mainly the UK at the time) could have better held its ground (Delreux 2011). A number of smaller Member States also complained that the EU 'could have gone a bit higher'.[5] Criticism aside, the EU had ultimately pushed the US up to a comparable target. Yet, this also meant that its internal burden-sharing agreement was now void and would have to be renegotiated. Crucially, the EU was successful in ensuring that the Kyoto Protocol included 'bubbles' within which parties were allowed to jointly meet their mitigation obligations (Babiker *et al.* 2002). Overall, its negative stance towards differentiation was unattainable, given that, as Schunz (2014, p. 106) notes, the EU had delivered itself, through its own 'bubble', 'the best argument for its opponents'.

Third, the US had successfully pushed for flexibility in the timescale in which national reduction targets would need to be achieved (Brown 2002). The EU proposal had been for targets to be met by 2010, with 7.5 per cent of the cut to be achieved by 2005. Instead of a single year, the Kyoto Protocol stipulated that parties could meet their objectives during a five-year averaging period, that is, 2008–12. The EU had only been able to insert a soft provision in Article 3.2, according to which each party 'shall, by 2005, have made demonstrable progress in achieving its commitments' (UNFCCC 1997b, p.3). Finally, the US had been able to secure the incorporation of all six major greenhouse gases, as opposed to the EU and Japanese 'three-gas' approach. As Royden notes (2002, p. 442), these three additional gases accounted 'for one percent of the [U.S.] seven percent reduction'. In summary, the only major US objective that was not achieved, because of opposition from G-77/China, was that of securing the meaningful participation of developing countries. The EU had supported the G-77/China by invoking the Berlin Mandate, even though it had (unsuccessfully) promoted the idea of a review process that would discuss developing country commitments for the post-2012 period (Schunz 2014). Soon after Kyoto, the Clinton administration announced that barring developing country participation, it had no intention of submitting the Kyoto Protocol to the Senate for ratification.

With respect to the EU, apart from compromising on the majority of its positions (Jordan and Rayner 2010), it also became embroiled in what became known as the 'EU bunker'. Changing positions and agreeing to new proposals on the table required the assent of the majority of the Member States, many of which would often even need to seek advice and guidance from their national capitals. As a result, prolonged intra-EU negotiations between the Member States and the Commission during COP-3 left the EU 'hardly able to react to outside developments, let alone take the initiative to steer events' (Oberthür and Ott 1999, p. 268). For instance, during the final dramatic night at Kyoto, EU ministers were holding internal consultations to establish a common position on the CDM while the plenary was concurrently deliberating on the final text (Grubb and Yamin 2001). When the EU 'informed the Chairman of their opposition to the pre-budget crediting of emission reductions, the decision had already been taken and could not be reopened' (Oberthür and Ott 1999, p. 90).

Another complication the EU's negotiating performance during Kyoto related to the limited capacity of the Luxembourgian Presidency to handle the negotiations, which intrinsically involved complex issues spanning several levels. Negotiations had to be conducted by a troika of the Netherlands, as Luxembourg's predecessor, and the UK, as its successor. This allowed UK Deputy Prime Minister John Prescott to readily take advantage of his country's diplomatic clout and assert leadership in the COP arena (Oberthür and Ott 1999). The UK's efforts to dominate over the EU agenda caused 'certain annoyance among some of the bigger Member States'. As one interviewee recalled:

> It was as much an attitude as anything. It was this sense that I know the Americans, I get along well with Al Gore, so I will do the negotiations because I can talk to the Americans and you cannot. I can do it, you can't. And that meant that the Germans and others were afraid that he was going to go and sell the EU case cheaply to some of the other major players.[6]

Various Member States were also concerned that the UK had a 'private agenda' and there was also 'a fear that he would bully the Dutch and the Luxembourgers into moving along his path'.[7] Apparently unsatisfied by the troika's performance, Germany expressed its unwillingness to provide it with the flexibility required to respond in a timely way to 'new positions and red herrings', notably those of the US (ENB 1997c, p. 15).

To conclude with Kyoto, a couple of main points need to be made about the EU. First, it misperceived the US preference structure on a number of fronts and entered the fray with aspirations that were perceived as 'unrealistically high' (Underdal 1998, p. 113). Consequently, it had to greatly compromise its positions on most fronts to reach a negotiated settlement. An interviewee described the EU's performance in Kyoto as a sequel of 'retreats, retreats, retreats'.[8] While reputational concerns were obviously important for the EU, leaving Kyoto without a deal was simply not a choice. As Underdal (1998) notes, process-generated stakes tend to impede rather than facilitate progress towards agreement. However, there are cases where they can actually provide 'positive opportunities' (p. 115). Kyoto, as well as Rio in 1992, were two such cases. In both there was pressure on many parties that were mindful of sustainability issues to 'do well' and reach an agreement (p. 115). In such cases, Underdal (1998, p. 115) notes, a party might accept 'measures it would otherwise not have supported'.

The second point is that the EU was again proposing a 'politically inadequate solution design model'. While its proposals on targets and mechanisms derived from sustainability principles, they were again dismissed on fairness and feasibility grounds by the US. Interestingly, even though it was the EU that was the main proponent of ambitious emissions targets, its proposals represented a politically inadequate solution design model even for its own Member States. Even EU officials were critical at the time of the fact that while the EU advocated for a 15 per cent reduction target, the burden-sharing agreement's combined commitments only added up to a reduction of 9.2 per cent. As one of them noted, the 15 per cent target was not a 'particularly credible one, as it would have been extremely difficult, if not impossible, to share this 15 percent between the Member States at the time'.[9]

Such misalignment between words and deeds had caused considerable uncertainty and mistrust among parties on past occasions, and would continue to do so in the future, greatly compromising the EU's credibility as a result.

The aftermath of Kyoto

Following the intensive talks at Kyoto, negotiations entered a phase of low activity. Most countries needed time to evaluate the final agreement. For the EU, the Kyoto Protocol, although a major step forward, admittedly fell short of its proposals and expectations. It was essentially a fiendishly complex framework, which needed to be clarified (see Environment Council 1998a). The May 1998 G-8 Summit in Birmingham reached a similar conclusion, with the final communiqué stating:

> As the Kyoto protocol says, to supplement domestic actions, we will work further on flexible mechanisms such as international market-based emissions trading, joint implementation and the clean development mechanism, and on sinks. We aim to draw up rules and principles that will ensure an enforceable, accountable, verifiable, open and transparent trading system and an effective compliance regime.
>
> (G-8 1998, para.11)

The Birmingham G-8 is also notable in that the participating EU Member States agreed that during the forthcoming COP-4 in Buenos Aires they should work 'with all countries to increase global participation in establishing targets to limit or reduce greenhouse gas emissions' (G-8 1998, para.11). The communiqué also noted that COP-4 should consider the adoption of voluntary efforts and commitments from developing countries (G-8 1998, para.11). European G-8 leaders at the Birmingham Summit, compelled by the realization that without increasing global participation the US would never ratify Kyoto, formally agreed to the text of the communiqué. As an interviewee noted, 'what we were looking for at the time was to satisfy the US demand'.[10] Interestingly, the negotiating text at Kyoto did contain until very late in the process a provision for developing countries to take on a voluntary target of their own choice at any time (Jacoby *et al.* 1998). This provision, while supported by several developing countries, was eventually removed because of strong opposition from key G-77 countries, such as China and India.

A clearer picture of the EU position at the time is offered by the proceedings of the March 1998 Environment Council. Apart from calling for increased global participation, EU officials expressed regret that the Kyoto Protocol did not include a wide range of legally binding PAMs. They stressed for the nth time that domestic action should provide the main means of meeting the commitments under the Protocol, which meant that a 'concrete ceiling' on the use of flexible mechanisms would need to be defined (Environment Council 1998a, para. 11). More importantly, despite the EU and its Member States being ready to sign the Protocol to signal their continuing commitment to achieving its objective, the same was not so with its ratification. The latter was to be withheld until satisfactory progress had been made on a number of outstanding issues, particularly in relation to the operation of flexible mechanisms (Delreux 2011). The EU, unwilling to subscribe to obligations still partly unknown, wanted first to ensure that these mechanisms provided 'real, cost effective, and verifiable environmental benefits and did not create loopholes that undermined the objectives of the Protocol' (Environment Council 1998a, para. 5).

A few months later, the June 1998 Environment Council announced the EU's revised burden-sharing agreement (see Table 4.4). With this new agreement, the EU was moving from an objective of –15 per cent for three gases to an objective of –8 per cent for six gases. Yet the combined commitments in the first, pre-Kyoto, burden-sharing agreement (1997) only added up to a reduction of 9.2 per cent, with PAMs expected to cover the difference. Most Northern and Central European countries therefore saw their commitments being slightly

Table 4.4 The EU burden-sharing agreement (June 1998) (%)

Member State	Internal Commitment	Member State	Internal Commitment
Belgium	−7.5	Luxembourg	−28
Denmark	−21	Netherlands	−6
Germany	−21	Austria	−13
Greece	+25	Portugal	+27
Spain	+15	Finland	0
France	0	Sweden	+4
Ireland	+13	UK	−12.5
Italy	−6.5	EU total	−8

Source: Environment Council (1998b).

reduced, apart from the Netherlands and Austria, whose targets were basically halved. Given that it had presided over the first agreement, the decision of the Netherlands to move to a significantly lower target not only attracted wide-spread criticism from several other Member States, but also gave a signal to some of them, such as Germany, Belgium and Denmark, to follow suit (Andersson and Mol 2002). It was only the cohesion countries that fared worse, as they were essentially told that they would need to implement stricter mitigation policies instead of relying on emission reductions achieved in the richer northern Member States (Dessai and Michaelowa 2001).

COP-4 (Buenos Aires)

From this point onwards, climate change negotiations entered a far more technical and complicated phase. The task of making sense of Kyoto's provisions began at COP-4 in Buenos Aires (2–13 November 1998). The conference started with an intense debate. A US-backed Argentinian proposal suggested developing nations could undertake voluntary commitments if they so wished. Most developing countries vehemently opposed the proposal on the grounds that it would create a new category of parties under the UNFCCC (ENB 1998). China also made a distinction between developing country 'survival emissions' and developed country 'luxury emissions' (ENB 1998). The EU, in an effort not to antagonize either side, noted that while targets for the first commitment period of the Kyoto Protocol only applied to Annex I parties, the question of 'broadening commitments in the long term [was] necessary and unavoidable', given that 'commitments of Annex I countries alone [would] not be sufficient to meet the ultimate objective of the Convention' (UNFCCC 1998, p. 8). It further proposed that the COP President make a decision on how to proceed forward, but lack of consensus resulted in the item being eventually dropped from the agenda (Tangen 1999). A few days later, however, Argentina and Kazakhstan unilaterally announced that they would soon take on voluntary commitments, a move which the US hailed as 'historic' and a step towards the 'meaningful participation' of developing countries, and prompted it to sign the Kyoto Protocol in New York the following day (ENB 1998). Senator Hagel was quick to note though, that the Senate would never ratify an agreement which excluded developing countries from *legally binding* commitments (Boehmer-Christiansen and Kellow 2002). 'In signing the Kyoto Protocol,' Hagel further said, 'the President blatantly contradicts the will of the US Senate' (ENB 1998, p. 13).

The major divisions among parties in Buenos Aires centred on the flexibility mechanisms. The EU, in an effort to ensure their supplementarity, called for limits ('caps') on their use to promote domestic emissions reductions. Such limits were opposed by the newly formed Umbrella Group (JUSCANZ plus Russia and Ukraine), with Stuart Eizenstat, chief negotiator of the US at COP-4, pointing out that the US would 'fight on the beaches and in the trenches' against them, thereby quoting a famous Winston Churchill World

War II dictum (Oberthür and Ott 1999, p. 288). On a counter-attack against the EU, Canada and the US noted that there 'was no ceiling on transfers of assigned amounts under Article 4 (bubble)' (ENB 1998, p. 8). Further disputes were averted by the decision to postpone agreement on the Kyoto mechanisms and other issues until COP-6 in 2000.

The main outcome of COP-4 was the adoption of the 'Buenos Aires Plan of Action' (BAPA), which stated that the parties should aim to resolve by COP-6 a list of outstanding issues concerning the Kyoto Protocol. These included questions around compliance modalities, technology transfer, as well as the financial and flexibility mechanisms. A further COP-4 decision addressed the issue of carbon sinks, with parties, given the topic's complexity and contentiousness, agreeing to defer agreement until after the IPCC had issued its special report on forestry and sinks in May 2000 (Kaiser 1998). Waiting for this report before adopting any new decisions on sinks had been specifically requested by the EU shortly before COP-4 (see Environment Council 1998c). Agreement on the core issues had been postponed until 2000. While most negotiators viewed COP-4 as having maintained the momentum, no decisions had been taken that could mollify the US Senate's outright hostility towards the Protocol, thereby leaving little room for optimism that the Kyoto Protocol would soon enter into force (Reiner 1999). Yet, the announcements of Argentina and Kazakhstan, the former's partially influenced by its intention to join the OECD, led many to believe that G-77/China unity was hanging on by a thread and that it would not be long before this group broke up into new constellations (Biermann 2005; Tangen 1999).

From the EU's point of view the BAPA was considered a satisfactory result. The December 1998 Environment Council noted that

> it can be seen as a significant success of the European Community and its Member States that the elaboration of a compliance system within the same time frame as for the development of the Kyoto mechanisms ... [was] included in the work-plan.
>
> (Environment Council 1998d)

Its performance at COP-4 had been problematic, however. Prolonged intra-EU negotiations 'paralyzed the whole process' at times, with internal divergence with respect to the Kyoto mechanisms preventing the EU from submitting a single paper on the flexibility mechanisms during COP-4 (Tangen 1999, p. 176). The source of this divergence was that Member States were divided with respect to the supplementarity of Kyoto mechanisms. Despite all Member States agreeing that there should be a 'concrete ceiling' on the use of the mechanisms, they could not agree on a figure or approach. Sweden, Finland, the Netherlands and Ireland argued in favour of a less stringent formula, while others, such as Austria, Germany and Denmark, supported a strict 50 per cent cap on the use of emissions trading, JI and CDM (ENDS 1999; Oberthür and Ott 1999). As Yamin (2000, p. 60) observes, divergence in opinion could be partly explained by the fact that a number of Member States, such as Denmark and the UK, had set up domestic emission trading schemes, meaning that they had an interest in keeping international emissions trading as free of 'bureaucratic constraints' as possible. The Commission and the European Parliament also appeared divided on the issue. Whereas the former had strongly supported a cap in June 1998, it looked more uncertain and willing to re-examine the issue by September (ENDS 1998a). Likewise, while the latter's Environment Committee had voted against a cap on 4 September, the plenary called for one on 16 September (ENDS 1998b).

Jordan and Rayner (2010) note that this debate over supplementarity actually stemmed from a growing realization among Member States of the costs of implementing their Kyoto targets. A number of Member States 'were on the retreat post-Kyoto', not even allowing the Commission to take the initiative in developing the policy measures necessary for the task at hand (Oberthür and Ott 1999, p. 148). Although EU emissions were again on the rise, reluctance from the Council and allocation of inadequate financial and other resources were often cited by Commission officials as the reason behind this stalemate (Jordan and Rayner 2010). As an interviewee noted:

> There was to a great extent a realization on the part of a lot of countries, including EU ones, which had taken on substantial commitments, that they hadn't really had a very close heart-to-heart conversation with their treasuries and finance ministers, so nobody had actually calculated what the potential bill was on the kind of agreement that came out of Kyoto. And there was a realization that this was something which would not be easy to pay for.[11]

COP-5 (Bonn)

Following COP-4, two technical workshops on protocol issues (carbon sinks and the Kyoto mechanisms), as well as the official sessions of the UNFCCC Subsidiary Bodies, were held in preparation for COP-5. BAPA's generous timeline gave a pretext to most parties to defer consideration of substantive issues until later (ENB 1999b). Despite COP-5 (October/November 1999) being 'a rather lackadaisical technical meeting', it did have moments of political fervour (Dessai 2000, p. 193). The aim of the Finnish Presidency of the EU for COP-5 had been for parties to move the process forward by concluding a draft negotiating text. Opposition from other parties put an end to the EU's aspirations. The G-77/China deemed such a move premature on the grounds that parties were still at the stage of 'making submissions, noting convergence/divergence and synthesizing views' (ENB 1999a, p. 8). For the Umbrella Group, there was equally no such need for a draft, since a negotiating text was a 'living document that would go through several drafts' (ENB 1999a, p. 8).

Regarding the issue of the compliance mechanism, parties, including the EU, agreed that its committee should have both a facilitative and an enforcement branch whose functions would include ensuring compliance through binding consequences known in advance, as well as promoting compliance by assisting those parties that were facing difficulties in complying (ENB 1999a). The EU argued that a strict, credible and legally binding compliance procedure would be a prerequisite for setting up a functioning market for emissions trading (Ott 2001). Another important development during COP-5 was a call by a number of parties, including the EU and Japan, but not the US, Australia and Canada, to set the 2002 Johannesburg Rio + 10 meeting as a self-imposed deadline for Kyoto's entry into force (Dessai 2000).

Discussions on the Kyoto mechanisms proceeded at a much slower pace, with the EU attracting anew the criticism of the Umbrella Group for seeking to impose limits ('caps') on their use. An important difference this time was that the EU had put a percentage number on its proposed cap. Following prolonged internal negotiations, the Member States in favour of greater flexibility gave ground by agreeing to a 50 per cent cap on the Kyoto mechanisms (ENDS 1999). This position failed to result in a rapprochement with the US, which expressed its disappointment that the EU was attempting to limit 'one of the most effective tools' available to mitigate climate change (ENDS 1999).

Considerable attention was given to the CDM, with the most notable development relating to a proposal by countries with large nuclear industries, such as France, the UK, Japan, the US and Canada, for nuclear power to qualify for the CDM (Pearce 1999). Developing countries with nuclear industries, such as China and India, were viewed by them as a potential source of new contracts for nuclear reactors. China and India wholeheartedly supported this proposal, while several European countries, especially Germany, Austria and Ireland, as well as environmental NGOs, vehemently rejected it (Dessai 2000). As Denmark's environment minister, Svend Auken, noted at COP-5: 'the CDM is about clean development and nuclear energy has no place' (cited in Brown 2000). Developing countries at large, particularly those in the Pacific and Africa, sided with these EU Member States, fearing that CDM investments would concentrate in nuclear projects. The support of France and the UK for nuclear power contradicted the official EU negotiating position and highlighted the inconsistencies and lack of coordination between EU Member States and their national policies. Nuclear power as an issue was also deferred to COP-6.

At the close of COP-5, the dates for COP-6 were set as 13–24 November 2000 in The Hague. Although most Umbrella Group countries preferred early 2001 in order to avoid the COP coinciding with the US Presidential elections, the position of the G-77/China in favour of November 2000 eventually prevailed. This increased the possibilities of the US being represented at The Hague by a 'lame duck administration, even if it proved to be succeeded by one of the same party' (Boehmer-Christiansen and Kellow 2002, p. 77). As it turned out, the election debacle in Florida would cast a shadow across COP-6.

Notes

1 As Downie (2014) notes, the final agreement covered only a 10 per cent target owing to great opposition from cohesion countries who feared that their share under a 15 per cent target would be too high. The final compromise was engineered by the then Danish Environment Minister, Svend Auken.
2 Interview No. 15 (Former Commission official).
3 Interview No. 15 (Former Commission official).
4 Interview No. 15 (Former Commission official).
5 Interview No. 1 (Member State official – Former Head of Delegation).
6 Interview No. 14 (Former Commission official).
7 Interview No. 14 (Former Commission official).
8 Interview No. 1 (Member State official – Former Head of Delegation).
9 Interview No. 15 (Former Commission official).
10 Interview No. 9 (Commission official). This point was also made by interviewee No. 15 (Former Commission official).
11 Interview No. 14 (Former Commission official).

References

Andersson, Magnus and Arthur P.J. Mol (2002). The Netherlands in the UNFCCC process – leadership between ambition and reality. *International Environmental Agreements: Politics, Law and Economics* 2 (1): 49–68.

Andresen, Steinar and Shardul Agrawala (2002). Leaders, pushers and laggards in the making of the climate regime. *Global Environmental Change* 12 (1): 41–51.

Babiker, Mustafa H., Henry D. Jacoby, John M. Reilly and David M. Reiner (2002). The evolution of a climate regime: Kyoto to Marrakech and beyond. *Environmental Science & Policy* 5 (3): 195–206.

Biermann, Frank (2005). Between the USA and the South: strategic choices for European climate policy. *Climate Policy* 5 (3): 273–90.

Boehmer-Christiansen, Sonja and Aynsley Kellow (2002). *International environmental policy: interests and the failure of the Kyoto process.* Cheltenham: Edward Elgar.

Brown, Donald A. (2002). *American heat: ethical problems with the United States' response to global warming.* Lanham: Rowman & Littlefield.

Brown, Paul (2000). UK hopes to win carbon credits deal with China. *The Guardian,* 23 May. Available at: www.guardian.co.uk/uk/2000/may/23/nuclear.world.

Delreux, Tom (2011). *The EU as international environmental negotiator.* Farnham: Ashgate.

Dessai, Suraje (2000). The Fifth Conference of the Parties to the United Nations Framework Convention on Climate Change: an advancement or derailment of the process? *Colorado Journal of International Environmental Law & Policy* 11 (2): 193–208.

Dessai, Suraje and Axel Michaelowa (2001). Burden sharing and cohesion countries in European climate policy: the Portuguese example. *Climate Policy* 1 (3): 327–41.

Downie, Christian (2014). *The politics of climate change negotiations: strategies and variables in prolonged international negotiations.* Cheltenham: Edward Elgar.

ENB (1997a). Report of the Meetings of the FCCC Subsidiary Bodies: 20–31 October 1997. *Earth Negotiations Bulletin* 12 (66): 1–17.

ENB (1997b). Report of the Meetings of the Subsidiary Bodies to the Framework Convention on Climate Change 28 July – 7 August 1997. *Earth Negotiations Bulletin* 12 (55): 1–14.

ENB (1997c). Report of the Third Conference of the Parties to the United Nations Framework Convention on Climate Change: 1–11 December 1997. *Earth Negotiations Bulletin* 12 (76): 1–16.

ENB (1998). Report of the Fourth Conference of the Parties to the UN Framework Convention on Climate Change: 2–13 November 1998. *Earth Negotiations Bulletin* 12 (97): 1–14.

ENB (1999a). Summary of the Fifth Conference of the Parties to the Framework Convention on Climate Change: 25 October – 5 November 1999. *Earth Negotiations Bulletin* 12 (123): 1–16.

ENB (1999b). Summary of the Tenth Session of the FCCC Subsidiary Bodies: 31 May – 11 June 1999. *Earth Negotiations Bulletin* 12 (110): 1–16.

ENDS (1998a). Commission joins EU fight for climate cap, 16 September.

ENDS (1998b). MEPs reinstate call for climate gas trading cap, 17 September.

ENDS (1999). USA slams EU Kyoto trading cap plan, 19 May.

Environment Council (1997a). *Environment Council Press Release*, 60 No. 6309/97, Brussels, 3 March.

Environment Council (1997b). *Environment Council Press Release*, 204 No. 9132/97, Brussels, 19 June.

Environment Council (1998a). *Environment Council Press Release*, 78 No. 6894/98, Brussels, 23 March.

Environment Council (1998b). *Environment Council Press Release*, 205 No. 09402/98, Luxembourg, 16 June.

Environment Council (1998c). *Environment Council Press Release*, 323 No. 11603/98, Luxembourg, 6 October.

Environment Council (1998d). *Environment Council Press Release*, 453 No. 14134/98, Luxembourg, 20 December.

G-8 (1998). Communiqué, Birmingham, 17 May. Available at: www.g8.utoronto.ca/summit/1998birmingham/finalcom.htm.

Grubb, Michael and Farhana Yamin (2001). Climatic collapse at The Hague: what happened, why, and where do we go from here? *International Affairs* 77 (2): 261–76.

Grubb, Michael, Christiaan Vrolijk and Duncan Brack (1999). *The Kyoto Protocol: a guide and assessment.* London: Royal Institute of International Affairs.

Gupta, Joyeeta (2014). *The history of global climate governance.* Cambridge: Cambridge University Press.

Höhne, Niklas, Sina Wartmann, Anke Herold and Annette Freibauer (2007). The rules for land use, land use change and forestry under the Kyoto Protocol – lessons learned for the future climate negotiations. *Environmental Science & Policy* 10: 353–69.

Jacoby, Henry D., Ronald G. Prinn and Richard Schmalensee (1998). Kyoto's unfinished business. *Foreign Affairs* 77 (4): 54–66.

Jordan, Andrew and Tim Rayner (2010). The evolution of climate policy in the European Union: a historical perspective. In Jordan, Andrew, Dave Huitema, Harro van Asselt, Tim Rayner and Frans Berkhout (eds) *Climate change policy in the European Union: confronting the dilemmas of mitigation and adaptation?* Cambridge: Cambridge University Press, 52–80.

Kaiser, Jocelyn (1998). Pollution permits for greenhouse gases? *Science* 282 (5391): 1025.

Newell, Peter (1998). Who 'CoPed' out in Kyoto? An assessment of the Third Conference of the Parties to the Framework Convention on Climate Change. *Environmental Politics* 7 (2): 153–9.

Oberthür, Sebastian and Hermann E. Ott (1999). *The Kyoto Protocol: international climate policy for the 21st century.* Berlin: Springer.

Ott, Hermann E (2001). The Bonn Agreement to the Kyoto Protocol – paving the way for ratification. *International Environmental Agreements: Politics, Law and Economics* 1 (4): 469–76.

Pearce, Fred (1999). Dirty dealing. *New Scientist* 164 (2212): 12.

Reiner, David M. (1999). Progress at Buenos Aires? *Environment* 41 (10): 4.

Royden, Amy (2002). U.S. climate change policy under President Clinton: a look back. *Golden Gate University Law Review* 32 (4): 415–78.

Schreurs, Miranda A. (2002). *Environmental politics in Japan, Germany, and the United States.* Cambridge: Cambridge University Press.

Schunz, Simon (2014). *European Union foreign policy and the global climate regime.* Brussels: P.I.E. Peter Lang.

Szarka, Joseph (2011). France's troubled bids to climate leadership. In Wurzel, Rüdiger K.W. and James Connelly (eds) *The European Union as a leader in international climate change politics.* London: Routledge, 112–28.

Tangen, Kristian (1999). The climate change negotiations: Buenos Aires and beyond. *Global Environmental Change* 9 (3): 175–8.

Underdal, Arild (1998). Leadership in international environmental negotiations: designing feasible solutions. In Underdal, Arild (ed.) *The politics of international environmental management.* Dordrecht: Kluwer, 101–27.

UNFCCC (1996a). Implementation of the Berlin Mandate, FCCC/CP/1996/Misc.2/Add.2.

UNFCCC (1996b). Implementation of the Berlin Mandate, FCCC/CP/1996/Misc.2/Add.4.

UNFCCC (1997a). Implementation of the Berlin Mandate, FCCC/CP/1997/Misc.1.

UNFCCC (1997b). Kyoto Protocol to the United Nations Framework Convention on Climate Change. New York: United Nations.

UNFCCC (1998). Second Review of the Adequacy of Article 4.2(a) and (b), FCCC/CP/1998/MISC.6.

Yamin, Farhana (2000). The role of the EU in climate negotiations. In Gupta, Joyeeta and Michael Grubb (eds) *Climate change and European leadership: a sustainable role for Europe?* Dordrecht: Kluwer, 47–66.

5 From collapse to revival

Few major developments took place during the year that elapsed between the Bonn and The Hague COPs. Prior to Bonn, the October 1999 Environment Council had asked the Commission to put forward a list of priority actions and policies that would enable the EU to meet its 8 per cent reduction target (Environment Council 1999). In response, the European Climate Change Programme (ECCP) was launched in June 2000. Its primary goal was to identify the costs and benefits of different emission reduction measures in *inter alia* the energy, transport and industry sectors, by the summer of 2001.

In another development, the June 2000 Environment Council overcame resistance from the UK, France and Finland to exclude nuclear power from the CDM until Kyoto was ratified (ENDS 2000a; see also Szarka 2011). On the international front, a flurry of formal and informal workshops led to progress on a number of outstanding technical issues, including inventories, reporting and monitoring. Yet progress, politically, remained disappointingly slow (Ott 2001a). By late 2000, and following the September sessions of the Subsidary Bodies in Lyon, observers began to openly question whether COP-6 would succeed. Whilst some negotiating text had emerged, it remained tentative at best as it was 'riddled with brackets' (ENB 2000b, p. 1). For instance, the 125-page text on flexibility mechanisms with which parties had arrived in Lyon ballooned to 200 pages by the time they departed (ENB 2000b). Following that meeting, the EU attacked the Umbrella Group for failing to advance the negotiations by engaging in them constructively. At least it could claim some success in that the G-77/China had given 'overwhelming and vocal support' for the first time to the EU position on supplementarity (ENDS 2000b; see also Michaelowa and Schwarze 2001).

Progress was painfully slow. A lack of urgency was unmistakable. Climate change was limited to 'a few speeches and footnotes' at the September 2000 UN Millennium Summit of World Leaders in New York (Ott 2001a, p. 280) and was seldom mentioned in the final communiqué of the G-8 Summit held in Okinawa, Japan, in July 2000 (G-8 2000). With most complex issues unresolved, the chances for COP-6 to succeed appeared very bleak indeed. In just a few weeks, parties would have to achieve something they had failed to do in the last three years of negotiations: reach an agreement. The question was: would they be able to pull this off?

COP-6 (The Hague)

Keen to avoid a foreseeable stalemate, Jan Pronk, the Dutch environment minister and President-designate of COP-6, announced early in the process that he would submit a compromise paper should the negotiations fail to yield a result (Ott 2001a). LULUCF (Land Use, Land-Use Change, and Forestry) or additional sink activities in the first commitment period under Protocol Article 3.4, and sinks in CDM, became the first points of contention (ENB 2000a). Under the Kyoto Protocol, parties could include reductions achieved through changes in forests' sinks since 1990. If the US 'planted new forests after 1990, it could get credit for the amount of carbon stored in the new forest against the Kyoto target' (Brown 2002, p. 188). Prior to The Hague, however, the US pressed for the right to use its existing forests' ability to 'remove carbon from the atmosphere as a credit against [its] 7 percent reduction target' (Brown 2002, p. 188). This proposal had been tabled just three months prior to the COP when the US had proposed that parties should get credits 'for carbon absorption from all managed lands, under the "catch all" land use Article 3.4' (Grubb 2001a, p. 833). This 'creative accounting' amounted to nearly 300 million tons of carbon a year (300MtC/yr), eliminating in a single stroke almost all of the US's mitigation requirements (Michaelowa and Schwarze 2001, p. 118). This proposal 'raised howls of outrage' (Grubb 2001a, p. 833). The EU and developing countries accused the US of wanting credit for doing nothing (Brown 2002).

Supplementarity was the second critical outstanding issue, but progress there in the months preceding The Hague had been equally disappointing. So was the case with respect to other agenda items such as technology transfer or compliance. Unable to bridge their difference at The Hague, and with only one day left of the conference, Pronk submitted his compromise paper to untie this Gordian knot.

With respect to additional sink activities under Article 3.4, the Pronk note suggested including grazing land management, cropland management, forest management, and revegetation in the first commitment period, in essence allowing parties to count ordinary business-as-usual agricultural practices as climate protection measures (Ott 2001a). Furthermore, the Pronk proposal also included sinks in the CDM, again contrary to the explicitly stated positions of the EU and most of the G-77/China. The former had been keen to ensure that the definition of sinks was not broadened to the extent sought by the US. Of concern was that the proposal lacked any safeguards for forestry activities, such as 'the protection of old-growth forests, principles of sustainable forestry or the protection of biodiversity' (Ott 2001b, p. 171). Without such safeguards the impacts on the environment and indigenous peoples could be devastating, as including sinks in the CDM in this way did not preclude, *inter alia*, gaining emission credits by converting native forests into industrial plantations (Ott 2001a). On the positive side, the proposal did exclude nuclear power from the CDM.

Regarding the other 'crunch' issue of supplementarity, the Pronk paper did not set a cap on the use of the flexibility mechanisms as sought by the EU. Instead, it stated that parties should 'meet their emission commitments *primarily* through domestic action' (ENB 2000a, p. 13, emphasis added). Despite this formulation conforming broadly to the EU's negotiating position, it was nevertheless rejected by the US as it ran counter to its demand for unlimited emissions trading.

On the final night of the negotiations and with hopes at their nadir, the UK Deputy Prime Minister John Prescott, in a move reminiscent of Michael Howard's successful attempt back in 1992, left the negotiating room in an attempt to directly strike a deal with the US. Several Member States were aware of the fact that The Hague represented a unique opportunity to strike a deal with the US before the new Bush administration came in (Kjellén 2008). Prescott managed to reach a deal only to see it slip out of his hands at the last minute. According to the compromise, the US would be prepared to let sinks account for just 75 million tons of its mandated reduction, while no sinks would be included in the CDM and there would be no quantitative cap on the flexibility mechanisms (Boyd *et al.* 2008; Dessai 2001). Prescott presented his breakthrough to the rest of the Member States but, after some hesitation, Germany, France and the Scandinavian countries declined it on the grounds that, as the French environment minister said, 'the British [had] made too many concessions' (Boehmer-Christiansen and Kellow 2002, p. 79). Various Member States were simply against any attempt by the US to allow for maximum use of flexibility mechanisms (Downie 2014). Infuriated, Prescott stormed out of the conference room shouting he was 'gutted', making headlines across the world (Dessai 2001, p. 142). Adding salt to the wound, a number of Member States dismissed his efforts as an 'unauthorized British demarche' (Vogler 2002, p. 3).

With no agreement in sight, Pronk suspended the ministerial negotiations until an unspecified future date. Interestingly, most parties blamed the US's 'unreasonable position on forests' for the COP's failure (Brown 2002, p. 39). Mechanisms and sinks were not the only issues left unsolved (e.g. finance, technology transfer, adaptation and compliance) (ENB 2000a). Pronk had intended to achieve convergence on these as well, but only made matters worse, as many parties were sceptical towards his proposals (ENB 2000a). The whole package had crumbled at COP-6.

Why did The Hague negotiations fail?

The Hague COP marked the first instance in which a discrete negotiation round under the UNFCCC failed to result in an agreement. It presents the first opportunity one gets to apply Underdal's framework so as to unpack the reasons behind this disappointing outcome. For Underdal, a number of factors can account for why a negotiation failed – from inaccurate information, uncertainty, and process-generated stakes to politically inadequate solution design models.

Starting with inaccurate information (i.e. **zone of agreement**), the EU in The Hague adopted a rigid bargaining approach and arguably overestimated the preference structure of the US. When this occurs, Underdal (1983, p. 189) notes, a party 'may optimistically insist on a solution that actually falls outside the Opponent's acceptance zone, thus contributing to deadlock'. A slight chance does exist that overestimation can lead to a party obtaining a deal that is 'marginally better for itself than what it would have settled for' (p. 189). Regrettably for EU interests, it was the former that materialized. The EU adamantly refused to compromise its positions on supplementarity and the flexibility mechanisms until the very end, thus contributing to the collapse of the talks. The EU in The Hague, as one interviewee noted, 'envisaged a deal on the level of detail and level of ambition that was just not possible'.[1] As a Commission official explained:

> At that point in time in The Hague the EU still wanted both and was not ready to compromise on the LULUCF side. It was LULUCF that broke the negotiations. Because people wanted to maintain supplementarity and at the same time also have their wishes on LULUCF. Because what the British did with the US was to find some compromise on the forest side which would have been acceptable to the US and the UK, but was not acceptable to the majority of the EU's Member States.[2]

Apart from overestimating the preference structure during The Hague COP, the EU was under the impression that the US misperceived the EU's own. When this occurs, Underdal (1983, p. 190) suggests, there are two eventualities: (a) either your opponent believes that you demand more than you actually do – an image with which you are obviously satisfied and will try to confirm or reinforce, or (b) you are under the impression that your opponent perceives you to be 'softer' than you really are – an image you are unhappy with and will try to modify by at least being 'very reluctant to make accommodative moves that might strengthen that image'.

Jan Pronk, although a minister of an EU Member State, was accused by his European colleagues of going too far in trying to satisfy the demands of the Umbrella Group (Dessai 2001). If so, why did the US reject the deal? The US delegation, as Ott (2001a) notes, could not have expected other parties to grant it *both* unlimited use of the mechanisms *and* the inclusion of additional Article 3.4 sink activities. The most convincing explanation is that the US was looking for a compromise too. It was hoping for a compromise where other parties accepted unlimited use of the flexibility mechanisms as a precondition. The US was not willing to accept some of both. Perhaps the US thought that by introducing a new 'surprise' issue on which it would demonstrate its willingness to compromise, it could soften opposition towards the one issue it really cared about. As the Prescott-Loy compromise (see below) demonstrated, the US was willing to compromise on sinks, but not on mechanisms. In this respect, US rejection of Pronk's paper does make sense. Past experience had taught the US that the EU would eventually 'budge and give its consent to a complete erosion of its position' (Ott 2001b, p. 175). Yet, it did not work that way in The Hague. The EU adopted a rigid stance and had not adequately defined the range of compromise solutions it would be willing to subscribe to. As an interviewee remarked:

You only know what a compromise will look like if you can actually get your own people on board and then say, right, okay, this is what we would like, and this is what we think might work. And then you go to the other parties and say let's shape this. It was very difficult for the EU to achieve this in The Hague.[3]

Interviewees agreed that the EU was accustomed to compromises, especially given it is the main instigator for this whole UNFCCC process. In The Hague, however, 'it was just too much; there is a limit also for Europe'.[4] Various EU officials were of the opinion that the EU had conceded too much flexibility at Kyoto – a mistake that should not be repeated in The Hague (Downie 2014). Some ministers, especially Green Party ones, felt antagonized by what they perceived as a 'take it or leave it' attitude by the US. Whereas the EU was prepared to sign deals in the past that went beyond its initial position, Downie (2014) reasons that the predominance of hardliners within the Environment Council explains why the EU failed to reach an agreement in The Hague.

Failure to identify a zone of agreement was also due to the high degree of **uncertainty** surrounding the COP. The Hague COP took place amidst the legal controversy over the US election with the recount in Florida. Thus, various EU actors seriously debated the merits of a compromise with the outgoing US administration.[5] An interviewee reflected that EU Member States were divided on how to approach the COP negotiations because of this and were uncertain as to whether the EU should signal its willingness to compromise given the next US administration might be 'tougher' than the outgoing one.[6]

Low levels of trust were also explicit in interviewee commentaries. Mistrust amongst parties had increased markedly in the run-up to The Hague because of the US's position on forestry. Intra-EU trust levels had also hit an all-time low. For instance, the French environment minister Dominique Voynet did not enjoy the trust of her own government. Interviewees recalled that she attended COP meetings with 'two watchdogs'.[7] Being from the Green Party, the French President's office wanted to ensure Voynet did not agree to anything that might upset the French nuclear industry.[8]

The decline in trust was exacerbated when – as in Rio and Berlin before – some Member States played the role of individual pushers. Not only did the UK pursue its traditional 'special relationship' with the US, but France also followed suit by negotiating compromises with developing countries which lacked EU backing (Grubb and Yamin 2001). John Prescott's initiative was heavily criticized by his EU colleagues:

The UK obviously started to act when they got the feeling that the French did not act. But how could we relate to something a single Member State had put forward? John Prescott was not the EU President; the French were. We were just not coordinated at all.[9]

This 'chaotic situation'[10] led smaller EU Member States to protest at being cut off from all this back-channel discussion.[11] This point was stressed by another interviewee, who was also critical of the UK's actions:

> Prescott tried to do a private deal with the Americans instead of doing it properly; do it in stages, bring the ideas back to the table, get EU consensus. It is difficult, it takes time, but it works! And it won't work if you do not do it this way, because people feel they have been shut out of the discussion.[12]

A parallel could be made here: the EU is like the whole regime in microcosm because of the way in which smaller players can feel excluded.

Reputational pressures, or what Underdal (1983; 1991) calls **process-generated stakes,** were another reason why an agreement failed to materialize in The Hague. At that time, the EU presidency had rotated to France, with Green Party Environment Minister Dominique Voynet leading the EU delegation whilst Jürgen Trittin, a Green Party 'fundamentalist', represented Germany. Both ministers were heavily influenced by constituency concerns and maintained hard-line positions, even if this made it harder to reach an agreement with the Umbrella Group (Reiner 2001). By 2000, green parties were members of coalition governments in five out of the (then) 15 Member States (Germany, France, Belgium, Finland and Italy). These Green ministers were also supported by environment misters in the Netherlands and Denmark, meaning that they were well placed to steer the Environment Council discussions and argue in favour of taking a hard line in negotiations (Downie 2014).

Finally, the EU's negotiating approach introduced a tension between what is scientifically 'appropriate' to do and what is politically 'acceptable' or 'feasible'. Underdal (1983; 1991) calls this the **'politically inadequate solution design model'.** For him, a 'good' solution to a collective policy problem is one that meets three main criteria: efficiency, fairness and feasibility. Efficiency refers to a solution that provides a real basis for an ecologically sound regime. Solutions that satisfy scientific standards often fall outside the settlement range, however (Underdal 1983; 1991).

Many of the EU ministers defended their strong positions on supplementarity and forests because this ensured the Protocol agreed with scientific recommendations (Downie 2014). Attempts by US negotiators following Kyoto and up to The Hague to maximize the use of flexibility mechanisms and forestry credits were met with fierce EU resistance. The Europeans accused the US of trying to undermine the environmental integrity of the Protocol. The US, by contrast, argued that their long-running experience with emission trading schemes had demonstrated the feasibility and effectiveness of such policy instruments. Furthermore, the US highlighted that the EU had benefited enormously from internal 'hot air' and had no right to complain or refuse another party a similarly favourable treatment. The political instability flagged up by the EU, where the UK's fuel switch led to unemployment and Germany's reunification became an extremely expensive affair, failed to appease dissenters (Gupta and van der Grijp 2000).

Other causes

In addition to Underdal's four factors, there were a number of additional, mainly procedural ones that were also highlighted by interviewees as having contributed to failure. The first one was Pronk's idea to put ministers personally in charge of negotiations during the final days. This was 'impossible negotiating; it was the wrong setting'.[13] Interviewees agreed that the issues involved were too technical for ministers to understand:

> The questions involved were very controversial. You cannot leave them for the ministers to negotiate. Technical people had worked on these documents for months and knew all the ambiguous words. Ministers on the other hand had only looked at the documents for a few hours at best. You simply cannot do that.[14]

An additional complication was that the great majority of ministers, especially from developing countries, 'did not like to negotiate. They had never negotiated in multilateral contexts; they had always been represented by officials based in New York and other places, who were better informed about the situation.'[15]

Other factors were more EU-specific. Interviewees were highly critical of Voynet's decision prior to The Hague to remove key people from the French negotiating team and replace them with 'a bunch of people nobody knew'.[16] Up to that point, it had been a unit under the President's office that led the negotiations. 'Everybody had got to know them; after a while you build confidence, you know?'[17] Voynet's decision to appoint people of her own choice was problematic, as 'we did not know the people that were supposed to lead us; and this was a problem.'[18] More experienced negotiators were offended:

> She sidestepped the President's office and took in a number of inexperienced and – I would say – rather arrogant young people from the Green Party who would tell us how things were![19]

Another EU-specific factor related to the 'EU bunker' phenomenon, which again made its appearance. EU ministers were still deliberating on the Pronk note, despite others having already communicated their amendments and the final night's negotiations having commenced (Grubb and Yamin 2001). In the context of climate change talks, the above complication resulted in the EU spending too much time in internal negotiations and too little time on formulating its position vis-à-vis the US, let alone reaching out to other parties or groups (Grubb and Yamin 2001). This was acknowledged at the highest levels of EU governance when the EU presiding minister, Dominique Voynet, in her final remarks to the plenary, confessed:

> I discovered many things in this conference. I discovered other groups in this process. For the first time I found myself engaged in in-depth discussion

with other Parties. It is not enough to meet just once a year … we need to build up relationships with other Parties.

(cited in Grubb and Yamin 2001, p. 274)

Her remarks caused analysts to wonder what 'on earth had she being doing for the previous two years' (Grubb and Yamin 2001, p. 274).

To conclude, The Hague, much to the delight of the media, witnessed some rather very undiplomatic exchanges between the ministers of the Member States. Prescott blamed Voynet for the collapse of the negotiations. He suggested the French minister was exhausted and was unable to follow the negotiations properly and got 'cold feet' over the proposed deal. Voynet did admit that she found the negotiations so tiring that it was hard to retain the mindfulness to follow the process and properly explain the key negotiating points to the rest of her EU partners. Interviewees also highlighted that during the final crucial hours Voynet 'collapsed' and subsequently 'came under attack' by EU colleagues for her ineffectiveness.[20] Voynet, however, argued that she had been well aware of the fact that the proposed agreement represented an inadequate deal before rejecting it, and further responded to Prescott characterizations by calling him 'macho' (Henley and White 2000, p. 1). It would not be an overstatement to suggest that for the EU, The Hague represented the nadir of nearly a decade of problematic negotiations on the climate change regime. Interviewees described it as the EU's 'worst moment'[21] in the UNFCCC talks, even surpassing Copenhagen in 2009:

It was a greater failure in The Hague because the cohesion of the Union is a necessary element in any kind of agreement within the environmental field. And we did not succeed to keep together in a good fashion. And this I regret very much. In Copenhagen the EU at least stuck together. Cohesion was maintained. And this was an achievement if you consider that in The Hague we were the EU-15, but in Copenhagen we had expanded considerably.[22]

The aftermath of The Hague

The collapse of COP-6 in The Hague came as a huge shock to the EU, especially given the slim prospects of the new Bush administration engaging constructively in future negotiations. Prescott raised this exact point, albeit without success (Egenhofer and Cornillie 2001). In any case, following COP-6 the outgoing Clinton administration invited the EU for a new round of negotiations before handing over power to George W. Bush, with the plan being for delegates from key EU and Umbrella Group countries to meet in December in Ottawa so as to prepare the ground for a subsequent ministerial-level conference in Oslo. The EU delegation put forward a proposal containing a number of key positions on which it was prepared to negotiate without preconditions (see Environment Council 2000), including:

- a limited opening of Article 3.4 sinks with a tight cap for the first commitment period;
- no sinks in the CDM in the first commitment period;
- mechanisms used only insofar as parties are legally bound by the compliance regime;
- domestic action as the primary part of each Annex I parties' efforts.

In other words, the EU adopted a more flexible stance on sinks, but stood firm on supplementarity (see Environment Council 2000). But Ottawa did not go well. While initially the atmosphere for an agreement appeared positive, EU actors progressively became sceptical as to whether a deal with the outgoing US administration at such a late stage would actually represent the best way forward. As an EU official who participated in this meeting noted, 'my instructions were not favourable to a deal; I had to see to it that there would not be an agreement.'[23] Negotiations broke down and the Oslo meeting was cancelled. The lead US negotiator, Under-secretary of State Frank E. Loy, said: 'Not only were pending issues not resolved, but old issues were brought back to the table. Further progress depends on a reasonable and coordinated position from the European Union' (cited in Hill 2000, p. C11). The EU replied by underlining that 'it was not going for a deal at any price' (Environment Council 2000). Thinking retrospectively, an EU official remarked:

> And I think for us in my delegation it was a relief that things happened this way. And when you look at the brutal way in which Bush afterwards managed this issue, it would have been a serious mistake to have tried to make a deal with the Clinton outgoing administration. I think it would have complicated the situation more than it would have helped.[24]

A month later, President Bush officially entered the White House. When asked about the prospects of the Kyoto Protocol, EU Environment Commissioner Margot Wallström commented that she felt 'a bit worried', but then added that President Bush should be judged 'on his actions' (Planet Ark 2001). Sensing the difficulties ahead, the EU adopted a more flexible stance, with the March 2001 Environment Council avoiding reference to sinks and simply noting with respect to supplementarity that 'the implementation of the Kyoto protocol must lead to real reductions in greenhouse gas emissions, supported by a credible compliance and liability system' (Environment Council 2001a, para.3).

Even so, prospects for COP-6bis, scheduled for May–June 2001, did not appear particularly bright. In the run-up to the polls, President Bush had referred to Kyoto as a 'bad deal for America and Americans' (Jacoby and Reiner 2001, p. 303). Condoleezza Rice, his new national security adviser, had also criticized Kyoto in an article published in *Foreign Affairs* in December 2000. 'Whatever the facts on global warming,' she wrote, 'a treaty that does not include China and exempts "developing" countries from tough standards while penalizing American industry cannot possibly be in America's national interest' (Rice 2000, p. 48).

The US had not pulled out of negotiations, however. An EU official recalled, 'the signals that we had got were that President Bush would not be so bad.'[25] During a March 2001 G-8 environment ministers' meeting in Trieste, Italy, it was noted in the final communiqué that G-8 countries would 'strive to reach agreement on the outstanding issues' (G-8 2001, para. 5; see also Kjellén 2008). The German environment minister Jürgen Trittin even stated that 'all ministers delivered today a clear desire for an agreement. I am particularly pleased that the new US administration endorsed this path' (ENDS 2001c). US officials in Trieste sounded 'relatively optimistic and constructive; obviously they were not aware of what was [concurrently] happening at official level back home' (see also Foerstel 2010).[26] A few days later, on 13 March 2001, President Bush sent a letter to Senators Hagel, Helms, Craig and Roberts in which he argued:

> As you know, I oppose the Kyoto Protocol because it exempts 80 percent of the world, including major population centres such as China and India, from compliance, and would cause serious harm to the US economy. The Senate's vote, 95–0, shows that there is a clear consensus that the Kyoto Protocol is an unfair and ineffective means of addressing global climate change concerns.
>
> (in Dessai *et al.* 2003, p. 187)

Bush's move generated a wave of criticism, with even Canada and Japan expressing disappointment. The EU stated that 'a global strategy to tackle climate change is an integral part of relations with the United States' (Dessai *et al.* 2003, p. 187). Note here that the letter was apparently sent without other Member States being consulted – a move that had angered the French which were pushing for a tougher response (ENDS 2001a). An exploratory delegation was also sent to Washington in April 2001, albeit in vain as Condoleezza Rice made a strongly worded statement noting that 'Kyoto is dead' (Kluger 2001, p. 30). After receiving 'a slap in the face' in Washington (Dessai *et al.* 2003, p. 188), the EU decided at the initiative of the Swedish Presidency to change its approach by dispatching a high-level mission to a number of key capitals, including Ottawa, Moscow, Tehran, Tokyo and Beijing, to gather support for the Kyoto Protocol. The message brought back was that the Kyoto Protocol could be saved (Grubb 2001b). The meeting in Tehran was described as 'quite successful', paving the way for the fruitful cooperation between the EU and the G-77/China in Bonn a few months later (Iran held the Presidency of the G-77/China at the time).[27] The EU's investment in relationship-building with other parties or groups was positively commented upon as representing a remarkable political transformation, given that the EU had until then primarily exerted its energy in internal deliberations (Grubb 2001b). Another important development, internal this time, was the decision to change the structure of the troika to include the European Commission so as to achieve greater coordination and continuity in the lead negotiating team.

In April, COP President Pronk, after reviewing comments received from parties on his 2000 proposal, released a new one to be discussed at informal ministerial consultations in New York on 20–21 April, held in preparation for COP-6bis in July. From the EU's point of view, Pronk's proposal, although welcomed, contained provisions which required further changes (European Commission 2001c). Nevertheless, while the EU maintained that the implementation of the Kyoto Protocol should lead to 'significant, real domestic reductions' in Annex I countries, it did signal its willingness, in the context of an overall package, to 'discuss supplementarity with other parties and to show flexibility about how to tackle this issue' (European Commission 2001c).

Such a debate was never going to be held, though, as in June 2001 the Bush administration declared the Protocol 'fatally flawed in fundamental ways' and formally withdrew the US from the Kyoto agreement. Apart from excluding developing nations from any commitments, President Bush argued that complying with the mandates of the Kyoto Protocol 'would have a negative economic impact, with layoffs of workers and price increases for consumers. And when you evaluate all these flaws, most reasonable people will understand that it is not sound public policy' (Bush 2001, p. 547). The potential cost was estimated in the vicinity of 1–2 per cent of GDP by 2010, a rate deemed equivalent to the 1970s oil shock (Lisowski 2002).

Despite this setback, the EU refused to start over with negotiating a new international climate treaty. The EU had invested too much time, effort, and reputation in Kyoto and was determined to make it work irrespective of the US's participation (Hovi *et al.* 2003). To do so, the EU adopted a twofold strategy. First, it would provide a 'good' example internally by swiftly ratifying the Protocol. Second, it would employ its entire diplomatic arsenal in pushing the reluctant 'Gang of Four' – Australia, Canada, Japan and Russia – to do likewise (Hovi *et al.* 2003). For instance, diplomatic missions were sent to Canberra and Tokyo. These succeeded in convincing the Japanese to come on board, but fared less well with the Australians. The Japanese were even determined to try to convince the US to return to the Kyoto process, with President Bush and Japanese Prime Minister Koizumi actually meeting in Camp David, albeit in vain (Parry 2001). In view of the US's rigid stance, the EU Heads of State and Government expressed their determination during the June 2001 EU–US summit in Gothenburg, Sweden, to ratify the Protocol by 2002 and asked President Bush to give his assurance – which he willingly gave – not to block progress during COP-6bis, 'unless US interests were adversely affected or undesirable precedents were created' (Wirth 2002, p. 649). Interviewees explained that the two US 'red lines' were that any agreement related to the Protocol did not (i) affect the Convention (to which the US was a party), and (ii) adversely affect the US economy.[28]

Again in June, and only a few days before COP-6bis, the Commission released its first report on the ECCP, which proposed over 40 measures to contribute to the EU Kyoto target, including a framework directive for an EU Emissions Trading Scheme and a directive on biofuels (see European Commission 2001b). The last important event prior to COP-6bis was the June Environment

Council, which summarized the EU position for Bonn, but also signalled its preparedness 'for compromises' (Environment Council 2001b). The Environment Commissioner, Margot Wallström, left the window open for postponing the Protocol's five-year commitment period beyond 2008–12 if this would convince the US to return to the negotiating table (ENDS 2001b).

The Bonn surprise

The omens for success in Bonn were not good. Most observers actually predicted the end of the Kyoto Protocol and a 'descent into environmental anarchy' (ENB 2001, p. 13). Interestingly, COP-6bis coincided with the G-8 Summit in Genoa. In Bonn there were protesters, agonizing over Kyoto's future (Athanasiou and Baer 2001). COP-6bis commenced with an updated version of Pronk's COP-6 compromise package, which had been released shortly before the meeting. Within a few days, parties managed – to the astonishment of observers – to reach agreement on almost all issues except compliance.

Swift progress was greatly facilitated by the fact that the EU, desperate not to fail, had arrived in Bonn prepared to make as many compromises as would be required to secure an agreement (Bodansky 2001).[29] Following the US exit, the 'Gang of Four' was in an extremely strong bargaining position, given that the rules for entry into force of the Kyoto Protocol required 55 parties to the Convention to ratify the Protocol, including Annex I parties accounting for 55 per cent of that group's CO_2 emissions in 1990 (see Table 5.1). Consequently,

Table 5.1 Annex I party shares of CO_2 emissions in 1990

Party	%	Party	%
Australia	2.1	Latvia	0.2
Austria*	0.4	Liechtenstein	0.0
Belgium*	0.8	Luxembourg*	0.1
Bulgaria	0.6	Monaco	0.0
Canada	3.3	Netherlands*	1.2
Czech Republic	1.2	New Zealand	0.2
Denmark*	0.4	Norway	0.3
Estonia	0.3	Poland	3.0
Finland*	0.4	Portugal*	0.3
France*	2.7	Romania	1.2
Germany*	7.4	Russia	17.4
Greece*	0.6	Slovakia	0.4
Hungary	0.5	Spain*	1.9
Iceland	0.0	Sweden*	0.4
Ireland*	0.2	Switzerland	0.3
Italy*	3.1	UK*	4.3
Japan	8.5	USA	36.1
*EU-15 Combined	24.2		

Source: UNFCCC (2002).

Japan's 8.5 per cent, Russia's 17.4 per cent, Canada's 3.3 per cent and Australia's 2.2 per cent had taken on a whole new importance.

The G-77/China faced a similar dilemma. Without a Protocol there would
be no funds. It was only natural for an alliance to emerge. Scrutiny of the conclusions of the two Environment Council meetings prior to Bonn reveals that
the EU courted the G-77/China for some time. The June 2001 meeting, for
instance, noted that the EU would 'seek further consultations with G77-part-
ners to work together on central issues such as technology transfer, capacity
building and action on adaptation' (Environment Council 2001b). This new
alliance went on to offer the 'Gang of Four' such large concessions that they
could not back out without facing the danger of being pilloried by both the press
and civil society. The EU compromised its positions to such an extent that *The
Economist* (2001, p. 77) wrote that it proved 'willing more or less to give away
the store'.

Starting with the Kyoto mechanisms, the most crucial political choices
regarding emissions trading, JI and the CDM were resolved in Bonn. The EU
dropped completely any requirement of supplementarity and no quantitative
cap on the use of the mechanisms was placed. In a submission prior to Bonn,
the EU had argued that the use of the flexibility mechanisms should 'not exceed
reductions achieved through domestic actions' (UNFCCC 2001a, p. 128). Even
so, the final agreement only stated that 'the use of mechanisms shall be supplemental to domestic action and that domestic action shall constitute a *significant
element* of the effort made by each Annex I Party to fulfil Protocol Article 3.1'
(UNFCCC 2001b, p. 42, emphasis added). In what was a trade-off for greater
EU flexibility on sinks (see below), it was further agreed that Annex I parties
were 'to refrain from' using nuclear power for activities under the CDM or JI
(UNFCCC 2001b, p. 43). With respect to sinks in the CDM, it was agreed that
afforestation and reforestation would be the only eligible LULUCF projects
during the first commitment period.

Turning to LULUCF, the other main issue that had led to failure in The
Hague, the 'Gang of Four', taking advantage of its strong bargaining position,
managed to emerge triumphant in Bonn, with Article 3.4 sinks being freely
allocated to Canada, Japan and Russia (Afionis and Chatzopoulos 2010). Forest
management, cropland management, grazing land management and revegetation were all added to the already eligible LULUCF activities under Article 3.4
(UNFCCC 2001b, p. 45). With respect to forest management activities (e.g.
conservation of existing forests), it was decided that they should be capped, with
a forest management cap for each Annex B party other than the US being
established in an Appendix Z to the Bonn Agreement (see UNFCCC 2001b,
p. 47). Unlike forest management, there was no cap for agricultural management, an omission which could create a great loophole for the 'Gang of Four'
(Dessai *et al.* 2003). 'We would have preferred to have fewer sinks in the deal,'
the head of the EU delegation admitted, 'but I prefer an imperfect living agreement to a perfect one that doesn't exist' (ENDS 2001d). Finally, it was decided
that the SBSTA would deal with a number of contentious methodological

issues, such as non-permanence, additionality, leakage, uncertainties, and socio-economic and environmental impacts (ENB 2001).

With the Bonn COP about to conclude, Russia threatened to unravel the whole pact when it questioned the validity of the numbers in Appendix Z and asked for a doubling of its percentage. To protect the agreement, the EU agreed to a provision being introduced that provided for 'a reconsideration of the numerical values upon request of a country' (Ott 2001c, p. 473). In summary, the overall formula that was finally agreed upon in Bonn severely compromised the environmental integrity of the Protocol, as the Bonn Agreement would now lead to reductions in emissions of about 2.5 per cent (Ott 2001c). Japan's 6 per cent reduction target under the Kyoto Protocol shrank to only 1 per cent, while Canada, instead of a 6 per cent reduction target, was allowed to increase its emissions by 5 per cent (Benedick 2001).

Compliance turned out to be one of the most contentious issues to be discussed in Bonn and the last to be resolved. The EU, a supporter of a legally binding compliance system, had to compromise its positions once again in the face of opposition from Japan, Russia and Australia, which were in favour of a softer legal regime. The EU was able to secure an agreement to postpone a decision on this matter until the Kyoto Protocol had entered into force, but other components of the compliance system were decided upon. The consequences for non-compliance were one of them, with the final decision stipulating that 'for every tonne of emissions by which a Party exceeds its target, 1.3 tonnes will be deducted from its assigned amount for the subsequent commitment period' (Ott 2001c, p. 474). As a deterrent to non-compliance, the EU had supported a ratio of deductions to shortfalls as high as two to one, while other parties preferred setting the multiplier closer to one (Wirth 2002).

The composition and voting procedure of the Compliance Committee was another hotly contested issue, with the EU taking the position that Annex I countries should control the Committee and that, to do so, a clear majority of the seats in the enforcement branch and at least 50 per cent of the seats in the facilitative branch would be necessary (European Commission 2001a). To achieve that balance, the EU proposed that the enforcement branch should consist of seven members, five nominated by Annex I parties and two nominated by non-Annex I parties (UNFCCC 2001a). According to the final decision, both branches would comprise ten members: one from each of the five UN regional groups, one from a small island state and two from Annex I and non-Annex I countries respectively (UNFCCC 2001b). In other words, developing countries would hold a small majority.

Closing with issues relating to finance, three new funds for developing countries were established in Bonn, two under the UNFCCC and one under the Kyoto Protocol – all to be managed by the GEF. These were the Special Climate Change Fund (SCCF), the Least Developed Countries Fund (LDCF), and the Adaptation Fund (under the Protocol). The EU, along with Canada, Iceland, New Zealand, Norway and Switzerland, committed to contributing annually $410 million by 2005, with this level to be reviewed in 2008 (ENB 2001). As

Kjellén (2008) reports, this financial pledge greatly facilitated agreement with developing countries.[30] Analysts at the time seriously doubted whether these funds would develop into an effective tool for developing countries, given they were voluntary, poorly funded and managed by the GEF, a body that was highly controversial in the eyes of developing countries because of its north-dominated agenda (Najam *et al.* 2003; see also Huq 2002).

Explaining Bonn

Why was Bonn a success? And what had changed since The Hague? For Bodansky (2001) there are a number of reasons. First, unlike in The Hague, compromise proposals in Bonn were put forward at an early stage. Following The Hague, the EU realized that a second failure would be fatal to the Kyoto Protocol and had ample time to 'analyse and digest' potential compromises (p. 48). Second, the US exit facilitated progress, given that in The Hague the US 'felt it had to win on virtually every issue to have even a prayer of overcoming Senate opposition to Kyoto' (p. 48). With the US out, parties had more room to manoeuvre and reach compromises. Not having to accommodate the US's appetite for sink credits, the EU could satisfy the lesser demands for such credits by Japan and Canada. Finally, perhaps the most decisive factor had been President Bush's attitude. His unilateral rejection of Kyoto had 'stuck in other countries' craws' (p. 48) and, instead of dealing a deathblow to Kyoto, his decision had the opposite effect. The Nigerian delegate received a rousing ovation when he declared that the Bonn Agreement represented a 'triumph for multilateralism over unilateralism' (ENB 2001, p. 14). Closing with the US presence in Bonn, it refrained from obstructive tactics, with its delegation attending all sessions but not actively participating in the discussions. Pronk even thanked the US for its 'constructive' silence (Benedick 2001, p. 73).

While the EU had been instrumental through sustained diplomatic efforts to ensure the survival of the Kyoto Protocol, this came at great cost as far as the environmental integrity of the agreement was concerned. The EU had strived to protect that integrity by proposing a cap on the use of the Kyoto mechanisms, as well as minimizing the use of sinks as a climate measure. In the end it was forced to water down its positions by succumbing to demands by the 'Gang of Four' for greater flexibility, as well as to calls by developing countries for additional finance, in order to save Kyoto (Jordan and Rayner 2010). For the 'Gang of Four', supporting the Bonn agreement made absolute sense, as its members could derive symbolic benefits by raising their international profile, as well as material benefits through the flexibility mechanisms (Schunz 2014).

Notes

1 Interview No. 2 (Member State official – Former Head of Delegation).
2 Interview No. 9 (Commission official).
3 Interview No. 14 (Former Commission official).

4 Interview No. 2 (Member State official – Former Head of Delegation).
5 Interviews No. 2 and No. 3 (Member State officials – Former Heads of Delegation).
6 Interview No. 13 (Member State official – Former Head of Delegation).
7 Interview No. 1 (Member State official – Former Head of Delegation); Interview No. 10 (Member State official – Head of Delegation); Interview No. 13 (Member State official – Former Head of Delegation).
8 Interview No. 14 (Former Commission official).
9 Interview No. 2 (Member State official – Former Head of Delegation).
10 Interview No. 13 (Member State official – Former Head of Delegation).
11 Interview No. 1 (Member State official – Former Head of Delegation).
12 Interview No. 14 (Former Commission official).
13 Interview No. 2 (Member State official – Former Head of Delegation).
14 Interview No. 1 (Member State official – Former Head of Delegation).
15 Interview No. 3 (Member State official – Former Head of Delegation).
16 Interview No. 2 (Member State official – Former Head of Delegation).
17 Interview No. 2 (Member State official – Former Head of Delegation).
18 Interview No. 2 (Member State official – Former Head of Delegation).
19 Interview No. 3 (Member State official – Former Head of Delegation).
20 Interview No. 1 (Member State official – Former Head of Delegation).
21 Interview No. 3 (Member State official – Former Head of Delegation).
22 Interview No. 2 (Member State official – Former Head of Delegation).
23 Interview No. 3 (Member State official – Former Head of Delegation).
24 Interview No. 3 (Member State official – Former Head of Delegation).
25 Interview No. 3 (Member State official – Former Head of Delegation).
26 Interview No. 3 (Member State official – Former Head of Delegation).
27 Interview No. 2 (Member State official – Former Head of Delegation); Interview No. 13 (Member State official – Former Head of Delegation).
28 Interview No. 13 (Member State official – Former Head of Delegation).
29 Interview No. 13 (Member State official – Former Head of Delegation).
30 This point was also stressed by interview No. 10 (Member State official – Head of Delegation).

References

Afionis, Stavros and Ioannis Chatzopoulos (2010). Russia's role in UNFCCC negotiations since the exit of the United States in 2001. *International Environmental Agreements: Politics, Law and Economics* 10: 45–63.

Athanasiou, Tom and Paul Baer (2001). Bonn and Genoa: a tale of two cities and two movements. *Foreign Policy in Focus*, August. Available at: http://fpif.org/bonn_and_genoa_a_tale_of_two_cities_and_two_movements/.

Benedick, Richard E. (2001). Striking a new deal on climate change. *Issues in Science and Technology* 18 (1): 71–6.

Bodansky, Daniel (2001). Bonn voyage: Kyoto's uncertain revival. *The National Interest.* Fall: 45–55.

Boehmer-Christiansen, Sonja and Aynsley Kellow (2002). *International environmental policy: interests and the failure of the Kyoto process.* Cheltenham: Edward Elgar.

Boyd, Emily, Esteve Corbera and Manuel Estrada (2008). UNFCCC negotiations (pre-Kyoto to COP-9): what the process says about the politics of CDM-sinks. *International Environmental Agreements* 8 (2): 95–112.

Brown, Donald A. (2002). *American heat: ethical problems with the United States' response to global warming.* Lanham: Rowman & Littlefield.

Bush, George W. (2001). Global climate change: making commitments we can keep and keeping commitments we can make. *Vital Speeches of the Day* 67 (18): 546–9.

Dessai, Suraje (2001). Why did The Hague Conference fail? *Environmental Politics* 10 (3): 139–44.

Dessai, Suraje, Nuno S. Lacasta and Katharine Vincent (2003). International political history of the Kyoto Protocol: from The Hague to Marrakech and beyond. *International Review for Environmental Strategies* 4 (2): 183–205.

Downie, Christian (2014). *The politics of climate change negotiations: strategies and variables in prolonged international negotiations.* Cheltenham: Edward Elgar.

Egenhofer, Christian and Jan Cornillie (2001). Reinventing the climate negotiations: an analysis of COP6. CEPS Policy Brief No. 1, March. Available at: www.ceps.eu/system/files/book/102.pdf.

ENB (2000a). Summary of the Sixth Conference of the Parties to the Framework Convention on Climate Change. *Earth Negotiations Bulletin* 12 (163): 1–19.

ENB (2000b). Summary of the Thirteenth Sessions of the Subsidiary Bodies of the UN Framework Convention on Climate Change: 4–15 September 2000. *Earth Negotiations Bulletin* 12 (151): 1–16.

ENB (2001). Summary of the Resumed Sixth Session of the Conference of the Parties to the UN Framework Convention on Climate Change: 16–27 July 2001. *Earth Negotiations Bulletin* 12 (176): 1–15.

ENDS (2000a). EU agrees "strong" climate talks position, 23 June.

ENDS (2000b). EU downbeat after global climate talks, 19 September.

ENDS (2001a). EU leaders reiterate commitment to Kyoto, 26 March.

ENDS (2001b). EU "open to deadline delay", 11 July.

ENDS (2001c). G8 green ministers keep climate ball rolling, 5 March.

ENDS (2001d). Kyoto climate protocol comes back to life, 23 July.

Environment Council (1999). *Environment Council Press Release*, 299 No. 11654/99, Luxembourg, 12 October.

Environment Council (2000). *Environment Council Press Release*, 486 No. 14668/00, Brussels, 18–19 December.

Environment Council (2001a). *Environment Council Press Release*, 93 No. 6752/01, Brussels, 8 March.

Environment Council (2001b). *Environment Council Press Release*, 201 No. 9116/01, Luxembourg, 7 June.

European Commission (2001a). EU position for the Bonn conference on climate change. Briefing Paper, July 6: 1–8.

European Commission (2001b). European Climate Change Programme, Report – June 2001. Available at: www.cepco.es/Uploads/docs/ECCP%20report.pdf.

European Commission (2001c). The EU troika on the high-level consultations on Climate Change in New York 21st April 2001, 23 April 2001. Available at: http://europa.eu/rapid/press-release_MEMO-01-147_en.htm.

Foerstel, Herbert N. (2010). *Toxic mix? A handbook of science and politics.* Santa Barbara, CA: Greenwood Publishing Group.

G-8 (2000). Okinawa Summit of the Eight. Communiqué, Okinawa, 23 July. Available at: www.g8.utoronto.ca/summit/2000okinawa/finalcom.htm.

G-8 (2001). G8 Environment Ministers Communiqué, Trieste, Italy, 24 March. Available at: www.g8.utoronto.ca/environment/2001trieste/communique.html.

Grubb, Michael (2001a). Cold shower in a hot climate: climate change responses on the knife-edge. *Energy Policy* 29 (11): 833–6.

Grubb, Michael (2001b). The UK and European Union: Britannia waives the rules? *German Foreign Policy in Dialogue* 2 (6): 9–12.

Grubb, Michael and Farhana Yamin (2001). Climatic collapse at The Hague: what happened, why, and where do we go from here? *International Affairs* 77 (2): 261–76.

Gupta, Joyeeta and Nicolien van der Grijp (2000). Perceptions of the EU's role: is the EU a leader? In Gupta, Joyeeta and Michael Grubb (eds) *Climate change and European leadership: a sustainable role for Europe?* Dordrecht: Kluwer, 67–82.

Henley, Jon and Michael White (2000). Prescott the 'macho man' refuses to back down. *Guardian*, 28 November.

Hill, Patrice (2000). Warming alert; GOP upset by attempt to revive gases treaty. *Washington Times*, 9 December.

Hovi, Jon, Tora Skodvin and Steinar Andresen (2003). The persistence of the Kyoto Protocol: why Annex I countries move on without the United States. *Global Environmental Politics* 3 (4): 1–23.

Huq, Saleemul (2002). The Bonn-Marrakech agreements on funding. *Climate Policy* 2 (2–3): 243–6.

Jacoby, Henry D. and David M. Reiner (2001). Getting climate policy on track after The Hague. *International Affairs* 77 (2): 297–312.

Jordan, Andrew and Tim Rayner (2010). The evolution of climate policy in the European Union: a historical perspective. In Jordan, Andrew, Dave Huitema, Harro Van Asselt, Tim Rayner and Frans Berkhout (eds) *Climate change policy in the European Union: confronting the dilemmas of mitigation and adaptation?* Cambridge: Cambridge University Press, 52–80.

Kjellén, Bo (2008). *A new diplomacy for sustainable development: the challenge of global change.* New York: Routledge.

Kluger, Jeffrey (2001). A climate of despair, *Time* 157 (14): 30–35.

Lisowski, Michael (2002). Playing the two-level game: US President Bush's decision to repudiate the Kyoto Protocol. *Environmental Politics* 11 (4): 101–19.

Michaelowa, Axel and Reimund Schwarze (2001). Beyond COP6: the need for extended flexibility. In Schwarze, Reimund, John O. Niles and Eric Levy (eds) *Law and economics of international climate change policy.* Dordrecht: Kluwer, 117–131.

Najam, Adil, Saleemul Huq and Youba Sokona (2003). Climate negotiations beyond Kyoto: developing countries concerns and interests. *Climate Policy* 3 (3): 221–31.

Ott, Hermann E. (2001a). Climate change: an important foreign policy issue. *International Affairs* 77 (2): 277–96.

Ott, Hermann E. (2001b). Global climate. In Jutta Brunnée and Ellen Hey (eds) *Yearbook of international environmental law* 11, (2000). Oxford: Oxford University Press, 166–77.

Ott, Hermann E. (2001c). The Bonn Agreement to the Kyoto Protocol – paving the way for ratification. *International Environmental Agreements: Politics, Law and Economics* 1 (4): 469–76.

Parry, Richard (2001). Blair pressed over role in Kyoto treaty. *Independent*, 2 July.

Planet Ark (2001). EU says worried by possible Bush stance on climate, 25 January. Available at: www.planetark.org/dailynewsstory.cfm?newsid=9611.

Reiner, David M. (2001). Climate impasse: how The Hague negotiations failed. *Environment* 43 (2): 36–43.

Rice, Condoleezza (2000). Promoting the national interest. *Foreign Affairs* 79 (1): 45–62.

Schunz, Simon (2014). *European Union foreign policy and the global climate regime.* Brussels: P.I.E. Peter Lang.

Szarka, Joseph (2011). France's troubled bids to climate leadership. In Wurzel, Rüdiger K.W. and James Connelly (eds) *The European Union as a leader in international climate change politics*. London: Routledge, 112–28.

The Economist (2001). What next, then? *The Economist* 360 (8232): 77.

Underdal, Arild (1983). Causes of negotiation 'failure'. *European Journal of Political Research*, 11 (2): 183–95.

Underdal, Arild (1991). International cooperation and political engineering. In Nagel, Stuart (ed.) *Global policy studies: international interaction toward improving public policy*. Basingstoke: Palgrave Macmillan, 98–120.

UNFCCC (2001a). Note by the President of COP 6 – Views from Parties. FCCC/CP/2001/MISC.1.

UNFCCC (2001b). Report of the Conference of the Parties on the Second Part of its Sixth Session, Held at Bonn from 16 to 27 July 2001. FCCC/CP/2001/5.

UNFCCC (2002). A Guide to the Climate Change Convention and its Kyoto Protocol, Bonn, Climate Change Secretariat. Available at: https://library.conservation.org/Published%20Documents/2002/Guide%20to%20Climate%20Change%20Convention.pdf.

Vogler, John (2002). In the absence of the hegemon: EU actorness and the global climate change regime. Paper presented at the Australian National University, 3–4 July.

Wirth, David A. (2002). The Sixth Session (Part Two) and Seventh Session of the Conference of the Parties to the Framework Convention on Climate Change. *American Journal of International Law* 96 (3): 648–60.

6 Waiting for Russia

Following on from the 2000 ECCP Report, the Commission brought forward in October 2001 a package of three broad initiatives to tackle climate change, comprising a proposal to ratify the Kyoto Protocol, a proposal to establish an emissions trading scheme, as well as a list of priority actions the Commission would implement during the next two years in the areas of energy, transport and industry (European Commission 2001). This 'Kyoto Package' clearly underpinned the EU's credibility and leadership role in the climate negotiations, raising hopes that the Protocol could actually enter into force by the end of 2002. COP-7 in Marrakech (29 October–10 November 2001), the first to be held in an African country, was considered as a crucial step to this direction. Its purpose would be to translate the political decisions made in Bonn into legal decisions the COP could then adopt. However, the 'Gang of Four' viewed it as another opportunity to extract further concessions from the EU and further reduce their actual domestic emission reduction requirements.

COP-7 (Marrakech)

Starting with sinks, Russia, which had registered an objection during COP-6bis in Bonn (see Chapter 5), succeeded in doubling its ceiling for forest management credits, with the EU and the G-77/China giving in so as to avoid further unravelling the agreement. An interviewee described Russia as an 'unguided missile'. As he went on to say, 'the Russians had no use for these credits. It was all about prestige. That, you know what? We are still important.'[1]

Turning to the flexibility mechanisms, a key debate concerned whether parties could 'bank' emissions units from one commitment period to another. Under the Kyoto Protocol, if a party had emission units (known as Assigned Amount Units or AAUs) to spare, it could either bank them or sell them via emissions trading to parties that were over their targets. Other emissions units that could be traded or sold under the Kyoto Protocol's emissions trading scheme included those generated by a JI or CDM project – Emission Reduction Units (ERUs) and Certified Emission Reductions (CERs) respectively.

In Marrakech, however, the 'Gang of Four' pushed for full flexibility, that is, banking of all the aforementioned credits, plus those from domestic sinks. The

EU and the G-77/China argued that banking the vast amount of sink credits into the second commitment period equated to extending a major loophole into a period during which the climate regime would have 'to go global and, presumably, become more serious' (Baer and Athanasiou 2001). In the end, however, the 'Gang of Four' prevailed, as the final compromise created a new unit, called Removal Unit (RMU), for emission credits from sink projects under Articles 3.3 and 3.4. An RMU could not be banked and could be used only to meet a party's emission target for the commitment period in which it was generated. Yet, all this was simply a façade, since transfer of credits (i.e. AAUs, ERUs, CERs and RMUs) between Annex I parties was unrestricted, meaning that a party was perfectly allowed to exchange non-bankable units for bankable ones and thus save the former (den Elzen and de Moor 2002). In other words, a party could transfer RMUs to another party to help it meet its target and buy in exchange CERs or ERUs – a form of credit 'laundering'. Note here that banking of CERs and ERUs was decided to be limited to 2.5 per cent of the assigned amount, a limit which was nevertheless deemed quite generous (Wirth 2002).

Closing with compliance, Marrakech saw extended controversy over whether there should be a binding link between compliance and eligibility to participate in the flexibility mechanisms. The EU, for instance, had argued that loss of such eligibility should be triggered following failure to submit annual sink inventories (ENB 2001). Japan rejected the EU proposal as it had traditionally opposed a binding compliance regime, while Russia was concerned that its lack of capacity to meet strict reporting requirements could jeopardize its potential for selling its substantial surplus of carbon credits to other developed countries, mainly Umbrella Group members (Dessai *et al.* 2003; Boyd and Schipper 2002). The 'Gang of Four' was ultimately successful in preventing any clear linkage from being made. The EU gave in, thereby losing the battle for bringing into force a legally binding compliance instrument.

To conclude, even though the Marrakech Accords largely fulfilled the BAPA, the Protocol's environmental integrity had nevertheless been further compromised, as according to projections it would lead to emission reductions of only about 2.2 per cent (Ott 2001). Some analysts have even argued that the EU's compromising mentality was primarily driven by its consideration of 'political benefits associated with leadership, rather than a sense of responsibility for the global environment' (Hovi *et al.* 2003, p. 19).

Momentum is lost

The adoption of the Marrakech Accords paved the way for EU ratification and potential subsequent entry into force of the Kyoto Protocol, which the EU had hoped could take place in time for the September 2002 Johannesburg World Summit on Sustainable Development (WSSD). As the Protocol would come into effect 90 days after the date of deposit of the last necessary instrument of ratification, all Member States and the EU had to deposit theirs by the start of June 2002. Indeed, all 16 instruments of ratification were simultaneously deposited at the UN Headquarters in New York in May 2002, despite some earlier anxiety that Italy and, above all, Greece might not complete the necessary procedures in time. Shortly afterwards Japan also ratified, meaning that all that was left in order for the Protocol to enter into force during the WSSD was Russia's ratification. President Putin, however, put an end to the EU's wishful thinking when he announced that Russia would ratify the Kyoto Protocol, but not in time for the WSSD (Afionis and Chatzopoulos 2010). Another blow came from Australia in July 2002, which sided with the US in opting not to ratify Kyoto on the grounds that doing so would cost jobs and damage the economy.

Two months later, it was Canada's turn to give the EU serious cause for concern. During a meeting in Madrid, Jean Chrétien, Canada's Prime Minister, told EU ministers that he would not be able to ratify unless certain elements were clarified. Chrétien, despite the sizeable concessions his country had managed to secure in Bonn and Marrakech, had reportedly come under considerable pressure from Canadian energy interests not to ratify the Protocol (Pearce 2002). Consequently, Chrétien demanded credits under the protocol for exporting hydroelectric power and natural gas to the US. The Canadian argument went like this: gas replaces coal in US power stations, burning gas produces less CO_2 than burning coal, ergo, the US's contribution to global warming is reduced thanks to Canada. Apparently, the EU found Canada's argument quite infuriating: 'We are totally fed up with the games the Canadians are playing,' an aide to Environment Commissioner Margot Wallström told reporters (Pearce 2002, p. 16).

Back to international negotiations, the sixteenth sessions of the Subsidiary Bodies to the Convention (SBSTA/SBI) were held in Bonn (5–14 June 2002). This meeting is worth mentioning as it was there that certain parties, most notably the EU, Switzerland and Norway, put forth the argument that as a result of the findings of the IPCC's 2001 Third Assessment Report (TAR), negotiations should start focusing on long-term objectives and future commitments – a discussion dismissed by China and others as 'premature and unfair' (ENB 2002b, p. 12). COP-8 would see more of this debate.

Another controversial development concerned Canada's demand for credits because of its substantial exports of hydro and natural gas energy to the US (Jacob 2002). Canada, even though opposed by the G-77/China, the EU and Norway, succeeded in its objective of having its proposal set for further discussion at the next session of the Subsidiary Bodies (to be held in conjunction with COP-8). Russia, a substantial exporter of natural gas, found the Canadian proposal to be 'interesting, generous and worthy of further study' (EPL 2002a, p. 203). This Russian backing sent 'shivers down the spines' of several delegates, especially those of the EU, who started to fear that Russia, like Canada, would demand further concessions in order to ratify the Protocol (ENB 2002b, p. 13).

Moving on, it was during the October 2002 Environment Council held in Luxemburg that the strategy of the Danish Presidency for COP-8 began to take shape. The Council recognized that the first commitment period of the Kyoto

Protocol was an important initial step, but that further action would be required in the period after 2012 to ensure the achievement of the ultimate objective of the Convention (Environment Council 2002a). COP-8, therefore, the Council concluded, constituted an important opportunity for parties to initiate a process aiming at

> cutting global emissions significantly as well as broadening and enhancing participation in the long-term [...] based on full and balanced partnership, while taking into account common but differentiated responsibilities and respective capabilities, and taking into account the necessity to move towards a globally equitable distribution of greenhouse gas emissions.
>
> (Environment Council 2002a)

COP-8 (New Delhi)

As parties arrived in New Delhi to attend COP-8 (23 October–1 November 2002), it was clear from the outset that focus had shifted from 'negotiation to implementation' (EPL 2002b, p. 18). Parties had already resolved most issues relating to modalities and rules in Bonn and Marrakech and the formal COP-8 agenda thus consisted mostly of outstanding secondary and technical issues (e.g. the CDM and the newly created developing country funds) (Schunz 2014; C2ES 2002). The Indian government, however, had far-reaching ambitions for the conference it was hosting. Up to then, COPs had been almost exclusively preoccupied with developed countries' concerns, with developing country interests largely marginalized (Najam *et al.* 2003). It was high time developing countries had their COP – a COP in which for once their demands and concerns would top the agenda. COP-8, therefore, was viewed by India as an opportunity to 'marry climate policy and sustainable development' (Ott 2003, p. 262). Yet, most developed countries, headed by the EU, thought differently, arguing that mitigation should remain the regime's primary focus, with parties stepping up efforts to determine what further future steps should be taken post-2012 to ensure effective action. This proposal met with resistance from developing countries, which argued back that Annex I parties should better focus on implementing their own commitments first. When the dust settled, the informal 'Green Alliance' – an alliance that had previously cooperated closely on key COPs (e.g. Berlin, Bonn and Marrakech) – was a thing of the past (Ott 2003). As an EU interviewee noted, the EU 'was crucified in Delhi for this demand'.[2]

Negotiations in New Delhi focused on the wording of the final declaration, with the EU issuing a statement outlining what it believed should constitute its most important elements (European Council 2002). First, parties should agree on how to reduce global emissions beyond 2012. Second, parties should note with deep concern the scientific findings of the IPCC's TAR in the Delhi Declaration, including the fact that the global climate is changing as a direct result of anthropogenic activities. Third, parties that had not yet ratified Kyoto should be strongly urged to do so as soon as possible. The EU, in an effort to somewhat 'sweeten' the pill for developing countries, noted *inter alia* that it would welcome the Delhi Declaration addressing the interlinkages between climate change and sustainable development, as combating the former was an essential requirement for the latter.

The first draft of the Delhi Declaration presented by the Indian President of the COP did not meet EU expectations, as apart from not linking the TAR's findings with the need for broader post-2012 participation, it even failed to mention the Kyoto Protocol (UNFCCC 2002a; see also Ott 2003). Instead, it focused on issues of poverty eradication and sustainable development, adaptation, and implementation of current commitments by developed countries (C2ES 2002). The draft prompted strong objections from the EU, but despite support from Japan and Canada, it failed to secure a reference to 'wider participation' after 2012 in the final text (EPL 2002b, p. 19). Surprisingly enough, China and India were not alone in opposing the EU and its allies, as their stance had been embraced by the most unlikely of allies, the US. Probably considering itself no longer bound by its 2001 pledge, the US shifted its strategy to one of actively preventing the Protocol from entering into force. According to Harlan Watson, the US chief negotiator, 'it would be unfair … to condemn developing nations to slow growth by insisting that they take impractical and unrealistic greenhouse gas targets' (Jacquemont 2003, p. 19). Developing countries remained adamant in their rejection of the EU proposal, despite the Danish EU Presidency's plenary statement that the EU was 'not talking about imposing emission reduction targets' on developing countries, but simply about establishing 'a forward-looking process' to consider what actions should be taken after 2012 (C2ES 2002).

Ultimately, the final text of the Delhi Ministerial Declaration was much closer to the position of developing countries, as no reference to future steps was made. In summation, the Declaration urged remaining parties to ratify the Kyoto Protocol, noted that economic development and poverty eradication were the 'first and overriding priorities' of developing countries, stressed that adaptation and technology transfer required urgent attention and recognized 'with concern' the findings of the TAR, which confirmed that significant cuts in global emissions would be necessary to meet the ultimate objective of the Convention (UNFCCC 2002b, pp. 1–3). Even though the Declaration was adopted by consensus, the EU and other developed countries expressed their disappointment that it did not establish a future vision. NGOs on their part complained that it merely recycled the text of the Johannesburg Plan of Implementation of Sustainable Development (Jacquemont 2003). The same point was also made by Depledge (2006, p. 7), who dismissed the COP-8 Ministerial Declaration as a prime example of 'text recycling', given that half of its operative paragraphs were based on 'text reproduced from the UNFCCC itself, or the [WSSD] Plan of Implementation'. Although a weak agreement, it was felt imperative that COP-8 adopted a declaration so as not to share the fate of COP-6 in The Hague. The EU (especially France and Germany) had to exert immense pressure on other parties to adopt even this weak declaration (Ott 2003). European diplomats justified their decision to give ground on the premise that the EU did not want to encourage Russia to use the COP's failure to adopt a declaration as an excuse for further delaying its ratification of the Protocol (EPL 2002b).

Developing countries and the US, on the other hand, overwhelmingly endorsed the Delhi Declaration. Nigeria, a country that only 15 months previously had declared that the 2001 Bonn Agreement represented the 'triumph of multilateralism over unilateralism', now thanked the US for being a 'constructive force' in the negotiations (C2ES 2002). While COP-8 had been overshadowed by the heated debate over the Delhi Declaration, delegates did manage to resolve a number of mostly technical and procedural issues, relating among others to the Executive Board of the CDM, reporting requirements, and funding for the least developed countries (LDCs). Other issues, however, proved somewhat more controversial, with Canada's proposal on clean energy exports being one of them. With the support of New Zealand, Poland, Russia and Slovenia, Canada requested the Secretariat to ask competent organizations to 'analyze the role of trade in cleaner energy in meeting the objective of the UNFCCC and the Protocol' (ENB 2002a, p. 7). The EU, supported by G-77/China, Switzerland and the US, strongly opposed Canada's request, with many observers being of the opinion that the US had sided with the EU only in order to deter Canada from ratifying the Protocol. Parties, however, were unable to adopt any decisions on this issue because of the insistence of Saudi Arabia that there be an analysis of the adverse economic effects on oil-producing countries of clean energy exports, as well as of mitigation response measures in developed countries (ENB 2002a). In other words, OPEC was requesting monetary compensation for lost oil revenues (Barnett and Dessai 2002). This met with strong resistance from both the EU and Canada and negotiations consequently reached a standstill.

Finally, another controversial debate took place with respect to organizational arrangements. Confident that Russia would soon ratify, most parties were under the impression that the first COP serving as the Meeting of the Parties (COP/MOP-1) would be held in conjunction with COP-9 in Milan. Given the substantial overlap in the agendas of the UNFCCC and the Kyoto Protocol, the Secretariat and most of the parties, including the EU, Japan and Canada, had proposed holding one combined session for both COP and COP/MOP (EPL 2002b). The US and Australia, however, wanting to ensure that their contributions would be used to support only the UNFCCC process, insisted on holding separate sessions under the rationale that:

a   The parties not ratifying the Kyoto Protocol are supposed to attend COP/MOP sessions as observers, which is not appropriate for the Ministerial level session.
b   The legal entities of the COP/MOP are different (EPL 2002b, p. 20).

The latter point was strongly opposed by the EU, which argued that while, in legal terms, the COP and the COP/MOP each remained responsible for deciding the conduct of their own affairs, they could still draw up and adopt agendas foreseeing joint meetings without compromising this responsibility (UNFCCC 2002). To distinguish between their competences, the EU proposed that the Secretariat clearly demarcate in the agenda issues relevant only to the COP, issues relevant only to the COP/MOP and issues common to both. Unable again to reach consensus, parties decided to forward the issue to the next sessions of the Subsidiary Bodies.

The EU at COP-8

Following COP-8 a number of important developments took place, such as the political agreement reached in December 2002 to establish an emissions trading scheme within the EU. As Ott (2003) observes, the debacle over the CO_2/ energy tax made the adoption of this directive an even greater success. Again in December, Canada ratified the Kyoto Protocol – a move attributed, among other reasons, to Prime Minister Chrétien's need for greater support in Parliament (see Harrison 2007). On a negative note, the change in US attitude was a major reason for concern. Unlike in Bonn and Marrakech, where it had adopted a low profile, in COP-8 the US had successfully sided with OPEC in order to stall progress on various issues. Vogler and Bretherton (2006, p. 17) described this turn in US policy as an attempt to 'undermine EU leadership by opportunistically supporting developing countries'. An EU interviewee argued that this alliance between the US, the Arabs, the Indians and the Brazilians was detrimental. 'If the Americans had not intervened,' they argued, 'we could have at least started discussing this topic.'[3]

A second negative development was the sudden cooling of relations between the EU and the G-77/China. The literature is quite critical of the EU in this respect, positing that there had been absolutely no need for this to have taken place. The argument, in other words, is that the strategy of the Danish Presidency had backfired by pushing the EU's closest ally into the arms of the US. According to Article 3.9 of the Kyoto Protocol, the COP/MOP should initiate a process for considering post-2012 commitments at least seven years before the end of the first commitment period, that is, in 2005. Consequently, there had been no particular reason for the Danish Presidency to have pressed the issue of developing countries' commitments at such an early stage. Depledge (2006, p. 5) even points out that it was because of the EU's 'clumsiness' that its relationship with the G-77/China had reached an 'all-time low'. As the G-77/China had served as a close ally during the critical previous two COPs, various analysts had argued at the time that the EU 'might have been better advised to remain calm and to allow COP-8 to have been turned into a forum for developing country concerns' (Ott 2003, p. 268).

According to EU diplomats, they had embarked on this strategy only out of fear of losing precious momentum while awaiting ratification by Russia (Ott 2003). In addition, the sentiment among EU officials had been that it was high time for developing countries to engage actively and constructively in a discussion on mitigation action during the second commitment period. Without them the climate regime would simply not be effective. 'It was quite obvious,' an interviewee argued, that the EU was 'carrying this on its back, almost alone. The US was out, Russia was doing its own thing and while all this was happening China was emerging as a great emitter.'[4] Feelings of frustration were also expressed by other interviewees, who noted a feeling within the EU of having 'been taken advantage of; everybody got from us whatever they wanted in Bonn and Marrakech and nobody wanted to give anything back in return.'[5] 'Clearly,' another interviewee said, 'many developing countries were just hiding behind the US, saying that if the US is not taking on any commitments and if Russia is not showing signals of ratifying Kyoto, how can you expect us to do anything?'[6]

In any case, the December 2002 Environment Council expressed the view that the political results of COP-8 had been 'inadequate in dealing with the urgent issue of longer-term reductions of greenhouse gas emissions' (Environment Council 2002b). Months prior to COP-8, Müller (2002) had noted this emerging divide between developed and developing countries and the fundamental differences in their perception of the climate change problem itself. While the former held an 'ecological view' of the problem, solvable via allocating emission mitigation targets, the latter perceived it as a 'human welfare problem' that was 'not life-style-, but life-threatening' (p. 242). In his view, the failure on the part of developed countries to allow COP-8 to make this link between climate change policy and sustainable development was a missed opportunity.

Heading towards ratification

At COP-8, Russia had given conflicting signals on the likely timing of a ratification decision. As a result, all diplomatic efforts in 2003 were devoted towards Russia. In March, an EU delegation, including Environment Commissioner Margot Wallström, was dispatched to Moscow to push Russia to speed up, but to no avail. Delegates attending the eighteenth sessions of the Subsidiary Bodies to the Convention (June 2003) had their attention fixed on that exact question and in particular to the Third World Conference on Climate Change (WCCC) to be held in Moscow in September 2003 (ENB 2003a). This could perhaps explain why 'attendance was low, energy lower, and accomplishments minimal' (Jacob 2003, p. 309). In an interesting, but nevertheless marginal/secondary, development, the US demanded again that the Secretariat's budget be divided in two in order to ensure that monetary contributions from non-parties to the Protocol would not be used to fund Protocol activities (ENB 2003a). The EU argued back that such a position was misplaced, since the purpose of all the activities undertaken by parties, whether under the Convention itself or under the Kyoto Protocol, were directed towards the fulfilment of the ultimate objective of the Convention (European Council 2003).

Far more interesting in terms of developments was the WCCC. As the Russians preferred the conference to focus solely on scientific issues, the EU had struggled to have even the word 'Kyoto' included anywhere in the resolution that Russia submitted to ask for UN backing of the event (Grubb 2003, p. 475). Rather ambiguously, President Putin in his opening speech noted that Russia was preparing ratification and would take a decision when ready. He even recalled a Russian joke that

> for a northern country like Russia, it won't be that bad if it gets 2 or 3 degrees warmer. Maybe it would even be better – we would spend less on fur coats and other warm things, and agriculture specialists say our grain production will increase, and thank God for that.
>
> (Peake 2004, p. 52)

Apparently, some participants took the joke seriously, since Putin had to address the conference again in order to reassure that he did not accept the 'climate-change-is-good-for-Russia' line (Grubb 2003, p. 476). Overall, instead of offering clarity, Moscow's WCCC further clouded the situation. Grubb (2003, p. 477) even used Churchill's famous words to summarize the (political) outcome of the conference: 'I cannot forecast to you the actions of Russia. It is a riddle wrapped in a mystery inside an enigma.' The EU–Russia Summit, held in Rome one month prior to COP-9 (6 November 2003), and assisted by a Troika visit, would offer no clarity either.

COP-9 (Milan)

COP-9 was held in Milan, Italy, from 1–12 December 2003, with the reason for holding it late in the year having been to allow Russia's Parliament more time to (hopefully) ratify the Protocol (Peake 2004). With most substantive issues having been resolved in previous conferences, COP-9's agenda was relatively light, with negotiations focusing on three main unresolved issues: funding of the UNFCCC Secretariat, funding for developing countries (including economic diversification) and the criteria for sinks projects under the CDM.

To begin with, the question of the UNFCCC Secretariat's budget was resolved in Milan. Parties decided that the Secretariat's total budget of US$35 million for the 2004–05 period would include US$3.3 million for Kyoto 'preparatory activity', with the US announcing that it would hence reduce its contribution by its proportionate share (21 per cent) of the US$3.3 million (C2ES 2003). Regarding the other issue that had caused friction during COP-8, parties decided that the first session of the COP serving as the meeting of the parties to the Kyoto Protocol would be held in conjunction with the session of the COP.

The second unresolved problem related to financial issues and the recently-created funds. The SCCF had been set up to finance activities in areas including adaptation, technology transfer, energy and transport, plus assist oil-exporting countries to diversify their economies. Conflict arose when the EU argued that financial transfers should be tied to the regular fulfilment of reporting obligations, that is, national communications and national adaptation programmes of action (NAPAs). Given that many developing countries had yet to submit their initial national communications, the EU had hoped that its proposal would encourage the non-Annex I parties in question to conform. This met with strong G-77/China opposition on the grounds that it would raise additional obstacles to the efforts of developing countries to secure funding through the SCCF. The G-77/China argued instead that national development plans and any other relevant information should be sufficient for identifying activities that could be funded under the SCCF. In a compromise much closer to the demands of developing countries, it was decided that the SCCF would support activities taking into account 'national communications or national adaptation programmes of action, and other relevant information provided by the applicant Party' (UNFCCC 2003b, pp. 11–12).

With regard to the LDCF, parties decided that NAPAs would be funded on a full-cost basis. LDCs, however, failed to secure a decision from Annex I parties for full-cost funding of adaptation projects in their territories through the GEF. Problematically, adaptation projects seldom fall squarely within the scope of the UNFCCC, often having components that include other aspects of development, such as disaster preparedness, water management, desertification prevention, or biodiversity protection. As Annex I parties argued, projects identified by NAPAs would likely resemble straightforward development, when they were willing to only fund the 'climate-proofing of such activities' (Dessai *et al.* 2005, p. 111). In the view of the EU, the newly-created climate funds could complement other bilateral and multilateral development assistance channels, but not substitute them (UNFCCC 2003a). COP-10 would see more of this debate.

Agreement on economic diversification proved elusive. Under UNFCCC Article 4, paragraph 8, parties were urged to: (i) give full consideration to the needs of highly vulnerable countries (e.g. small island states or countries with low-lying coastal areas); and (ii) take into account the impact of mitigation measures on their economies, as well as on the economies of countries 'highly dependent on income generated from the production, processing and export, and/or on consumption of fossil fuels and associated energy-intensive products' (UNFCCC 1992, p. 15). Yet, coupling economic diversification of rich OPEC countries with the adaptation needs of poor countries was deemed unacceptable by the EU (Dessai *et al.* 2005). With no breakthrough in sight, this controversial issue was postponed for COP-10.

The final main controversial issue related to sinks in the CDM. Back in Marrakech, parties had agreed that only afforestation and reforestation projects would be eligible under the CDM. However, concrete definitions and modalities on various issues, such as non-permanence, the reference year for reforestation activities, leakage, and environmental and socio-economic impacts, were still lacking. Non-permanence refers to the unavoidable fact that carbon sequestered by a forest is at a continuous risk of being released back into the atmosphere, either as a result of human activities (i.e. logging) or natural disasters (i.e. fires). To tackle this, parties decided, on the basis of a proposal tabled by the EU back in New Delhi, to create two new types of tradable certificates: tCERs (temporary CERs), which expired at the end of the commitment period following the one during which they were issued; and lCERs (long-term CERs), which were valid for the project's full crediting period (Boyd et al. 2008). The main difference therefore lay in their expiring time and the flexibility they thus allowed project proponents and developers. Parties could pay less and buy compliance through tCERs for only one commitment period, or invest more in lCERs and buy compliance until the end of the project's crediting period, which can be between 20 and 60 years (see Dutschke et al. 2005). In other words, as Höhne et al. (2007b, p. 359) note, 'acquiring an lCER is equivalent to acquiring a string of regularly renewed tCERs.' In the former case, transaction costs are lower, as you only have to buy them once, instead of every five years. The risks though are higher, as lCERs run greater dangers of becoming invalid as a result of, for example, a forest fire.

With respect to the reference year for reforestation activities, Canada, as well as a number of Latin American and African parties, had argued in favour of having 1999 instead of 1989 as the baseline for reforestation activities, the rationale being that lack of land use data before 1999 would prevent several countries, especially LDCs, from being eligible for forestry-CDM activities (Dessai et al. 2005). The EU, AOSIS, Malaysia and Brazil successfully opposed this proposal by arguing that changing the definitions on afforestation and reforestation agreed in Decision 11/CP.7 would 'go against the coherence of the policy making process' (Boyd et al. 2004, p. 3). One, however, could plausibly argue that the decision back in COP-7 to change Russia's numerical figure in Appendix Z was an example of a previously approved Decision that was changed as a result of political bargaining (Boyd et al. 2004).

Accounting for leakage was another contested issue. Negative leakage refers to the situation where a project removes emissions in one place but increases them outside of its boundaries (e.g. fossil fuel substitution leads to a decline in fuel prices and a rise in fuel use elsewhere). Leakage can also be positive, as when a successful project leads to removals taking place outside of its boundaries (e.g. a successful forestry CDM project impacts positively on the carbon sequestration of adjacent forests). Accounting for leakage is therefore a rather complex exercise, as a project developer needs to monitor for impact beyond the project's geographical boundaries, as well as over time (Boyd et al. 2004). Some parties, such as Canada, favoured accounting for both positive and negative leakage, while others, such as the EU, Brazil and Norway, were against. The accounting complications were clearly illustrated by a hypothetical case provided during the negotiations of two neighbouring projects concurrently claiming credits for positive leakage in a third adjacent area (Boyd et al. 2004). In the final decision, accounting for leakage was excluded, with project participants being simply urged to design afforestation or reforestation activities under the CDM in such a manner as to minimize (negative) leakage (Boyd et al. 2008; UNFCCC 2003c).

Environmental and socio-economic impacts represented the final controversial issue with respect to sinks in the CDM. To begin with, all parties were in agreement that every project design document (PDD) for forestry activities under the CDM would need to include impact assessment information on environmental impacts (i.e. hydrology, soils, risk of fires, pests and diseases), as well as on socio-economic impacts (i.e. local communities, indigenous peoples, land tenure, local employment, food production, cultural and religious sites, and access to fuelwood and other forest products) (UNFCCC 2003c). What sparked controversy was whether to exclude or include genetically-modified organisms (GMOs) in sink projects. The EU was in favour of banning them, but had to overcome the resistance of the US. As a compromise, it was agreed that the PDDs would clearly state whether GMOs were being used in a sink project and leave it up to the developing countries involved to decide in accordance with their national laws whether or not to host such a project. Moreover, since PDD information would be publicly available, concerned purchasers could refrain from buying CERs generated from such projects – a provision that also applied to the use of non-local (invasive) tree species in afforestation and reforestation projects (Ott and Santarius 2004).

Evaluating Milan

The above decisions on sinks in the CDM completed the last outstanding issues relating to the BAPA, which in itself was a historical milestone. The EU stressed for its part that the decision was 'balanced and reflected progress toward implementing the Protocol' (ENB 2003b, p. 5). Despite having compromised on environmental and socio-economic impacts, the final text did reflect, to a large extent, its positions. Moreover, the fact that the issue of future participation of developing countries in the climate regime was kept out of the political negotiations in Milan warded off the danger of renewed conflict (see COP-8) between the EU and the G-77/China. As Höhne *et al.* (2007a, p. 11) note, the EU kept silent on this matter as it 'did not want to repeat the negative experience of COP-8'. Parties even decided not to adopt any type of declaration, mandate or similar document in Milan, with the high-level segment of the COP simply concluding with a COP President's 'Summary' (Dessai *et al.* 2005). COP-9, however, had ended with the Russian government giving conflicting signs as to its Kyoto Protocol ratification intentions. While at the beginning of the conference one of President Putin's economic advisors had announced in Moscow that Russia would not ratify the Protocol in its present form, the Kremlin soon afterwards denied this statement, reassuring the international community of Russia's intent to move towards ratification (Ott and Santarius 2004).

Notes

1 Interview No. 13 (Member State official – Former Head of Delegation).
2 Interview No. 9 (Commission official).
3 Interview No. 1 (Member State official – Former Head of Delegation).
4 Interview No. 2 (Member State official – Former Head of Delegation).
5 Interview No. 1 (Member State official – Former Head of Delegation).
6 Interview No. 9 (Commission official).

References

Afionis, Stavros and Ioannis Chatzopoulos (2010). Russia's role in UNFCCC negotiations since the exit of the United States in 2001. *International Environmental Agreements: Politics, Law and Economics* 10: 45–63.

Baer, Paul and Tom Athanasiou (2001). Climate change after Marrakech: should environmentalists still support the Kyoto Protocol? *Foreign Policy in Focus*, December. Available at: www.foreighpolicy-infocus.org/.

Barnett, Jon and Suraje Dessai (2002). Articles 4.8 and 4.9 of the UNFCCC: adverse effects and the impacts of response measures. *Climate Policy* 2 (2–3): 231–9.

Boyd, Emily and Emma Lisa Schipper (2002). The Marrakech Accord – at the crossroad to ratification: Seventh Conference of the Parties to the United Nations Framework Convention on Climate Change. *Journal of Environment & Development* 11 (2): 184–90.

Boyd, Emily, Esteve Corbera and Manuel Estrada (2008). UNFCCC negotiations (pre-Kyoto to COP-9): what the process says about the politics of CDM-sinks. *International Environmental Agreements* 8 (2): 95–112.

Boyd, Emily, Esteve Corbera, María Gutiérrez and Manuel Estrada (2004). The politics of afforestation and reforestation activities at COP-9 and SB-20. Tyndall Briefing Note No. 12, November. Available at: www.tyndall.ac.uk/sites/default/files/note12.pdf.

C2ES (2002). Conference of the Parties 8 (COP 8): Climate Talks in New Delhi. November. Available at: www.c2es.org/international/negotiations/cop-8.

C2ES (2003). Ninth Session of the Conference of the Parties to the UN Framework Convention on Climate Change (COP-9) Milan, Italy. December. Available at: www.c2es.org/international/negotiations/cop-9.

den Elzen, Michael G.J and André P.G. de Moor (2002). Analyzing the Kyoto Protocol under the Marrakech Accords: economic efficiency and environmental effectiveness. *Ecological Economics* 43 (1–2): 141–58.

Depledge, Joanna (2006). The opposite of learning: ossification in the climate change regime. *Global Environmental Politics* 6 (1): 1–22.

Dessai, Suraje, Lisa F. Schipper, Esteve Corbera, Bo Kjellén, Maria Gutiérrez and Alex Haxeltine (2005). Challenges and outcomes at the Ninth Session of the Conference of the Parties to the United Nations Framework Convention on Climate Change. *International Environmental Agreements* 5 (2): 105–24.

Dessai, Suraje, Nuno S. Lacasta and Katharine Vincent (2003). International political history of the Kyoto Protocol: from The Hague to Marrakech and beyond. *International Review for Environmental Strategies* 4 (2): 183–205.

Dutschke, Michael, Bernhard Schlamadinger, Jenny L.P. Wong and Michael Rumberg (2005). Value and risks of expiring carbon credits from afforestation and reforestation projects under the CDM. *Climate Policy* 5: 109–25.

ENB (2001). Summary of the Seventh Conference of the Parties to the UN Framework Convention on Climate Change: 29 October – 10 November 2001. *Earth Negotiations Bulletin* 12 (189): 1–16.

ENB (2002a). Summary of the Eighth Conference of the Parties to the UN Framework Convention on Climate Change: 23 October – 1 November 2002. *Earth Negotiations Bulletin* 12 (209): 1–15.

ENB (2002b). Summary of the Sixteenth Session of the Subsidiary Bodies to the UN Framework Convention on Climate Change: 5–14 June 2002. *Earth Negotiations Bulletin* 12 (200): 1–13.

ENB (2003a). Summary of the Eighteenth Session of the Subsidiary Bodies to the UN Framework Convention on Climate Change: 4–13 June 2003. *Earth Negotiations Bulletin* 12 (219): 1–15.

ENB (2003b). Summary of the Ninth Conference of the Parties to the UN Framework Convention on Climate Change: 1–12 December 2003. *Earth Negotiations Bulletin* 12 (231): 1–19.

Environment Council (2002a). *Environment Council Press Release*, 320 No. 12976/02, Luxembourg, 17 October.

Environment Council (2002b). *Environment Council Press Release*, 379 No. 15101/02, Brussels, 9 December.

EPL (Environmental Policy and Law) (2002a). In Preparation for COP-8. *Environmental Policy and Law* 32 (5): 203.

EPL (Environmental Policy and Law) (2002b). Less than satisfactory results. *Environmental Policy and Law* 33 (1): 18–20.

European Commission (2001). Proposal for a Council Decision concerning the conclusion, on behalf of the European Community, of the Kyoto Protocol to the United Nations Framework Convention on Climate Change and the joint fulfilment of commitments thereunder. COM (2001) 579, Brussels.

European Council (2002). Statement by Denmark on Behalf of the European Community and its Member States: New Delhi, 25 October 2002 COP 8: General exchange of views on a Delhi Declaration. Available at: www.consilium.europa.eu/uedocs/cmsUpload/2002cop8COP-DelhiD.pdf.

European Council (2003). SBI 18: Agenda Item 10 (b) – Programme Budget for the biennium 2004–2005. 4–13 June. Available at: www.consilium.europa.eu/uedocs/cmsUpload/2003sbi18item10b.final.pdf.

Grubb, Michael (2003). Meeting report: the Moscow World Conference on Climate Change, Moscow, 30 September–3 October 2003. *Climate Policy* 3 (4): 475–7.

Harrison, Kathryn (2007). The road not taken: climate change policy in Canada and the United States. *Global Environmental Politics* 7 (4): 92–117.

Höhne Niklas, Gylvan Meira Filho, Jacques Marcovitch, Farhana Yamin and Sara Moltmann (2007a). History and status of the international climate change negotiations on a future climate agreement. BASIC Paper 15, September. Available at: www.basic-project.net.

Höhne, Niklas, Sina Wartmann, Anke Herold and Annette Freibauer (2007b). The rules for land use, land use change and forestry under the Kyoto Protocol – lessons learned for the future climate negotiations. *Environmental Science & Policy* 10: 353–69.

Hovi, Jon, Tora Skodvin and Steinar Andersen (2003). The persistence of the Kyoto Protocol: why Annex I countries move on without the United States. *Global Environmental Politics* 3 (4): 1–23.

Jacob, Thomas R. (2002). Report on UNFCCC Subsidiary Body Negotiations 16, Bonn, 5–14 June 2002. *Climate Policy* 2 (1–2): 255–8.

Jacob, Thomas R. (2003). Report on UNFCCC Subsidiary Body Meetings, Bonn, June 2003. *Climate Policy* 3 (3): 309–13.

Jacquemont, Frédéric (2003). A report on the Eighth Session of the Conference of the Parties. *Environmental Law Network International* 1: 18–24.

Müller, Benito (2002). A New Delhi mandate? *Climate Policy* 2 (2–3): 241–2.

Najam, Adil, Saleemul Huq and Youba Sokona (2003). Climate negotiations beyond Kyoto: developing countries concerns and interests. *Climate Policy* 3 (3): 221–31.

Ott, Hermann E. (2001). Global climate. In Jutta Brunnée and Ellen Hey (eds) *Yearbook of international environmental law* 11, (2000). Oxford: Oxford University Press, 166–77.

Ott, Herman E. (2003). Global climate. In Ulfstein, Geir and Jacob Werksman (eds) *Yearbook of international environmental law* 13, (2002). Oxford: Oxford University Press, 261–70.

Ott, Hermann E. and Tilman Santarius (2004). Global climate. In Ulfstein, Geir and Jacob Werksman (eds) *Yearbook of international environmental law* 14 (2003). Oxford: Oxford University Press, 272–9.

Peake, Stephen (2004). Delivering the Kyoto baby. *Refocus* 5 (1): 52–3.

Pearce, Fred (2002). Canada plays dirty. *New Scientist* 174 (2343): 16.

Schunz, Simon (2014). *European Union foreign policy and the global climate regime.* Brussels: P.I.E. Peter Lang.

UNFCCC (1992). *Framework Convention on Climate Change.* New York: United Nations.

UNFCCC (2002a). The Delhi Ministerial Declaration on Climate Change and Sustainable Development. Informal Proposal by the President, 28 October. Available at: http://unfccc.int/cop8/latest/delhidecl_infprop.pdf.

UNFCCC (2002b). The Delhi Ministerial Declaration on Climate Change and Sustainable Development. Proposal by the President. FCCC/CP/2002/L.6/Rev.1.

UNFCCC (2003a). Implementation of Article 4, Paragraphs 8 and 9, of the Convention – Matters Relating to the Least Developed Countries. CCC/SBI/2003/MISC.4/Add.1.

UNFCCC (2003b). Report of the Conference of the Parties on its Ninth Session, Held at Milan from 1 to 12 December 2003 – Addendum. FCCC/CP/2003/6/Add.1.

UNFCCC (2003c). Report of the Conference of the Parties on its Ninth Session, Held at Milan from 1 to 12 December 2003 – Addendum. FCCC/CP/2003/6/Add.2.

Vogler, John and Charlotte Bretherton (2006). The European Union as a protagonist to the United States on climate change. *International Studies Perspectives* 7 (1): 1–22.

Wirth, David A. (2002). The Sixth Session (Part Two) and Seventh Session of the Conference of the Parties to the Framework Convention on Climate Change. *American Journal of International Law* 96 (3): 648–60.

7 The Protocol enters into force

The uncertainty with respect to Russia's intentions would unexpectedly develop during this period into a real test for the resolve of EU solidarity and unity on Kyoto Protocol action. In December 2003, Italy and Spain, as a result of unrest in domestic industrial circles due to the imminent emissions trading scheme, explicitly referred to Kyoto as a threat to business during the Brussels European Council (ENDS 2003a). Loyola de Palacio, the Spanish Energy Commissioner, followed suit by stating that the EU needed a 'plan B' in case Russia refused to ratify, as it would be 'suicide' for the EU to implement Kyoto without Russian participation (Barnes 2010; ENDS 2003b). While Commission President Romano Prodi publicly rebuked de Palacio, the latter's views were echoed by Italy a few months later at the March 2004 Environment Council, where it called on its fellow Member States to make future mitigation action conditional on Russia signing up to the Protocol (King 2004; ENDS 2004a). Spain even suggested not using the term 'targets' when referring to post-2012 reductions (Costa 2011). With Finland having also expressed reservations, the Irish EU Presidency came under pressure to ensure that no negative signals concerning the EU's commitment to Kyoto surfaced during its term in office. It therefore pushed for all Member States to unanimously adopt a text underlining the importance the EU attached to the ratification process of the Kyoto Protocol and to its early entry into force. It was apparent, however, that urgent action towards somehow inducing Russia to ratify was needed if EU unity was to be maintained.

The key to untying this Gordian knot was Russia's ambition to join the WTO. As the price for its support, the EU had initially demanded that Russia raise its low gas prices and deregulate its natural gas industry, as the former in particular amounted according to the EU to a major subsidy to Russian producers of energy-intensive goods (Zimmermann 2007). In the final deal, reached at the May 2004 EU–Russia Summit in Moscow, the EU settled for an increase in prices by 2010 plus, critically, a Russian agreement to ratify the Protocol (Afionis and Chatzopoulos 2010; Henry and Sundstrom 2007; Bretherton and Vogler 2006). While the EU did get what it wanted (i.e. Kyoto Protocol ratification), there is no doubt as to who derived the most benefits out of the bargaining arrangement. As Kotov (2004, p. 165) notes, 'the economic benefits for Russia from WTO entry exceed by several-fold its potential losses from surpassing the Kyoto [emissions] targets'.

In any case, May 2004 was to be a historic month for the EU, as it witnessed its fifth enlargement (part I) with ten new nations: Cyprus, the Czech Republic, Estonia, Hungary, Latvia, Lithuania, Malta, Poland, Slovakia, and Slovenia. This fifth enlargement was to be completed with the accession of Bulgaria and Romania in January 2007 (part II). As far as international climate policy was concerned, the following points should be stressed. First, all 12 countries had ratified the Kyoto Protocol at the time of their accession. Second, the Central and Eastern European Member States already had their own Kyoto Protocol targets for the first commitment period of between 6 per cent (Hungary and Poland) and 8 per cent (all remaining countries). Since, because of Article 4.4 of the Protocol, the EU-15 had to stick to its own bubble for the first commitment period, the enlargement would only have an effect on the international status quo until after 2012. Third, Cyprus and Malta were non-Annex-I parties at the time and thus had no target, with Cyprus also being an AOSIS member (Pallemaerts and Williams 2006). Both though joined Annex I in 2013 and 2010 respectively. Fourth, emissions in all these countries were projected to stay significantly below 1990 levels, except in Slovenia, which would miss its target, and Hungary, which would just reach its commitment (EEA 2003). The Baltic States in particular were projected to achieve cuts in emissions of more than 50 per cent from 1990 to 2010 (European Commission 2003), thus endowing them with considerable volumes of surplus allowances with which to trade.

COP-10 (Buenos Aires)

In the run-up to COP-10, the October 2004 Environment Council had emphasized the need to consider the post-2012 framework and had noted that while mitigation of climate change remained the cornerstone of present and future climate change policies, the inevitability of climate change required that adaptation be also considered as another key element of such policies (Environment Council 2004a). This represented an interesting formulation of words if one considers the EU position during COP-8 in New Delhi. On 18 November 2004, Russia finally completed its ratification of the Protocol, which, in accordance to Article 25.1 provisions, represented the final one required for the Kyoto Protocol to enter into force. This would take place 90 days later, on 16 February 2005. Against this positive backdrop, it was imperative to ensure that the 'house was in order' in time (ENB 2004, p. 1). Another positive development came on the first day of the COP, when Canada decided to drop its insistence on credits for clean energy exports – an issue that had consumed considerable time and energy during the past couple of years (Ott *et al.* 2005).

The first main topic to be dealt with in Buenos Aires concerned the selection of the forum in which to discuss the way forward post-2012, with the main two options on the table being to carry out this debate within the framework of the COP or that of the COP/MOP. The first option was favoured by many, as it implied that the US would be able to participate in the deliberations as a fully-fledged party and not as simply an observer without the right to vote. Others, including the EU, were advocating the latter option as a safeguard against probable US vetoes (Ott *et al.* 2005). In order to initiate more concrete talks on post-2012 commitments, the host Argentine government took the lead by proposing two Seminars of Governmental Experts that would discuss 'future actions' and report back to COP-11 (C2ES 2004). The EU's Dutch lead negotiator dismissed the proposal as 'talks about talks about talks' (Ott *et al.* 2005, p. 85) and argued in favour of a more forward-looking process that would eventually lead to decisions on future steps (C2ES 2004). The US and the majority of developing countries rejected both the Argentine and EU proposals, with the US tabling a counter-proposal according to which there would only be one seminar with a focus on the implementation of existing national policies. The great majority of G-77/China parties were adamant that the seminar(s) should not act as a facade for a process that would lead to talks on future commitments for developing countries. The final decision, adopted following prolonged negotiations behind closed doors between Argentina, India, Brazil, the US and the EU, was rather weak and very much closer to the initial position of the US and the G-77/China. Specifically, parties were only able to agree on text stating that 'the proceedings of the Seminar will be made available by the Secretariat to Parties for their consideration, bearing in mind that this Seminar does not open any negotiations leading to new commitments' (ENB 2004, p. 14).

The second main issue on the agenda was adaptation – an issue that had been gaining in prominence ever since COP-8 in New Delhi. However, the linking by OPEC of the issues of adverse effects and the impact of the implementation of response measures had stalemated the talks for the past few years. As noted, the fact that both issues were dealt with under the same Article (4.8 and 4.9) gave OPEC blocking power over decisions that ignored OPEC funding demands. The EU remained unwilling to provide funding to wealthy OPEC countries and argued instead in favour of prioritizing the needs of the most vulnerable parties. The EU's objective at COP-10, therefore, was 'to have a decision text which [would] further facilitate those countries most at risk from the adverse effects of climate change, to develop the capacity required to adapt and cope with those adverse effects' (European Council 2005b, p. 18). Eventually, parties agreed on a spectrum of adaptation capacity-building actions (e.g. workshops, pilot projects etc.), packaged as the 'Buenos Aires Programme of Work on Adaptation and Response Measures' (see UNFCCC 2004).

While the Buenos Aires Programme acknowledges their needs, the demands of the oil-exporting countries were somewhat stunted, as OPEC countries were only able to secure funding for reporting requirements and two expert meetings (Ott *et al.* 2005). More importantly, however, COP-10 witnessed a schism within G-77/China, with OPEC countries being unable to count on the support of the LDCs and AOSIS. Having neglected their own interests in the past in order to maintain a unified position within the G-77/China, these two groups of countries would have no more. They successfully pushed for putting an end to the linking of the two issues, thus allowing future COPs to discuss adaptation to the impacts of climate change and adaptation to the impacts of response measures as separate agenda items (Ott *et al.* 2005).

The final major agenda item to be discussed related to financial issues. In particular, LDCs were unsuccessful for a second consecutive COP to secure a commitment for the full-cost funding of adaptation measures. LDCs repeatedly stressed the difficulty in finding and securing adequate co-financing, as well as the costly and cumbersome calculation of the additional costs, which resulted in the financial resources of the LDCF becoming in practice almost inaccessible. The EU's reply was that co-financing emphasized countries' sense of ownership over projects (ENB 2004). Eventually, the issue was forwarded to the next meeting of the Subsidiary Bodies.

Evaluation of COP-10

With the agreements on seminars and adaptation being rather weak, the official outcome of COP-10 was modest at best, while the unhelpful role of the US again gave rise to concern (see ENB 2004). There were, however, a number of positive developments, both inside and outside the UNFCCC process, which provided room for optimism. First, the sudden rift in the G-77/China was hailed by many as the start of a process that would bring about the end of the dominant role the OPEC countries had enjoyed until then within that group (Ott *et al.* 2005). Second, in an important deviation from US and Australian official federal policy, an increasing number of federal states there were beginning to take climate policy into their own hands by setting up emissions trading schemes (see *The Economist* 2004).

Turning to the EU, a number of issues arose from its performance at COP-10. To start with, recent disagreements between Member States resurfaced in Buenos Aires when the Italian Environment Minister again questioned the principle of legally binding targets (Michaelowa 2005). In particular, Italy broke EU ranks by repeatedly suggesting that post-2012 targets should be voluntary as an incentive for the US and major developing countries to re-embrace the agreement (ENDS 2004b). EU strategic planning was also problematic in another respect, given that COP-10, like COP-8 in New Delhi, had no mandate to discuss the future of the climate regime. Nevertheless, by supporting the Argentinean proposal on seminars, the EU had only succeeded in undermining its own prospects for establishing a 'strategic alliance' with key developing countries, pushing them instead into the arms of the US (Ott *et al.* 2005, p. 90). The EU position was that developed countries should continue to take the lead, but in order for climate change to be controlled effectively, action by developing countries, such as policies to improve energy efficiency, was also necessary

(Environment Council 2004b). What was abundantly clear at COP-10, however, was that certain parties were not at all ready to embark on post-2012 negotiations. China even stated that the (few) measures contained in its national climate change report would be its 'final word for the next two decades' (Michaelowa 2005, p. 2). By supporting Argentina, therefore, the EU had arguably fallen in the same trap as in New Delhi. Schunz (2014) notes that instead of leading, the EU found itself isolated and unable to exert influence.

Climate policy enters a new phase

In January 2005, the EU launched its emissions trading scheme, a policy instrument that covered roughly half of its CO_2 emissions and had at the time been termed as 'the most important piece of climate change legislation anywhere in the world to date' (Scott 2005, p. 13). A month later, the European Commission issued a communication on future climate change policies, which is notable for a number of reasons. First, the Commission reassessed the EU position on the optimum concentration level of greenhouse gases in the atmosphere by noting that in order for global average temperatures not to exceed 2°C above pre-industrial levels, concentration of greenhouse gases should stabilize well below the level of 550 ppmv (CO_2 equivalents). The Commission's argument was based on research findings that had indicated a level of 550 ppmv CO_2 equivalent to offer at most a one in six chance of respecting the 2°C target (European Commission 2005a). Surprisingly, however, the Commission did not define precise targets for reducing greenhouse gas emissions, arguing that the EU should 'explore options for a post-2012 strategy with key partners during 2005 before deciding on the position it [would] take in the upcoming negotiations' (European Commission 2005a, p. 11). In order to clarify this position further, the Commission's communication stated that:

> The reduction commitments that the EU would be willing to take under such a regime should depend on the level and type of participation of other major emitters. Therefore, the Commission is not recommending the adoption of a specific EU target at this stage.
>
> (p. 11)

The refusal to set targets soon led to criticisms of the EU having abandoned its leading role in fighting climate change (ENDS 2005). Environment Commissioner Stavros Dimas justified this approach on the grounds that he did not wish to 'scare off other countries' by setting targets at this moment (Jordan and Rayner 2010, p. 70). Instead of targets, the communication included a set of proposals on future EU strategy, both internally and externally. Internally, the Commission argued for the need to invest in intra-EU adaptation, which represented an area which had been largely neglected by Member States up until then, followed by measures to raise public awareness and promote promising mitigation technologies that either existed already or were at an advanced pilot stage (carbon storage, biofuels and others). Externally, the Commission argued that the EU should push for mitigation commitments in the aviation and maritime sectors, as well as ensure the maintenance in any post-2012 agreement of the successful structural elements of the Kyoto Protocol, such as emissions trading, emissions monitoring and reporting rules, and a multilateral compliance regime. Its most ground-breaking proposal, however, was for the EU to effectively bypass the UNFCCC and try to 'accelerate progress at the global level by discussing reductions among ... [a] smaller group of major emitters in a forum similar to the G8, in parallel with vigorous efforts to reach agreement in the UN context' (European Commission 2005a, p. 5).

In March, the EU environment ministers, while welcoming the Commission's communication, made recommendations that effectively went against it by setting out ambitious emissions reduction targets (15–30 per cent by 2020 and 60–80 per cent by 2050 of 1990 levels) for EU leaders to approve at their annual spring summit in Brussels a few weeks later (Environment Council 2005a). While EU heads of state and government agreed to aim for a 15–30 per cent cut in greenhouse gas emissions by 2020, they dropped the 60–80 per cent cuts proposed for 2050, at the insistence of Germany and Austria.

In May, the Seminar of Governmental experts, as agreed back in COP-10, was held in Bonn. Its goal was solely to encourage the informal exchange of information on adaptation and mitigation issues. As a matter of fact, the Secretariat and the chairpersons 'were at great pains' to emphasize the informal nature of the meeting, with Depledge (2006, p. 17) noting that presenters 'sat on red armchairs on a lowered podium, in a style more reminiscent of TV chat shows than intergovernmental talks'. In any case, parties did engage in an 'open, frank and broad-ranging' dialogue on actions taken to implement the UNFCCC and its Kyoto Protocol, but which did not lead to a narrowing of differences (ENB 2005c, p. 7). The Commission and a number of Member States (France, Germany, Finland and the Netherlands) presented on a variety of topics (e.g. emissions trading, technology transfer, aviation emissions, adaptation, etc.), while at the closing session EU delegates were asked to present their views on two key issues: technology transfer and adaptation/mitigation. On the former issue, Germany, on behalf of the EU, said the CDM should be strengthened without renegotiating the Marrakech Accords, while on the latter issue, Finland stressed that 'adaptation and mitigation are complementary, not alternative actions, and that the international approach to adaptation should be different to that on mitigation' (ENB 2005c, p. 6). Finally, Luxembourg showed interest for Brazil's Proalcool Programme, one of the world's most ambitious efforts to produce a renewable biomass fuel (ethanol from sugarcane) as an oil substitute.

Also in May, the twenty-second sessions of the Subsidiary Bodies were held in Bonn. These sessions are most notable for the draft decision on the LDCF, an issue that had caused much controversy during COP-10. Much of the debate during this meeting centred on an EU proposal, according to which 'funding from the LDCF should support priority adaptation activities identified in [NAPAs] that are "additional" to activities that would be undertaken to respond to climate variability' (ENB 2005a, p. 10). Even though LDCs noted again the difficulties associated with differentiating between climate variability and climate change, the final decision called for the development of a sliding co-financing scale for supporting activities identified in the NAPAs. Later on, the GEF proposed a sliding scale for co-financing according to which the LDCF would pay up to 75 per cent if project costs were under $250,000; 50 per cent if the cost was less than $2 million; 33 per cent if the cost was $2–5 million; and 20 per cent if the cost was over $5 million (see Mace 2005).

The G-8 Gleneagles 2005 Summit

The year 2005 was especially important to the UK, as it held the presidencies of both the G-8 and the EU. Consequently, Prime Minister Tony Blair had set high ambitions for the UK's double presidencies, with climate change and Africa being the two main priorities. Following the US 2001 withdrawal, the EU had primarily focused on 'saving' the Kyoto Protocol in Bonn and Marrakech, heading for swift ratification by 2002, and ensuring ratification of the agreement by the 'Gang of Four'. As a result, neither the EU nor any other international actor had been particularly active in formulating a strategy for re-engaging the US. However, as Vogler (2016, p. 140) notes, despite its 'animosity' with the US on this issue, the EU acknowledged that ensuring US participation was a *sine qua non* if the international community was to forge an effective climate regime. A strategy to this end was going to be unveiled by the UK in Gleneagles (see Grubb 2005).

The G-8 Gleneagles Summit in July 2005 is notable for a number of reasons. While world leaders neither agreed to any firm new targets, nor did the US embrace Kyoto, the final communiqué did state that: 'We know enough to act now and put ourselves on a path to slow and, as science justifies, stop and then reverse the growth of greenhouse gases' (G-8 2005). It was the first time that President Bush acknowledged the reality of anthropogenic climate change and the imperativeness of a swift response (Lesage *et al.* 2009).

Of notable political significance was also the G-8 agreement to create a 'Dialogue on climate change, clean energy and sustainable development', basically a forum where countries could share information and best practice. Participants to this dialogue, which was convened annually at the ministerial level up to 2008, included G-8 members as well as the EU and the 20 most important greenhouse gas emitters (minus Iran). The backbone of the Gleneagles commitments was the Gleneagles Plan of Action (GPOA), which contained a large set of commitments in a multitude of areas, such as, *inter alia* energy efficiency, buildings, transport, cleaner fossil fuels and renewables.

It should be stressed that the UK Presidency had no intention of bypassing the UNFCCC formal process, with Prime Minister Blair going to great lengths to make this abundantly clear in the final communiqué. Instead, the Dialogue was envisaged as a parallel process that would hopefully further action and cooperation between key countries. The EU, despite some initial scepticism, did eventually support the Blair initiative. As Vogler and Bretherton (2006, p. 18) note:

> Meetings of the G8 at Evian 2003 and Sea Island 2004 found common ground in treating climate change as a problem to be solved through technological innovation and this trend continued with the 2005 Gleneagles 'Plan of Action'. The EU supports this. Indeed, it must be part of the Lisbon Strategy for economic renewal, but it is not seen as an alternative to emissions reductions and carbon trading. Rather, the latter provides the necessary conditions for making low or non-carbon energy alternatives financially viable.

The fact that the US was again actively participating in climate change talks could only be seen as a positive development. As to why it won US approval, it should be noted that the GPOA contained nothing to which the US had not agreed to in the past (e.g. technology transfer). To those disappointed by the outcome of the Gleneagles Summit, Blair's response was that he believed it unwise to 'push an unwilling partner into a corner' (O'Riordan 2005, p. 3).

Yet, a few weeks after Gleneagles, the world community was taken by surprise when, during an Association of South East Asian Nations (ASEAN) Regional Forum meeting, six countries (US, Australia, Japan, China, India and South Korea) announced the Asia-Pacific Partnership on Clean Development and Climate (abbreviated as AP6). Like the Gleneagles Dialogue, this partnership would seek to advance cooperation between its members in developing and sharing a wide range of clean-energy and energy-efficient technologies, such as, liquefied natural gas, methane capture and use, clean coal, nuclear power and others. Interestingly enough, antipodal viewpoints have been expressed in the literature with respect to the AP6's role. Kellow (2006, p. 302), for instance, adopted a positive stance, arguing that as a result of its modest scope and limited number of parties it could prove a more 'effective policy instrument than Kyoto'. On the contrary, Friel (2005) approached the AP6 as yet another example of US unilateralism and defiance of multinational organizations, international law and important UN-based international agreements. Similarly, Athanasiou (2006, p. 47) interpreted the AP6 as a US move to undercut the G-8 process by negotiating a series of overlapping bilateral agreements in which it could 'manoeuvre freely' without the troublesome presence of 'grim climatologists' and, above all, Europeans. While the UN cautiously welcomed the agreement, the EU was more sceptical, expressing concern that the AP6 could undermine the Kyoto Protocol if it was used as an excuse by, for example, China and India to avoid enacting other climate change mitigation measures (Sissell 2005). While Canada joined later and the EU showed interest in being granted observer status, the AP6 was eventually discontinued in April 2011 because of its low problem-solving effectiveness (Andresen 2015).

With only a few months left until Montreal, the EU-15 was in the unpleasant position of having to admit that its emissions had not been substantially reduced, being just 1.7 per cent below 1990 levels (EEA 2005). Austria, Denmark, Ireland, Portugal and Spain were signalled as being among the worst performers. At the international front, the UK Presidency of the EU, obviously satisfied with the Gleneagles outcome, decided to apply the same strategy to China and India. Consequently, one of the major outcomes of the September 2005 China–EU Summit was the establishment of a Partnership on Climate Change, which would focus on clean coal technologies, energy-efficiency, energy conservation and renewable energy (European Commission 2005b). A few days later, at the EU–India Summit, the India–EU Initiative on Clean Development and Climate Change was launched, again with the aim of promoting the use of cleaner technologies.

The October 2005 Environment Council hailed the two agreements, describing them as examples of 'how economies in different stages of development can work together, through transfer of technology and building of capacity, to tackle climate change' (Environment Council 2005b). This meeting also outlined the EU's expectations of the forthcoming Montreal COP/MOP, stressing that it should deliberate on the issue of further commitments based on the provisions of Article 3(9) of the Kyoto Protocol, which provided that the first COP/MOP should initiate consideration of such commitments at least seven years before the end of the first commitment period.

The Montreal COP/MOP-1

While these developments were taking place, the international community was gearing up for COP/MOP-1 in Montreal – a conference whose host had increased its emissions by 24 per cent, putting it 30 per cent over its Kyoto commitment. Montreal signalled the start of a new era for international climate policy, given that negotiations on post-2012 emissions targets were to be initiated at least seven years before the end of the first commitment period, that is, no later than December 2005. Quite by chance, this coincided with COP/MOP-1. According to Stéphane Dion, Canadian Environment Minister and chair of the conference, the agenda was to be based on 'three-I's': 'implementation', 'improvement', and 'innovation'.

Implementation

The first issue on the agenda concerned the adoption of the Marrakech Accords. In legal terms, COP-7 in Marrakech had adopted only draft decisions which required formal adoption by the COP/MOP to enter into effect. Thus, COP-7 had simply forwarded the Accords to the COP/MOP for final adoption, under the understanding that parties, as part of a 'gentlemen's agreement', would adopt them as a whole at the first COP/MOP (Depledge and Grubb 2006). Four years later, parties formally adopted the 21 decisions comprising the Marrakech Accords, with the sole exception being the modalities of the compliance mechanism.

With respect to this later issue, Article 18 of the Kyoto Protocol clearly stated that any procedures and mechanisms entailing binding consequences should be adopted by means of an amendment. While Saudi Arabia was in favour of adopting the compliance mechanism by way of such an amendment, Japan, followed by New Zealand, preferred adopting it through a simple COP decision (ENB 2005b). As Müller (2006) notes, this went way beyond the narrow confines of a legalistic debate, as for penalties to be binding the compliance mechanism would need to be adopted as an amendment. The same, however, was not true for non-binding consequences – a recurrent Japanese demand – as a simple decision would suffice. In addition, an amendment required ratification by three-quarters of the parties in order to come into force – a process that would certainly not be over by 2008, that is, the start of the first commitment period. Furthermore, an amendment would only bind those parties that had ratified it, creating as a consequence two sets of countries (Wittneben et al. 2006). The Saudi proposal, therefore, amounted in practical terms to a derailment of the whole Kyoto process (Depledge and Grubb 2006).

The EU noted that without an operational compliance mechanism in place, parties would be unable to use the flexibility mechanisms or seek the support of the facilitative branch (European Council 2005a). Eager to ensure the compliance system became operational on time, it took a middle position by suggesting that the compliance mechanism be first adopted by way of a decision, followed by initiation of a process for amending the Protocol in accordance with Article 18 (ENB 2005b). China, the African Group and AOSIS all supported the EU proposal. The deadlock was eventually overcome when Canada and New Zealand presented a compromise proposal according to which the COP/MOP would 'approve and adopt' the compliance mechanism, while simultaneously launching a process, 'without prejudice to its outcome', for adoption by amendment, with a view to making a decision by COP/MOP-3 (ENB 2005b, p. 13). As to the binding nature of the above formulation, Rajamani (2008) posits that the Compliance Committee cannot apply binding consequences based on UNFCCC Decisions, which are by their own nature not legally binding. MacFaul (2005, p. 9) argues though that while, following Article 18, a decision could be argued to be non-binding, the fact that it was taken by consensus signalled the intent of all parties to abide by it, especially since it contained 'language of a mandatory nature'. To back up this argument, the example of the Non-compliance Procedure of the Montreal Protocol on Substances that Deplete the Ozone Layer (1987) was given, which, despite having been adopted by way of a decision, can nevertheless deliver binding rulings (Wittneben et al. 2006).

Funding for developing countries was another hotly contested issue, especially with respect to the Adaptation Fund. Negotiations there focused on two questions: co-financing and the Adaptation Fund's location in the GEF. As with the LDCF and the SCCF, the EU proposed a sliding co-financing scale for calculating additional costs, while it expressed its preference for the Adaptation Fund to be located at the GEF so as to ensure the coordination of project activities under all three funds (see UNFCCC 2005). Yet, several developing countries expressed concern about the fact that the AF, unlike its two other counterparts, operated under the Kyoto Protocol and not the UNFCCC. Consequently, fears were raised that locating it at the GEF could allow the US to exert undue influence on its operation (Bausch and Mehling 2006).

The adoption by the GEF in September 2005 of its Resource Allocation Framework (RAF) further polarized discussions, as many developing countries expressed concern regarding its adopted system for allocating GEF resources to recipient countries (Mace 2005). In particular, the RAF's two basic criteria were a 'country's potential to generate global environmental benefits', as well as whether it had appropriate national policies and an enabling environment in place to facilitate successful implementation of GEF projects (GEF 2005). Despite the EU viewing this framework as a step towards the modernization of GEF procedures, many developing countries perceived it as a formula that in essence rewarded large and fast-growing emitters (Müller 2006; European Council 2005a). Unable to agree, parties simply decided to organize a workshop to further discuss the specificities of the Adaptation Fund.

Improvement

The key element on the 'improvement' agenda was undoubtedly the poorly performing CDM, as many developing countries, as well as business, had repeatedly voiced their concerns over its overly bureaucratic nature and the cumbersomeness of its approval process to cope with an exponentially increasing stream of project proposal (Bausch and Mehling 2006). A first problem, according to the CDM Executive Board, was insufficient staff and funding. In order to boost the CDM's finances, parties decided to put a levy of US$0.10 to US$0.20 per CER for administrative expenses, with the first 15,000 CERs per project being charged a lower administrative fee of US$0.10 and the subsequent US$0.20 (ENB 2005b).

Another issue of concern to developing countries, especially African ones, was the uneven regional distribution of CDM projects and the strictness and complexity of the additionality principle. Regarding the former concern, the COP/MOP simply invited party submissions by the next meeting of the Subsidiary Bodies on 'systemic or systematic' barriers to a more equitable distribution of CDM projects (ENB 2005b, p. 12). On the latter issue, what especially came under heavy fire from developing countries was the controversial tool developed by the CDM Executive Board for clarifying the requirements for additionality, with many parties being of the opinion that the Board should be stripped of the authority to determine additionality (Wittneben *et al.* 2006). The EU, despite acknowledging that assessing additionality was indeed methodologically challenging, viewed the tool as a useful instrument and was against any removal of authority from the CDM Executive Board. According to the final compromise, authority on additionality would be left with the CDM Executive Board, while a call would be made for public input on new and innovative methods for demonstrating additionality, as well as on ideas for improving the existing tool (Bausch and Mehling 2006).

Innovation

Regarding negotiations under the Kyoto Protocol, discussions focused on Article 3.9 of the Kyoto Protocol, as the Montreal COP/MOP was the one required to initiate a process for negotiating post-2012 commitments. The G-77/China once again called for developed nations to take the lead and called for establishing an open-ended ad hoc working group of Kyoto parties that would complete its work by 2008. Proposals by leading Annex I parties were less substantive, being viewed as part of a 'strategic' manoeuvre to handle them a 'bargaining chip' on the question of which parties should take on commitments (Wittneben *et al.* 2006, p. 91). The EU, while recognizing that Annex I parties should continue to take the lead, simply invited parties to make submissions on issues to be considered in addressing Article 3.9 for further consideration at the twenty-fourth sessions of the Subsidiary Bodies (ENB 2005b). Japan went much further by noting that since emissions in non-Annex I countries were growing rapidly, COP-12 should start a review process of the UNFCCC with the aim of establishing an effective framework in which all parties would participate and take actions to realize the ultimate objective of the Convention.

Critically, however, both the EU and Japanese proposals suggested linking Article 3.9 to Article 9 of the Protocol, which called on parties to periodically review the Protocol and take appropriate action, with the first such review being scheduled for COP/MOP-2 (Spence *et al.* 2008; Depledge and Grubb 2006). Unlike Article 3.9, Article 9 does not explicitly refer to Annex I parties alone, causing the G-77/China to adamantly refuse any linkage between the two articles on the suspicion that the ulterior motive behind this suggestion was the use of the review as a pretext to raise the issue of developing country commitments. Parties were only able to reach a compromise that in reality simply deferred the issue for later. As a concession to developing countries, Annex-I parties accepted the establishment of an open-ended ad hoc working group, whereas the G-77/China had to abandon the 2008 timeline for the vague formulation that the ad hoc group should aim to complete its work in time to ensure that there would be no gap between commitment periods (Bausch and Mehling 2006). Regarding Article 9, parties simply agreed to submit proposals by September 2006 on how best to proceed under it.

Unlike negotiations under the Kyoto Protocol, negotiations under the Convention included parties that had not ratified the Protocol, namely the US and Australia. From the outset, these negotiations focused on President Dion's rather weak proposal for action under the Convention, according to which a series of workshops would be held to discuss approaches for long-term cooperative action to address climate change. However, Dion's proposal on a 'dialogue on long-term cooperative action' was met with suspicion by the US, the delegation of which was particularly sensitive to the use of the word 'dialogue', perceiving it to be an alternative term to 'negotiations' on a new treaty (Müller 2006). Unable to secure a breakthrough, the US delegation decided to walk out of the discussions as a sign of protest, with its lead negotiator, Harlan Watson, reportedly noting that 'if it walks like a duck, quacks like a duck, then it is a duck' (Bals *et al.* 2006, p. 5). Watson's infelicitous remark not only earned him a new nickname ('Duck' Watson), but also resulted in NGO representatives holding toy ducks out towards him throughout the duration of the Montreal COP/MOP (Bals *et al.* 2006).

The remaining parties decided to move on without the US, reaching an agreement on a draft decision on a dialogue on long-term action. At that point, the US delegation, in the face of complete international isolation, decided to return to the negotiating table with a 'take-it-or-leave-it' proposal, according to which the dialogue would be 'an open and non-binding exchange of views' and would 'not open any negotiations leading to new commitments' (Müller 2006, p. 26). It appears that the mediation of the UK Presidency of the EU was instrumental in convincing the US to sign up to the dialogue as, according to the UK Environment Secretary Margaret Beckett, there were 'conversations to and fro between London and Washington' in an effort to overcome the objections of the Americans to the text of the agreement. She then added:

> Once they saw what had been agreed overnight they realised that actually what we had all been telling them right the way through, which is that there was goodwill on the part of the negotiators of the world to re-engage the United States constructively, they looked at the text, they saw that was true. They then suggested some other minor amendments that would make it more comfortable for them and that is why, in the end, we got agreement.
>
> (cited in Müller 2006, p. 12)

This dialogue, which would focus primarily on adaptation, technology transfer and market-based opportunities, would take place in four workshops – the last to be held during COP-13 (Schipper and Boyd 2006).

An evaluation of COP/MOP-1

Montreal turned out to be a memorable milestone in the development of the climate regime, as there was substantial progress on all 'three-I's'. Apart from reaching a decision to initiate a process in an open-ended ad hoc group to consider further commitments by Annex I parties beyond 2012, the decision for a dialogue under the UNFCCC allowed for the constructive re-engagement of the US in the climate regime. As an EU interviewee noted:

> Our expectation at the time was mainly to keep the US in. Even if it is the wrong administration for an agreement, it is important that the technical people and the experts are kept in the process. And we were aware that things with the US could only come to a positive result following a change in the administration.[1]

Another positive development came from two heavily forested countries, Papua New Guinea and Costa Rica, who stressed the need to combat emissions resulting from deforestation (responsible for one-fifth of global carbon emissions). As *The Economist* (2006) noted, it appeared rather paradoxical at the time that the Protocol would allow for carbon credits from LULUCF projects (e.g. planting new forests), but not for protecting and preserving what forests were already there (see also Gupta 2014). Consequently, the two countries proposed either elaborating an optional Protocol under the UNFCCC or making forest conservation activities eligible under the CDM. The proposal received wide support, with the EU agreeing that the UNFCCC should seek ways to address tropical deforestation emissions, but pointing to a number of complex technical issues that needed to be tackled in advance, including modalities for monitoring and verifying emission cuts, provisions for tackling forest degradation, as well as definition of targets or baselines (ENB 2005b; see also Depledge and Grubb 2006; European Council 2005a).

To conclude with the EU, only positive remarks can be made of its performance at COP/MOP-1. The EU participated constructively in the negotiations, while also being instrumental in convincing the US to return to the negotiating table and agreeing to the COP dialogue. However, Depledge and Grubb (2006) wondered at the time about the willingness of the EU, Japan and other developed countries to concede so much by agreeing to unconditionally negotiate new emission targets for themselves, while settling for an informal COP dialogue that precluded any sort of future commitments on the part of developing countries or the US. As they noted (p. 559), this was either 'a remarkable leap of faith' or an effort on their part to exhibit leadership by providing some sort of reassurance that commitments would again figure in the post-2012 regime. Biermann (2005), however, views the EU's willingness to compromise as being part of its adopted strategy vis-à-vis the US. As he argues, the EU had two options: confrontation or conciliation. The former could entail the EU moving ahead on its own and making the Kyoto process develop into a success story, even by introducing – if needed – border carbon adjustments to deal with the question of the growing gap in the cost of energy in EU Member States and the US. The latter strategy, however, would require steps to bring the US back into the multilateral process via a soft UNFCCC-based dialogue, separate agreements outside the Kyoto framework (e.g. the Gleneagles Dialogue) or both. The drawback of opting for the conciliatory approach was that a US re-engagement would take place largely on Washington's terms and thus result in a softening of overall environmental policy ambition. In the end, the EU espoused the conciliatory viewpoint.

Note

1 Interview No. 12 (Commission official).

References

Afionis, Stavros and Ioannis Chatzopoulos (2010). Russia's role in UNFCCC negotiations since the exit of the United States in 2001. *International Environmental Agreements: Politics, Law and Economics* 10: 45–63.

Andresen, Steinar (2015). International climate negotiations: top–down, bottom–up or a combination of both? *International Spectator: Italian Journal of International Affairs* 50 (1): 15–30.

Athanasiou, Tom (2006). Too much of nothing. *Earth Island Journal* 20 (4): 46–7.

Bals, Christoph, Manfred Treber, Sven Anemüller, Dustin Neuneyer and Gerold Kier (2006). Results of the UN Climate Summit in Montreal: the community of states agrees upon concrete negotiation pathway for climate protection after 2012. Germanwatch Briefing Paper, January. Available at: http://germanwatch.org/rio/c11-hg06e.pdf.

Barnes, Pamela M. (2010). The role of the Commission of the European Union: creating external coherence from internal diversity. In Wurzel, Rüdiger K.W. and James Connelly (eds) *The European Union as a leader in international climate change politics*. London: Routledge, 74–91.

Bausch, Camilla and Michael Mehling (2006). Alive and kicking: the first meeting of the parties to the Kyoto Protocol. *Review of European Community & International Environmental Law* 15 (2): 193–201.

Biermann, Frank (2005). Between the USA and the South: strategic choices for European climate policy. *Climate Policy* 5 (3): 273–90.

Bretherton, Charlotte and John Vogler (2006). *The European Union as a global actor*. London: Routledge.

C2ES (2004). Tenth Session of the Conference of the Parties (COP) to the U.N. Framework Convention on Climate Change: December 6–17, 2004, Buenos Aires, Argentina. December. Available at: www.c2es.org/international/negotiations/cop-10/summary.

Costa, Oriol (2011). Spanish, EU and international climate change policies: download, catch up, and curb down. In Wurzel, Rüdiger K.W. and James Connelly (eds) *The European Union as a leader in international climate change politics*. London: Routledge, 179–94.

Depledge, Joanna (2006). The opposite of learning: ossification in the climate change regime. *Global Environmental Politics* 6 (1): 1–22.

Depledge, Joanna and Michael Grubb (2006). COP/MOP-1 and COP-11: a breakthrough for the climate change regime? *Climate Policy* 5 (5): 553–60.

Economist, The (2004). Welcome to Kyoto-land. *The Economist* 372 (8396): 57–8.

Economist, The (2006). Giving credit. *The Economist* 379 (8475): 40.

EEA (European Environment Agency) (2003). Most of central and eastern Europe to meet Kyoto targets. News release, Copenhagen, 2 December. Available at: www.eea.europa.eu/media/newsreleases/ghg-accession-en.

EEA (European Environment Agency) (2005). Annual European Community greenhouse gas inventory 1990–2003 and inventory report 2005 – Submission to the UNFCCC Secretariat. Technical Report No. 4/2005, Copenhagen. Available at: http://acm.eionet.europa.eu/reports/EEA_Techn_Rep_4_2005.

ENB (2004). Summary of the Tenth Conference of the Parties to the UN Framework Convention on Climate Change: 6–18 December 2004. *Earth Negotiations Bulletin* 12 (260): 1–16.

ENB (2005a). Summary of the Eleventh Conference of the Parties to the UN Framework Convention on Climate Change and First Conference of the Parties Serving as the Meeting of the Parties to the Kyoto Protocol: 28 November – 10 December 2005. *Earth Negotiations Bulletin* 12 (291): 1–20.

ENB (2005b). Summary of the Twenty-second Sessions of the Subsidiary Bodies of the UN Framework Convention on Climate Change: 19–27 May 2005. *Earth Negotiations Bulletin* 12 (270): 1–15.

ENB (2005c). Summary of the UNFCCC Seminar of Governmental Experts: 16–17 May 2005. *Earth Negotiations Bulletin* 12 (261): 1–7.

ENDS (2003a). Commitment test set for EU climate policy, 15 December.

ENDS (2003b). Prodi tries to hold the line on Kyoto Protocol, 17 December.

ENDS (2004a). Italy tests EU unity on Kyoto Protocol action, 2 March.

ENDS (2004b). World climate talks end in Buenos Aires, 20 December.

ENDS (2005). EU shows caution on future climate targets, 9 February.

Environment Council (2004a). *Environment Council Press Release*, 283 No. 12908/04, Luxembourg, 14 October.

Environment Council (2004b). *Environment Council Press Release*, 357 No. 15962/04, Brussels, 20 December.

Environment Council (2005a). *Environment Council Press Release*, 40 No. 6693/05, Brussels, 10 March.

Environment Council (2005b). *Environment Council Press Release*, 255 No. 12953/05, Luxembourg, 17 October.

European Commission (2003). Climate change: more action required from Member States to cut greenhouse gas emissions. *Press Release*, IP/03/1637, Brussels, 2 December.

European Commission (2005a). Communication from the Commission to the Council, the European Parliament, the European Economic and Social Committee and the Committee of the Regions. Winning the Battle against Global Climate Change. COM (2005) 35, Brussels.

European Commission (2005b). EU and China Partnership on Climate Change. *Press Release*, MEMO/05/298, Brussels, 2 September.

European Council (2005a). Eleventh Conference of the Parties (COP 11) to the United Nations Framework Convention on Climate Change (UNFCCC) in conjunction with the first session of the Conference of the Parties serving as the meeting of the Parties to the Kyoto Protocol (COP/MOP 1) (Montreal, 28 November to 9 December 2005) – Compilation of EU statements. Brussels, 21 December 2005.

European Council (2005b). Tenth session of the Conference of the Parties (COP 10) to the United Nations Framework Convention on Climate Change (UNFCCC) (Buenos Aires, 6–17 December 2004) – Compilation of EU statements. Brussels, 20 January 2005.

Friel, Howard (2005). With no one on their side. *Ecologist* 35 (7): 21.

G-8 (2005). Gleneagles Summit of the Eight. Communiqué, Gleneagles, 8 July 2005. Available at: www.g8.utoronto.ca/summit/2005gleneagles/.

GEF (Global Environment Facility) (2005). The GEF Resource Allocation Framework. GEF/C.27/Inf.8/Rev.1, October 17.

Grubb, Michael (2005). The G8 Gleneagles Summit: 6–8 July 2005. *Climate Policy* 5 (2): 233–4.

Gupta, Joyeeta (2014). *The history of global climate governance*. Cambridge: Cambridge University Press.

Henry, Laura A. and Lisa McIntosh Sundstrom (2007). Russia and the Kyoto Protocol: seeking an alignment of interests and image. *Global Environmental Politics* 7 (4): 47–69.

Jordan, Andrew and Tim Rayner (2010). The evolution of climate policy in the European Union: a historical perspective. In Jordan, Andrew, Dave Huitema, Harro Van Asselt, Tim Rayner and Frans Berkhout (eds) *Climate change policy in the European Union: confronting the dilemmas of mitigation and adaptation?* Cambridge: Cambridge University Press, 52–80.

Kellow, Aynsley (2006). A new process for negotiating multilateral environmental agreements? The Asia-Pacific climate partnership beyond Kyoto. *Australian Journal of International Affairs* 60 (2): 287–303.

King, Tim (2004). EU reaffirms support for Kyoto Protocol. *Irish Times*, 3 March.

Kotov, Vladimir (2004). The EU-Russia ratification deal: the risks and advantages of an informal agreement. *International Review for Environmental Strategies* 5 (1): 157–68.

Lesage, Dries, Thijs Van de Graaf and Kirsten Westphal (2009). The G8's role in global energy governance since the 2005 Gleneagles Summit. *Global Governance* 15: 259–77.

Mace, M.J. (2005). Funding for adaptation to climate change: UNFCCC and GEF developments since COP-7. *Review of European Community and International Environmental Law* 14 (3): 225–46.

MacFaul, Larry (2005). Adoption of procedures and mechanisms relating to compliance under the Kyoto Protocol: a guide. *Vertic Brief*, 6 November. Available at: www.vertic. org/media/assets/Publications/VERTIC_Brief_06.pdf.

Michaelowa, Axel (2005). Leaving the Kyoto oasis – the climate caravan moves on. *Intereconomics* 40 (1): 2–3.

Müller, Benito (2006). Montreal 2005: what happened, and what it means. *Oxford Institute for Energy Studies*, February. Available at: www.oxfordenergy.org/2006/03/ montreal-2005-what-happened-and-what-it-means/.

O'Riordan, Timothy (2005). Beyond Gleneagles. *Environment* 47 (7): 3.

Ott, Hermann E., Bernd Brouns, Wolfgang Sterk and Bettina Wittneben (2005). It takes two to tango – climate policy at COP 10 in Buenos Aires and beyond. *Journal for European Environmental & Planning Law* 2: 84–91.

Pallemaerts, Marc and Rhiannon Williams (2006). Climate change: the international and European policy framework. In Peeters, Marjan and Kurt Deketelaere (eds) *EU climate change policy: the challenge of new regulatory initiatives*. Cheltenham: Edward Elgar, 22–50.

Rajamani, Lavanya (2008). From Berlin to Bali and beyond: killing Kyoto softly? *International & Comparative Law Quarterly* 57 (4): 909–39.

Schipper, Lisa F. and Emily Boyd (2006). UNFCCC COP 11 and COP/MOP 1: at last, some hope? *Journal of Environment & Development* 15 (1): 75–90.

Schunz, Simon (2014). *European Union foreign policy and the global climate regime*. Brussels: P.I.E. Peter Lang.

Scott, Alex (2005). EU launches trading program for CO2 emissions. *Chemical Week* 167 (1): 13.

Sissell, Kara (2005). U.S. trade officials sign pact with Asian countries for clean technologies. *Chemical Week* 167 (25): 13.

Spence, Chris, Kati Kulovesi, María Gutiérrez and Miquel Muñoz (2008). Great expectations: understanding Bali and the climate change negotiations process. *Review of European, Comparative & International Environmental Law* 17 (2): 142–53.

UNFCCC (2004). Report of the Conference of the Parties on its tenth session, held at Buenos Aires from 6 to 18 December 2004 – Addendum. FCCC/CP/2004/10/Add.1.

UNFCCC (2005). Elements for a draft decision on the Adaptation Fund proposed by the United Kingdom of Great Britain and Northern Ireland on behalf of the European Community and its Member States. FCCC/SBI/2005/CRP.2.

Vogler, John (2016). *Climate change in world politics*. Basingstoke: Palgrave Macmillan.

Vogler, John and Charlotte Bretherton (2006). The European Union as a protagonist to the United States on climate change. *International Studies Perspectives* 7 (1): 1–22.

Wittneben, Bettina, Wolfgang Sterk, Hermann E. Ott and Bernd Brouns (2006). The Montreal Climate Summit: starting the Kyoto business and preparing for post-2012. *Journal for European Environmental & Planning Law* 2: 90–100.

Zimmermann, Hubert (2007). Realist power Europe? The EU in the negotiations about China's and Russia's WTO accession. *Journal of Common Market Studies* 45 (4): 813–32.

8 Heading towards success

During 2005 the UNFCCC regime had been reinvigorated by *inter alia* the agreement in principle to extend the terms of the Kyoto Protocol beyond 2012 and launch a dialogue on long-term cooperation to tackle climate change. The EU attempted to capitalize on the momentum and initiate a discussion on climate targets beyond the Kyoto Protocol commitment period. The March 2006 Environment Council, for instance, repeated the call for emissions reductions in the order of 15–30 per cent by 2020, but failed, because of resistance from Italy, to repeat another call it had made a year ago – that of pushing for 60–80 per cent emission cuts in developed countries by 2050. The Italians had 'massive problems on that point' and, as a result, the Council settled on a compromise in which the figure was omitted and replaced instead by mention of the need for 'substantial reductions in the order of at least 15 percent and perhaps by as much as 50 percent by 2050 compared to 1990 levels' (ENDS 2006d; see also Environment Council 2006a). Italian uneasiness can be easily explained by looking at its emissions. The burden-sharing agreement stipulated that Italy cut its emissions by 6.5 per cent. Instead, it had actually increased them by 12 per cent, thereby figuring high among the worst performers in the EU.

The next important events on the road to COP/MOP-2 in Nairobi were a series of meetings held in May 2006 in Bonn, including the first workshop of the UNFCCC Dialogue, the twenty-fourth sessions of the Subsidiary Bodies and the first session of the Ad hoc Working Group on Further Commitments for Annex I Parties (AWG). The Convention Dialogue Workshop provided a forum for parties to exchange views on the four themes included in Decision 1/CP.11 adopted in Montreal, namely advancing development goals in a sustainable way; addressing action on adaptation; realizing the full potential of technology; and realizing the full potential of market-based opportunities. The workshop had no binding or negotiated outcome, as these were precluded by its mandate. Nevertheless, a number of EU Member States noted that future discussions would need to be more focused and better structured (ENB 2006a). As with the 2005 Seminar of Governmental Experts, parties went to great lengths to stress the informality of the event, with 'the participants sat at round tables in a room that appeared at first glance to be set up more for a wedding party than for a dialogue on climate change' (ENB 2006c, p. 1). In both the Convention Dialogue Workshop and AWG-1, the EU argued that even though developed countries should continue taking the lead, they could not possibly mitigate climate change on their own as their share of global emissions was projected to decrease substantially over the coming decades, while that of developing countries was to substantially increase (UNFCCC 2006c; Young 2006). Japan argued that, in contrast to the Kyoto approach, the second commitment period should be based on sound scientific analysis and should not be solely a political exercise (ENB 2006a). The G-77/China rejected such calls and called instead for 'substantially stricter' commitments for developed parties during the post-2012 period, with details and rules of the second commitment period to be decided by 2008 at the latest (ENB 2006a, p. 3).

On other issues, the EU submission outlined a number of questions that needed to be urgently answered by parties, including: the length of future commitment periods, the role of flexibility mechanisms, and the inclusion of further sources of emissions, such as international bunker fuels. Eager to protect its emissions trading scheme, the EU was quite vocal about the need to ensure a global carbon market with a sound legislative and regulatory framework and long-term certainty (European Council 2006a). The most controversial issue on the agenda, however, concerned the modalities of the Adaptation Fund. While the SCCF and the LDCF had already been largely operationalized by that time, negotiations on the management and governance of the Adaptation Fund only started during the May 2006 Bonn meeting (Grasso 2011). The main divisive issue was whether or not the GEF should be managing the fund. It should be remembered at this point that unlike its two other counterparts, the Adaptation Fund fell under the Kyoto Protocol and not the Convention, thus placing it outside the influence of countries that had not ratified the former agreement, for example the US. What this also meant was that the EU served, for all intents and purposes, as the undisputed leader of the developed countries involved in deliberations on how this fund should be run (Okereke et al. 2007).

In general, the EU and its allies were of the opinion that the GEF should be in charge, so as to ensure minimization of transaction costs and complementarity with the SCCF and LDCF. The G-77/China's objections centred on the GEF's cumbersome disbursement procedures (i.e. incrementality and co-financing), as well as its undemocratic governance structure, which was dominated by donor governments. In addition, unlike the SCCF and LDCF, which were financed by donor countries, the Adaptation Fund was to be funded primarily through a 2 per cent levy on CERs traded under the CDM – funds, in other words, which developing countries regarded as 'their own money' (Grasso 2011, p. 370). They therefore argued that locating the fund in the GEF would not only be unfair in terms of procedural justice, but would also allow developed countries that had not ratified the Kyoto Protocol and were consequently ineligible to participate in the CDM to influence decision-making processes because of their great weight in the GEF (Grasso 2011; Okereke et al. 2007; Sterk et al. 2007). Negotiations proved unable to find common ground and finally culminated in a major rift between the EU and developing countries, resulting in the meeting being dissolved in acrimony.

Following these Bonn sessions, in June 2006 the EU set up another dialogue on climate change. At the annual EU–US summit in Vienna, a High Level Dialogue on Climate Change, Clean Energy and Sustainable Development was established, focusing among other things on 'experience with different market-based mechanisms' (European Council 2006c, p. 10). Stavros Dimas, the EU Environment Commissioner, drew particular attention to the willingness of the US to discuss international carbon trading, noting that: 'For the first time the US will come into a dialogue [on this]. It's a great change and a very important step towards our position' (ENDS 2006b). Interestingly, a few days later UK Prime Minister Tony Blair and Californian Governor Arnold Schwarzenegger announced they would explore the possibility of linking the EU's emissions trading scheme to a planned Californian one (Legge 2007; Jones 2006).

With the Nairobi COP/MOP in sight, the October 2006 Environment Council met to coordinate the EU position. Given that this was going to be the first COP taking place in Sub-Saharan Africa, EU officials did not discuss the issue of targets at length, stressing instead the need to finalize the Buenos Aires five-year programme of work on adaptation and the importance of promptly operationalizing the Adaptation Fund (Environment Council 2006b). Soon after, a number of interesting intra-EU developments took place. First, Italy's new centre-left government reversed its predecessor's opposition to deeper post-2012 emission cuts (see for example the Environment Councils of March 2004 and 2006), with Pecoraro Scanio, Italy's new Green Environment Minister, dismissing the Berlusconi administration's stance as having been an 'anomaly' to be soon followed by the adoption of a 'normal policy' (ENDS 2006c). A second interesting internal EU development followed in November 2006 when French Prime Minister Dominique de Villepin proposed the imposition of an EU carbon tax on imports from countries that did not take on post-Kyoto commitments, such as the US, Australia or emerging developing countries like China and India (Wiers 2008). Nelly Olin, the French Environment Minister, was to present the idea at the Nairobi COP/MOP, with a concrete proposal being put forward in the first half of 2007. Eventually, however, not much came out of this, due to concerns over increased carbon leakage or incompatibilities with established trade norms (Van Asselt and Brewer 2010).

The Nairobi COP/MOP-2

From 6–17 November 2006, world attention turned to Nairobi for a series of meetings, including COP/MOP-2, AWG-2 and the second Convention Dialogue workshop. Starting with the latter, advancing development goals in a sustainable way and realizing the potential of market-based opportunities were the two topics on the agenda. Highlights included Lord Stern's presentation of his ground-breaking new economic review (see Stern 2007), as well as a proposal by South Africa for developing countries to pledge to Sustainable Development Policies and Measures (SD-PAMs), which would simultaneously address national development objectives and climate change mitigation (C2ES 2006). Regarding the EU, its attention was focused on the market mechanisms, with Germany noting that the absence of a clear carbon price signal after 2012 could potentially discourage investments.

Turning to AWG-2, the EU's approach was based on a twofold strategy. First, it argued that before setting goals and targets, parties would first need to define a quantified shared goal (temperature or atmospheric concentration) that would guide their efforts (Okereke *et al.* 2007; Young 2006). The EU thus proposed that parties adopt a long-term vision of keeping temperature increase below 2°C compared with 1990 levels – a goal that the EU itself had embraced in 1996 (New *et al.* 2011; European Council 2006b). This was opposed by the G-77/China, which argued that defining long-term objectives was not within the AWG's mandate. As a result, the final conclusions did not contain a target date or temperature/atmospheric concentration objectives, but merely repeated the IPCC TAR's findings which stipulated that global emissions of CO_2 'have to be reduced to very low levels, well below half of levels in 2000, in order to stabilize their concentrations in the atmosphere' (UNFCCC 2006a, p. 5).

Second, the EU repeated its call for Article 3.9 on further commitments to be linked with the Kyoto Protocol's Article 9 review provisions. Regarding Article 3.9, while parties had agreed in Montreal that there should be no gap between the first and second commitment periods, they failed in Nairobi to set an end date for agreeing new targets, with preferences ranging from 2008 to 2010. Developing countries in general were in favour of 2008, while a number of Annex I parties, most notably Japan, supported gathering more scientific data before deciding on further commitments (Sterk *et al.* 2007). The EU held a similar position, arguing that it would need more time before committing to a timeline so as to better 'understand the means and tools that [would] be available to implement future commitments' (European Council 2006b, p. 7). In other words, the EU's underlining motive was to delay an agreement on a timeline so as to ensure that Articles 3.9 and 9 were dealt with in one package (Sterk *et al.* 2007). Ultimately, the G-77/China prevailed in battling against a formal link between the two articles, while no particular timeline was agreed upon in Nairobi.

The initial review of the Kyoto Protocol did take place in Nairobi, as demanded by Article 9, but was conducted in a rather perfunctory manner as no preparations had been made for it in advance. In fact, the Protocol was 'reviewed' with such haste that a BBC journalist wrote that 'many of us must have missed the review when we blinked' (Black 2006). The final decision simply states that even though

> the Kyoto Protocol has initiated important action and has the potential to make a decisive contribution to addressing climate change, […] a number of elements of the Kyoto Protocol, in particular adaptation could be further elaborated upon, and that the implementation of the Protocol could be further enhanced.
>
> (UNFCCC 2006b)

Turning to COP/MOP-2, contentious issues included: the modalities of the Adaptation Fund, the terms of the second Kyoto Protocol review, a proposal by Belarus to join Annex B, a Russian proposal for developing countries to take on voluntary emission targets, and finally the functioning of the CDM. Regarding the Adaptation Fund, realizing that a continuation of the 'GEF/not GEF' debate risked further polarization of the parties, the EU decided to 'go into listening mode' and accept the G-77/China suggestion to agree on the fund's overarching principles, modalities and governance first and postpone institutional arrangements for later COP/MOPs (Müller 2006, p. 4; see also Grasso 2011). The end result was Decision 5/CMP.2, which contains the principles and modalities of the Adaptation Fund, including among others the provision that non-Annex I parties would hold the majority in the fund's future governing body, following a one-country-one-vote rule (ENB 2006b; Sterk *et al.* 2007; Kulovesi *et al.* 2007).

Regarding the second Kyoto Protocol review, having been unsuccessful in linking Article 3.9 with the first review of the Kyoto Protocol under Article 9, the EU, supported by most other Annex I parties, tried anew by arguing in favour of setting 2008 as the date for the second review and explicitly linking this process to Article 3.9 negotiations (C2ES 2006). The EU went even further by noting that future periodic reviews should be carried out in a 'complete, thorough and efficient way', preferably via a dedicated Working Group (European Council 2006b, p. 20). The G-77/China argued that Article 9 was about 'review' and not 'revision' of the Protocol and sought assurances that the review would not result in new commitments for developing countries. The final compromise was closer to the G-77/China's position, as it was decided that the review would be conducted in 2008, as the EU wanted, but would not lead to any new commitments (ENB 2006b).

A third controversial issue concerned a proposal by Belarus, which even though an Annex I party, did not have a target under the Kyoto Protocol because of its status as an Economy in Transition (EIT) country. In Nairobi, Belarus asked for permission to join Annex B by taking on a target of reducing its emissions by 5 per cent below 1990 levels by 2008–12. The EU, as well as several other parties, expressed their scepticism, knowing full well that even a 5 per cent reduction target would grant Belarus substantial 'hot air', if taken into account that its emissions at the time were about 40 per cent below 1990 levels (Sterk *et al.* 2007). Belarus eventually compromised to a target of minus 8 per cent, together with a requirement to hold 7 per cent of its allowances in reserve, plus a commitment to use any revenue generated under emissions trading to finance further emission abatement measures (C2ES 2006). This decision constituted the first amendment of the Kyoto Protocol, but as of January 2016 it has still to come into effect as only 29 parties have ratified it. The EU in particular had clearly stated in Nairobi that its Member States would not ratify the amendment, thus making the amendment's passage a highly unlikely future scenario (Sterk *et al.* 2007).[1] Another controversial proposal was tabled by Russia, which since the Montreal COP/MOP had been arguing that developing countries should be allowed to take on voluntary targets (Bausch and Mehling 2006). In

Nairobi, the G-77/China remained firmly opposed to the Russian proposal, while the EU and Canada expressed their interest in exploring further the idea of voluntary commitments (ENB 2006b). With no agreement in sight, the issue was deferred to COP/MOP-3.

Turning to the CDM, an issue of great importance to African countries had to do with the regional distribution of CDM projects. Until then, only a minuscule percentage of CDM projects had been implemented in Africa, with about three-quarters being in large developing countries, such as China, India, Mexico and Brazil (Sterk *et al.* 2007). According to Kulovesi *et al.* (2007), the reason was investor preference for locales which offered low-risk and stable investment environments. To somehow remedy this injustice, the CDM Executive Board had *inter alia* recommended that parties cover the total costs of CDM projects in these countries. However, the EU, Japan and Canada objected to the creation of any new funds (Kulovesi *et al.* 2007). In the end, the UN Secretary-General Kofi Annan announced a new UN plan, called the 'Nairobi Framework', to help developing countries, especially in Africa, secure greater access to CDM funds, with the final decision simply encouraging Annex I parties to 'consider further initiatives, including financial support' (see Kulovesi *et al.* 2007, p. 257). The European Commission announced that Germany and Finland would invest in clean energy programmes in Africa (C2ES 2006). Yet, despite its high profile, the Nairobi Framework has reportedly failed to attain its overarching goals (see Byigero *et al.* 2010).

Finally, a number of other decisions were taken in Nairobi, including one setting the rules for the SCCF. Until then, the SCCF had been operational in the domains of adaptation and technology transfer, but not in that of economic diversification, a main point of disagreement between the EU and G-77/China in past COPs. The EU had continuously insisted that OPEC countries should only be provided with technical assistance to diversify their economies, arguing that it was up to their governments to put in place adequate measures to attract foreign direct investment and sustain investments in human and physical capital (see European Council 2005). Eventually, it was decided that developed countries would only provide technical and capacity-building assistance to oil-producing countries, as the EU had preferred.

The EU in COP/MOP-2

Unlike COP/MOP-1 in Montreal, the Nairobi COP did not result in any major breakthroughs (ENB 2006b). Even the outgoing UN Secretary-General Kofi Annan complained about the 'frightening lack of leadership' from governments (C2ES 2006). Turning to the EU, the Finnish Presidency argued that all the goals it had set for Nairobi were reached, with the EU being especially instrumental in driving progress in the adaptation domain (Enestam 2006). Indeed, following the confrontational May 2006 Bonn session, EU performance on this issue in Nairobi helped rebuild its strained relationship with developing countries, with many of them even praising the EU as being an 'honest broker' (Okereke *et al.* 2007, p. 17).

Yet, one could argue that there was no timetable agreed upon for adopting post-2012 commitments, with the G-77/China succeeding in dominating discussions in the AWG, as well as on the issue of the review of the Kyoto Protocol. Sterk *et al.* (2007, p. 147), in particular, are rather dismissive of the EU's stance, viewing it as not befitting a climate change leader eager to engage in coalition-building. As they argue:

> There was still much finger pointing and waiting for others to take the first step. True, developing countries were demanding a timetable for the AWG to agree on post-2012 commitments for Annex I countries while refusing to accept a timetable for the considerations in the Article 9 review process. This is inconsistent and obviously a negotiation strategy. But why did the Union have to respond with the same measure – demanding a timetable for the review process while refusing a deadline for the AWG negotiations?

The Finnish Presidency was further accused of not 'catalysing' EU leadership in Nairobi, leaving it to 'individual Member States to be more vocal about the EU's ambitions for the future' (EEB 2006, p. 5). It was the UK and Germany that 'did their best' by proposing a 30 per cent reduction in emissions for Annex I parties by 2020, while other Member States appeared divided on this issue (*New Scientist* 2006, p. 5). Germany in particular highlighted its hope that fellow EU Member States would eventually agree to a 30 per cent cut by 2020, and even went a step further by noting that it would be prepared to reduce its emissions by 40 per cent by that time (ENB 2006b). Finland found the German openness about EU positions towards the NGOs as being 'unhelpful', given that both were in the troika and Finland felt that the Germans were sidestepping it and making it harder for it to negotiate effectively with other parties.[2]

It was during the December 2006 Environment Council that the Finnish Presidency quite belatedly raised the issue of a post-2012 target for the EU. To begin with, Member States came forward with their proposed timeline for the completion of post-2012 negotiations, arguing in favour of 2009 at the latest. On target ambitiousness, however, agreement proved elusive. Several Member States, such as the UK, Germany, Italy and Sweden, supported by Environment Commissioner Stavros Dimas, favoured a 30 per cent target reduction by 2020, while Hungary, Slovakia, Poland, Spain and others took the position that the EU should wait for other Kyoto parties before making any 'hasty declaration of commitment' (ENDS 2006a). The latter were backed by EU Enterprise Commissioner Günter Verheugen, who had also recently taken a position against the EU unilaterally adopting any commitment larger than 15 per cent.

Gearing up for Bali

The post-Nairobi period found the EU seriously divided over the level of its post-2012 target. Unlike in 1996, where it was the Dutch Presidency that had led intra-EU burden-sharing negotiations, 2007 saw the European Commission taking over that role. In January, it proposed that the EU commit unilaterally to a 20 per cent target, further noting that the post-2012 framework should aim for a 30 per cent cut by developed countries (European Commission 2007b). This dual-target approach was hailed by Stavros Dimas as representing 'a set of ambitious, but realistic targets' (p. 1). In a second document, the European Commission (2007a) outlined a number of sub-targets that could allow the EU to cost-effectively meet its aforementioned unilateral pledge, including a 20 per cent improvement in energy-efficiency, a 10 per cent biofuels target, as well as a binding target to increase the contribution of renewable energy to 20 per cent of total EU energy consumption by 2020.

In the run-up to the February 2007 Environment Council, positions among Member States varied considerably. On the one hand, there were Denmark and Sweden pushing for a 30 per cent unilateral target, whereas on the other Poland and Hungary were expressing objections to the very idea of a unilateral EU target (ENDS 2007b). Others, such as Spain and Finland, were requesting more detailed information on how the 20 per cent unilateral target would be divided among Member States. The final Council conclusions endorsed both the Commission's unilateral and conditional proposed targets, as well as its sub-targets, while they also noted that developed countries should aim to collectively reduce their emissions by 60–80 per cent by 2050 of 1990 levels (see Environment Council 2007). In order to accommodate the concerns of Hungary and Poland, it was decided that Member States would continue using their existing Kyoto Protocol baselines, which in effect gave Hungary and Poland – the only Member States with a mid-1980 baseline – extra leeway to meet their post-2012 target (ENDS 2007b). On other issues, the Council's conclusions, while stereotypically repeating the need for adherence to the principle of common but differentiated responsibility, went one step further by noting that the moment had arrived for non-Annex I parties to meaningfully participate in the regime by at least 'reducing the emission intensity of their economic development' (Environment Council 2007, p. 9). Among others, SD-PAMs, an enhanced CDM and non-binding targets or sectoral approaches were identified by the Council as offering 'promising ways of enhancing the participation of these countries'.

Following the endorsement of the 2020 package by the European Council of March 2007, the next major event prior to Bali was a late March visit to Brussels by a fact-finding mission of Californian officials setting up that state's emissions trading scheme. Interestingly, there was increased optimism at the time of the potential of linking the EU emissions trading scheme to emerging US state-led initiatives, including the one by California, or the Regional Greenhouse Gas Initiative (RGGI), which covered at the time eight northeast and mid-Atlantic states (Legge 2007).

In May 2007, parties gathered in Bonn for yet another series of meetings, including AWG-3 and the third Convention Dialogue workshop. The EU formally tabled its recently adopted post-2012 mitigation target, followed again by a call on all major economies to join global efforts to reduce greenhouse gas emissions (UNFCCC 2007a). Parties in general refrained from referring to numerical reduction targets, with only the G-77/China, supported by the EU, proposing that Annex I parties reduce their emissions by as much as 25–40 per cent below 1990 levels (ENB 2007a; European Council 2007). Turning to the Dialogue, of notable importance was a suggestion by Brazil and South Africa that parties consider continuing the Dialogue in some strengthened format after Bali (ENB 2007a).

Two months later, the 2007 G-8 Summit was hosted by Germany at Heiligendamm on the Baltic Sea coast. However, only a few days before the meeting President Bush, in a move reminiscent of his establishment of the AP6 in 2005, had thrown most of his UNFCCC partners into confusion by announcing plans for yet another forum to discuss climate policy outside the UN, the Major Economies Meeting (MEM). According to the Bush initiative, the 15 largest greenhouse gas-emitting nations would be brought together for a series of meetings designed to explore technology-related ways of limiting global emissions by a set amount by 2050 (Andresen 2015). Despite rejecting both binding caps and carbon trading, the Bush initiative was welcomed by the UK, Japan, Australia and Canada, while Germany reacted more cautiously by calling on the US to adopt 'clear targets to reduce emissions' (ENDS 2007c). In a similar fashion, Environment Commissioner Stavros Dimas dismissed the US proposal as vague and 'the classic US line' (Harvey *et al.* 2007, p. 1). European Commission President Manuel Barroso stated that even though the US had 'crossed the Rubicon' in acknowledging the threat of climate change, technology by itself would fail to properly address the problem unless the US approbated the need for a global system of 'measurable, binding, enforceable targets' (Benoit and Williamson 2007, p. 8).

It was against this background that the Heiligendamm G-8 Summit commenced its deliberations in early July, with the German hosts hoping to extract some tangible concessions from the US President, such as an endorsement of the EU's 2°C objective, an expression of willingness to create a global carbon trading system or an agreement to a target of reducing emissions by 50 per cent by 2050 (ENDS 2007a). Ultimately, none of these objectives materialized, as the final summit communiqué merely noted that the US would 'consider seriously' the calls made by the EU and other countries to halve global emissions by 2050 (G-8 2007, p. 15). However, the G-8 did endorse the UN as the 'appropriate forum' for the conduct of future negotiations on climate change, and agreed on 2009 as a deadline for reaching an agreement on the Kyoto Protocol's future (p. 16).

The fourth Convention Dialogue workshop and AWG-4 in Vienna (August 2007) proved far more exciting in terms of outcomes. Regarding the former, the EU and several G-77/China parties, such as Brazil, praised it as having been a useful exercise and advocated for it to be turned into a formal negotiating body that would meet up to 2009 (Vihma 2009; ENB 2007b). Regarding AWG-4, talks focused on whether an indicative range for reduction objectives for Annex I parties should be determined, taking into account the scientific evidence contained in the IPCC's Working Group 3 report, published in May 2007. The EU in particular was in favour of parties agreeing to a text that (i) referenced the need to ensure that global emissions peaked in the next ten to fifteen years, followed by a reduction of 50 per cent by 2050, and (ii) recognized the IPCC's lowest stabilization scenario which required Annex I parties as a group to reduce emissions by a range of 25–40 per cent below 1990 levels by 2020 (Spence *et al.* 2008; Watanabe *et al.* 2008). Other developed parties, however, such as Canada, Russia and Japan, were opposed to the AWG determining initial indicative ranges of Annex I emission reduction objectives (ENB 2007b). For its part, the G-77/China was wary of the AWG citing as a target the IPCC's scenario of stabilizing the atmospheric concentration of CO_2 at 450 ppm (Aguilar 2007). As a result, the final AWG conclusions took note of the aforementioned ranges, acknowledging that they provided 'useful initial parameters for the overall level of ambition of further emission reductions by Annex I Parties' (UNFCCC 2007b, p. 5). The EU expressed its disappointment with this outcome, stating that it 'had come to Vienna prepared to go further in discussing emission ranges' (ENB 2007b, p. 6).

The Bali COP/MOP-3

Public awareness, attention and expectations for the Bali conference were high, fuelled by the publication in November of the IPCC's Fourth Assessment Report (AR4), which predicted that climate changes would be 'abrupt or irreversible' (IPCC 2007, p. 13). Also important was Al Gore's Oscar-winning documentary *An Inconvenient Truth*, which shared the 2007 Nobel Peace Prize with the IPCC (Vihma 2009). This momentum was further added to by the ratification of the Kyoto Protocol by Australia's new Prime Minister, Kevin Rudd, who had only a week before succeeded Kyoto-sceptic John Howard (Christoff 2008). The main two tasks that had been set for the Bali Conference were the finalization of the operational details of the Adaptation Fund and the definition of a post-2012 roadmap for the climate regime.

Contrary to expectations, negotiations on the Adaptation Fund proceeded smoothly, with an agreement being reached early in the first week. According to Müller (2008, p. 1), the EU's declaration that it 'would accept whatever model the G77 endorsed' had been instrumental. The final decision established an independent Adaptation Fund Board under the direct authority and guidance of the COP/MOP, which would serve as its operating entity. Developing countries would constitute a majority on the board, while it was also decided that the GEF would act as the secretariat on an interim basis and subject to periodic review (ENB 2007c). This was interpreted as a concession to the EU and Japan, which were keen on retaining some role for the GEF.

Negotiations under the AWG (from now on the AWG-KP) were also straightforward. The most controversial issue concerned two options for the articulation of the vision that should guide the AWG-KP's work. Canada and Russia were in favour of the final text merely making reference to the relevant paragraph numbers in the report of the Vienna session, while the EU and most developing countries insisted that the IPCC's findings should be spelled out anew (ENB 2007c; Watanabe *et al.* 2008). The EU was able to ensure an ambitious outcome, as it was the second version which was eventually adopted by the AWG-KP.

The EU, however, was not as successful in the negotiations that led to the adoption of the 'Bali Action Plan'. Undoubtedly, the most tangible outcome from COP/MOP-3 was the establishment of the 'Ad hoc Working Group on Long-Term Cooperative Action under the Convention' (AWG-LCA), in which both the US and developing countries would participate. As most parties had therefore preferred, the informal Dialogue established previously in Montreal was to be transformed into a fully-fledged negotiating body. Its mandate would be 'to enable the full, effective and sustained implementation of the Convention through long-term cooperative action, now, up to and beyond 2012, in order to reach an *agreed outcome* and adopt a decision at its fifteenth session' (UNFCCC 2007c, p. 2; emphasis added). Negotiations leading to this decision were rather contentious, with the main two stumbling blocks being the vision that should guide the process, as well as the nature of the commitments to be undertaken by developed and developing parties.

Regarding the former, the EU had insisted that the AWG-LCA process should mimic its AWG-KP counterpart and adopt as its ultimate objective the IPCC's indicative ranges that had been referenced in the Vienna conclusions only a few months ago. As a sign of determination, the German Environment Minister Sigmar Gabriel stated that he had not travelled to Bali 'just to decide that we would meet again next year', while Portugal, speaking on behalf of the EU, threatened to boycott Bush's MEM talks if no progress was made with numerical targets (Clémençon 2008, p. 74; see also Vihma 2009). Even so, the US was adamant in its opposition to start the post-2012 negotiations with 'some set of numbers' and, with the support of Russia, Canada and Japan, was ultimately successful in forcing the EU to drop its insistence on having preliminary emission reduction targets included in the preamble of the decision establishing the AWG-LCA (Clémençon 2008, p. 74; see also Spence *et al.* 2008). Instead, the IPCC's findings were relegated to a footnote, which does not directly reference the recommended 25–40 per cent range but merely refers to the pages of the IPCC report in which these are spelled out (Watanabe *et al.* 2008; Shamsuddoha and Chowdhury 2008). Removing these key points was perceived as having significantly weakened the Bali Action Plan, which merely states that 'deep cuts in global emissions will be required to achieve the ultimate objective of the Convention' (UNFCCC 2007c, p. 1). Nevertheless, this had been the first time the UNFCCC had quantitatively articulated dangerous climate change (Gupta 2014).

Turning to the actual commitments, unlike the 1995 Berlin Mandate which called for 'a protocol or another legal instrument', the Bali Action Plan's selection of words noted earlier (i.e. agreed outcome) clearly illustrated a lack of consensus among parties as to the legal form of the post-2012 agreement (Vihma 2009; Rajamani 2008). Developing countries were eager to have text that explicitly mentioned that Annex I parties should take on binding commitments, which was also what the US wanted of developing countries to start with. In the end, both were unsuccessful in their pursuits, with the final agreement calling developed countries to consider:

> Measurable, reportable and verifiable nationally appropriate mitigation commitments or actions, including quantified emission limitation and reduction objectives, by all developed country parties, while ensuring the comparability of efforts among them, taking into account differences in their national circumstances.
>
> (UNFCCC 2007c, p. 2)

Ott *et al.* (2008) viewed this language at the time as representing a major setback for US efforts to replace binding targets with voluntary pledges. Others argued though that by referring to 'actions' the agreement left the door open for developed countries adopting voluntary (soft) targets (Spence *et al.* 2008). Rajamani (2008, p. 910) expressed a similar position, noting that the Bali Action Plan allowed for the option of 'killing Kyoto softly'.

A major controversy broke out with respect to developing country commitments, which came close to causing the collapse of the conference. According to the final agreement, developing country parties were to consider:

> Nationally appropriate mitigation actions by developing country Parties in the context of sustainable development, supported and enabled by technology, financing and capacity-building, in a measurable, reportable and verifiable manner.
>
> (UNFCCC 2007c, p. 2)

This formulation, which had been tabled by India on behalf of the G-77/China, was initially rejected by the US, which insisted that in addition to technology, financing and capacity-building, *actions* should also be measurable, reportable and verifiable (Müller 2008). In plenary, the EU had declared its support for India's proposal, 'as a sign of the spirit of cooperation, compromise, and trust among us' (cited in Müller 2008, p. 5). With a full day behind schedule, South Africa urged the US to join the consensus by stressing the willingness of developing countries to actively participate in mitigation activities, something that was unheard of only a year ago. It then went on to clarify India's proposal by noting that 'measurable, reportable and verifiable' applied to developing country mitigation actions as well (Spence *et al.* 2008). Under great pressure, the US eventually backed down and accepted India's original formulation following some 'hasty phone calls to Washington' (Vogler 2016, p. 129).

Evaluating Bali

'Despite its rather timid language,' the Bali Action Plan was, as Ott *et al.* (2008, p. 93) note, 'a real achievement in real-world politics'. Müller (2008, p. 1) calls

Bali a 'very successful' conference, while Depledge (2008, p. 154) views it as a 'turning point'. Indeed, not only had the US been drawn back into the negotiating fold, but also developing countries had expressed their willingness to actively participate in nationally appropriate mitigation actions (NAMAs), thereby creating a sense of optimism for the future success of the climate regime. The post-Montreal strategy of the EU had thus been clearly vindicated, as it had arduously pursued both the aforementioned outcomes. As observers acknowledge, the EU's coalition with the G-77/China proved instrumental in ensuring Bali's success, with the deal on the Adaptation Fund having gone a long way towards raising the 'level of trust' between the two actors (Müller 2008, p. 2). The EU had been able to count on developing country support to steer the AWG-KP towards adopting a strong vision, while China had led the G-77 bloc in embracing the need for meaningful mitigation action, without committing to any sort of targets. Yet, the EU and other parties proved unable to counter the relative power and determination of the US, allowing it to substantially weaken the AWG-LCA process. This led some observers to question the logic behind its inclusion in this process (Christoff 2008). In addition, Ott *et al.* (2008) observed that alliances and ambitious mitigation targets aside, the EU would also need to exert leadership in the areas of technology transfer and finance, in both of which its performance up to that date had been rather poor.

Notes

1 Only the Czech Republic accepted the amendment in April 2007. France accepted it in August 2009 but withdrew it in October 2009.
2 Interview No. 8 (Member State official – Former Minister).

References

Aguilar, Soledad (2007). Elements for a robust climate regime post-2012: options for mitigation. *Review of European Community & International Environmental Law* 16 (3): 356–67.

Andresen, Steinar (2015). International climate negotiations: top–down, bottom–up or a combination of both? *International Spectator: Italian Journal of International Affairs* 50 (1): 15–30.

Bausch, Camilla and Michael Mehling (2006). Alive and kicking: the first meeting of the parties to the Kyoto Protocol. *Review of European Community & International Environmental Law* 15 (2): 193–201.

Benoit, Bertrand and Hugh Williamson (2007). EU greets new strategy cautiously. *Financial Times*, 1 June.

Black, Richard (2006). Climate talks a tricky business. *BBC News*, 18 November. Available at: http://news.bbc.co.uk/1/hi/sci/tech/6161998.stm.

Byigero, Alfred D., Joy Clancy and Margaret Skutsch (2010). CDM in sub-Saharan Africa and the prospects of the Nairobi Framework Initiative. *Climate Policy* 10: 181–9.

C2ES (2006). Twelfth Session of the Conference of the Parties to the UN Framework Convention on Climate Change and Second Meeting of the Parties to the Kyoto Protocol. November. Available at: www.c2es.org/docUploads/COP%2012%20Report.pdf.

Christoff, Peter (2008). The Bali roadmap: climate change, COP 13 and beyond. *Environmental Politics* 17 (3): 466–72.

Clémençon, Raymond (2008). The Bali road map: a first step on the difficult journey to a post-Kyoto Protocol agreement. *Journal of Environment & Development* 17 (1): 70–94.

Depledge, Joanna (2008). Crafting the Copenhagen consensus: some reflections. *Review of European Community and International Environmental Law* 17 (2): 154–65.

EEB (European Environmental Bureau) (2006). EEB Assessment of the Environmental Results of the Finnish Presidency of the EU, July to December 2006. Available at: www.eeb.org/publication/FI-Assessment-191206.pdf.

ENB (2006a). Twenty-Fourth Sessions of the Subsidiary Bodies of the UNFCCC and First Session of the Ad hoc Working Group under the Kyoto Protocol: 17–26 May 2006. *Earth Negotiations Bulletin* 12 (306): 1–16.

ENB (2006b). Summary of the Twelfth Conference of the Parties to the UN Framework Convention on Climate Change and Second Meeting of the Parties to the Kyoto Protocol: 6–17 November 2006. *Earth Negotiations Bulletin* 12 (318): 1–22.

ENB (2006c). Summary of the UNFCCC Dialogue on Long-Term Cooperative Action: 15–16 May 2006. *Earth Negotiations Bulletin* 12 (297): 1–4.

ENB (2007a). Fourth Sessions of the Ad hoc Working Group on Further Commitments for Annex I Parties under the Kyoto Protocol and Convention Dialogue: 27–31 August 2007. *Earth Negotiations Bulletin* 12 (339): 1–14.

ENB (2007b). Summary of the Thirteenth Conference of Parties to the UN Framework Convention on Climate Change and Third Meeting of Parties to the Kyoto Protocol: 3–15 December 2007. *Earth Negotiations Bulletin* 12 (354): 1–22.

ENB (2007c). Twenty-sixth Sessions of the Subsidiary Bodies of the UNFCCC and Associated Meetings: 7–18 May 2007. *Earth Negotiations Bulletin*, 12 (333): 1–18.

ENDS (2006a). Council debates post-2012 climate options, 18 December.

ENDS (2006b). EU and USA find common ground on climate change, 26 October.

ENDS (2006c). Italy returns to the fold on post-Kyoto rules, 8 November.

ENDS (2006d). Italy weakens ministerial climate resolution, 10 March.

ENDS (2007a). G8 backs post-2012 global climate agreement, 7 June.

ENDS (2007b). States back unilateral EU climate gas curbs, 20 February.

ENDS (2007c). World digests Bush climate policy pledge, 1 June.

Enestam, Jan-Erik (2006). Small step on climate. *New Scientist* 192 (2582): 20.

Environment Council (2006a). Environment Council Press Release, 58 No. 6762/06, Brussels, 9 March.

Environment Council (2006b). Environment Council Press Release, 287 No. 13989/06, Luxembourg, 23 October.

Environment Council (2007). Environment Council Press Release, 25 No. 6272/07, Brussels, 20 February.

European Commission (2007a). An energy policy for Europe. COM(2007) 1 final, Brussels, 10 January.

European Commission (2007b). Limiting global climate change to 2 degrees Celsius: the way ahead for 2020 and beyond. COM(2007) 2 final, Brussels, 10 January.

European Council (2005). Eleventh Conference of the Parties (COP 11) to the United Nations Framework Convention on Climate Change (UNFCCC) in conjunction with the first session of the Conference of the Parties serving as the meeting of the Parties to the Kyoto Protocol (COP/MOP 1) (Montreal, 28 November to 9 December 2005) – Compilation of EU statements. Brussels, 21 December 2005.

European Council (2006a). Information Note: Compilation of EU statements. Brussels, 1 June.

European Council (2006b). Information Note: Compilation of EU statements. Brussels, 29 November.

European Council (2006c). Vienna Summit Declaration, Vienna, 21 June. Available at: http://eeas.europa.eu/us/sum06_06/index_en.htm.

G-8 (2007). Communiqué, Heiligendamm, 7 June 2007. Available at: www.g-8.de/Content/EN/Artikel/__g8-summit/anlagen/chairs-summary,templateId=raw,property=publicationFile.pdf/chairs-summary.pdf.

Grasso, Marco (2011). The role of justice in the North–South conflict in climate change: the case of negotiations on the Adaptation Fund. *International Environmental Agreements: Politics, Law and Economics* 11: 361–77.

Gupta, Joyeeta (2014). *The history of global climate governance.* Cambridge: Cambridge University Press.

Harvey, Fiona, George Parker, David Pilling and Hugh Williamson (2007). European anger at Bush shift on climate. *Financial Times,* 2 June.

IPCC (2007). Climate change 2007: synthesis report. Available at: www.ipcc.ch/pdf/assessment-report/ar4/syr/ar4_syr_full_report.pdf.

Jones, George (2006). Blair cuts out Bush in deal with Schwarzenegger to set up carbon trading scheme. *Telegraph,* 1 August.

Kulovesi, Kati, María Gutiérrez, Peter Doran and Miquel Muñoz (2007). UN 2006 Climate Change Conference: a confidence-building step? *Climate Policy* 7 (3): 255–61.

Legge, Thomas (2007). An EU outlook on the future of the Kyoto Protocol. *International Spectator: Italian Journal of International Affairs* 42 (1): 81–93.

Müller, Benito (2006). Nairobi 2006: trust and the future of adaptation funding. *Oxford Institute for Energy Studies,* January. Available at: www.oxfordclimatepolicy.org/publications/documents/EV3825Jan.pdf.

Müller, Benito (2008). Bali 2007: on the road again! *Oxford Institute for Energy Studies,* February, Available at: www.oxfordclimatepolicy.org/publications/documents/comment_0208-2.pdf.

New, Mark, Diana Liverman, Heike Schroder and Kevin Anderson (2011). Four degrees and beyond: the potential for a global temperature increase of four degrees and its implications. *Philosophical Transactions of the Royal Society* A 369: 6–19.

New Scientist (2006). The climate won't wait. *New Scientist* 192 (2579): 5.

Okereke, Chukwumerije, Philip Mann, Henny Osbahr, Benito Müller and Johannes Ebeling (2007). Assessment of key negotiating issues at Nairobi climate COP/MOP and what it means for the future of the climate regime. Tyndall Centre for Climate Change Research Working Paper 106. Available at: www.tyndall.ac.uk/sites/default/files/wp106.pdf.

Ott, Herman E., Wolfgang Sterk and Rie Watanabe (2008). The Bali roadmap: new horizons for global climate policy. *Climate Policy* 8 (1): 91–5.

Rajamani, Lavanya (2008). From Berlin to Bali and beyond: killing Kyoto softly? *International & Comparative Law Quarterly* 57 (4): 909–39.

Shamsuddoha, Md. and Rezaul Karim Chowdhury (2008). The political economy of UNFCCC's Bali Climate Conference: a roadmap to climate commercialization. *Development* 51: 397–402.

Spence, Chris, Kati Kulovesi, María Gutiérrez and Miquel Muñoz (2008). Great expectations: understanding Bali and the climate change negotiations process. *Review of European, Comparative & International Environmental Law* 17 (2): 142–53.

Sterk, Wolfgang, Hermann E. Ott, Rie Watanabe and Bettina Wittneben (2007). The Nairobi Climate Change Summit (COP 12 – MOP 2): taking a deep breath before negotiating post-2012 targets. *Journal for European Environmental & Planning Law* 2: 139–48.

Stern, Nicholas (2007). *The economics of climate change: the Stern Review.* Cambridge: Cambridge University Press.

UNFCCC (2006a). Report of the Ad hoc Working Group on Further Commitments for Annex I Parties under the Kyoto Protocol on its second session, held at Nairobi from 6 to 14 November 2006. FCCC/KP/AWG/2006/4.

UNFCCC (2006b). Review of the Kyoto Protocol pursuant to its Article 9. FCCC/KP/CMP/2006/L.7.

UNFCCC (2006c). Views regarding Article 3, paragraph 9, of the Kyoto Protocol: Submissions from Parties. FCCC/KP/AWG/2006/MISC.1.

UNFCCC (2007a). Information and views on the mitigation potential at the disposal of Annex I Parties: Submissions from Parties. FCCC/KP/AWG/2007/MISC.1.

UNFCCC (2007b). Report of the Ad hoc Working Group on Further Commitments for Annex I Parties under the Kyoto Protocol on the first part of its fourth session, held at Vienna from 27 to 31 August 2007. FCCC/KP/AWG/2007/4.

UNFCCC (2007c). Revised draft decision-/CP.13 Ad hoc Working Group on Long-term Cooperative Action under the Convention Proposal by the President. FCCC/CP/2007/L.7/Rev.1.

Van Asselt Harro and Thomas Brewer (2010). Addressing competitiveness and leakage concerns in climate policy: An analysis of border adjustment measures in the US and the EU. *Energy Policy* 38: 42–51.

Vihma, Antto (2009). Friendly neighbor or Trojan horse? Assessing the interaction of soft law initiatives and the UN climate regime. *International Environmental Agreements: Politics, Law and Economics* 9: 239–62.

Vogler, John (2016). *Climate change in world politics.* Basingstoke: Palgrave Macmillan.

Watanabe, Rie, Christof Arens, Florian Mersmann, Hermann E. Ott and Wolfgang Sterk (2008). The Bali roadmap for global climate policy – new horizons and old pitfalls. *Journal for European Environmental & Planning Law* 5 (2): 139–58.

Wiers, Jochem (2008). French ideas on climate and trade policies. *Carbon and Climate Law Review* 1: 18–32.

Young, Thomas R. (2006). Limited progress on a multitude of fronts. *Environmental Policy and Law* 36 (3–4): 121–4.

9 The demise of the top–down approach

The ink had barely dried on the December 2007 Bali Action Plan when the Kyoto Protocol's first five-year commitment period officially kicked off on 1 January 2008. The international community, however, was soon to find itself in the midst of a financial crisis of epic proportions. Unaware of this, parties quickly commenced the demanding task of optimally organizing their work to meet the tight 2009 deadline for negotiating the key components of the post-2012 climate change regime. For the EU, 2008 presented an additional challenge: its Member States had to finalize an agreement on how to divide among themselves the effort of meeting the climate and energy targets they had unilaterally set back in March 2007.

Regarding the UNFCCC talks, the objective for the first few months of 2008 was to put in place a comprehensive work programme on how to advance the key elements of the Bali roadmap – that is, mitigation, adaptation, finance, technology transfer and a 'shared vision' for long-term cooperative action. The focus of the first few meetings was on organizational and procedural matters, the exchange of ideas among parties and the development of a text that could serve as a basis for negotiations. Various parties took advantage of the opportunity to table new issues and proposals, as well as revisit some of the older ones. The March/April 2008 sessions of the two AWGs, held in Bangkok, Thailand, certainly served this purpose for the EU, which circulated a number of recommendations aiming to improve the effectiveness of the UNFCCC. Among them were calls for adding new gases with great global-warming potential,[1] tackling international aviation and maritime transport emissions, as well as complementing existing project-based flexibility mechanisms with sector-based approaches. The latter proposal in particular generated considerable controversy. The EU's idea involved *inter alia* the introduction of legally binding or 'no-lose' sectoral emissions targets so as to leverage finance and technology deployment in developing countries, plus facilitate enhanced mitigation action by both developed and developing countries (UNFCCC 2008d). Under the 'no-lose' approach, for instance, developing country governments, with support from their developed country counterparts, could take on sectoral intensity targets and receive further credits and assistance in case of successful implementation. Such targets were regarded 'no-lose' as there would be no penalty for non-compliance. Similar proposals were circulated by other developed parties, such as Japan. As they lacked clarity at that stage, they were viewed with suspicion by various developing countries, notably China. In particular, their fear was that sectoral approaches could serve as a pretext for imposing mitigation commitments on them under the Kyoto Protocol (Depledge 2008).

This flurry of activity by all parties continued during the preparatory meetings in Bonn, Germany (June 2008) and Accra, Ghana (August 2008). The EU, for its part, presented more detailed proposals on its ideas with respect to the key elements of the Bali Action Plan. To start with, the EU called for greater emphasis on a shared vision, underlining the vagueness of the existing UNFCCC's ultimate objective and calling for its operationalization in light of scientific advances via the insertion of the 2°C target. Having a clear objective, the EU argued, could help to guide the mitigation efforts of the international community. On this topic, the EU underscored the need for developed countries to take the lead by agreeing to emissions reduction commitments in the order of 30 per cent by 2020, while ensuring the 'comparability of efforts' across all of them (i.e. including the US), as had been agreed the year before in Bali. When it came to developing countries, and light of the distinction made by the Bali Action Plan, the EU's position was that their nationally appropriate mitigation actions should result in ambitious deviations of emissions from business as usual, especially for the advanced developing countries. In singling out this group of countries, the EU's rationale was that their effective participation was a *sine qua non* if parties were to meet the objective of peaking global emissions before 2020 and achieving global emission reductions of at least 50 per cent by 2050, as outlined by the IPCC (UNFCCC 2008a).

The EU highlighted again the merit of sectoral approaches in transitioning towards a low-carbon society. Acknowledging the confusion and concern among all parties around the concept, the EU elaborated upon its preferred definition by outlining a number of market- and non-market-based options available to developed and developing parties alike.[2] This clarifying statement, however, did not prevent controversies from emerging between China and the EU, with the former successfully pushing for the final text to explicitly indicate that sectoral approaches should not lead to commitments for non-Annex I parties, or the imposition of new trade barriers (Depledge 2008; ENB 2008c). The US was also unsupportive of the EU position on sectoral approaches as a means through which to involve developing countries in global mitigation efforts. In particular, it was unwilling to subsidize large-scale energy-efficiency improvements in developing countries and argued instead that they should adopt legal commitments as part of an international climate agreement.

Regarding the other elements, the EU acknowledged the necessity of improving access to new additional and predictable financial flows, offering part of the revenues from the 2012 auctioning of allowances for aviation under the EU's emissions trading scheme for adaptation and mitigation purposes in developing countries. However, it also stressed that adaptation action should be primarily country-driven, highlighting the special role of national governments in incentivizing it. The EU furthermore underscored the critical role of the private sector in enhancing technologies for adaptation and mitigation, as well as in directing investment flows and mobilizing additional finance (UNFCCC 2008a). This EU emphasis on 'innovative financing' and private sector approaches was not very well received by developing country parties, which insisted that public funding and government-led implementation should predominate.

By the end of the Accra meeting in August 2008, it was evident that parties were playing a game of 'wait-and-see', with developing countries avoiding a debate on the scope of their mitigation responsibilities until their developed country counterparts had specified quantitative targets, and vice versa (ENB 2008b). Consequently, Accra only concluded with an agreement for the Secretariat to prepare for the Poznań COP an 'assembly document' listing all the ideas and proposals of the parties on the key elements of the Bali Action Plan (Kulovesi and Gutiérrez 2009), rather than a draft text to form the basis of subsequent negotiations.

The Poznań COP/MOP-4

From 1–12 December 2008, COP/MOP-2, plus the meetings of the AWGs and the Subsidiary Bodies, took place in Poznań, Poland. As expected, the event generated substantial interest, given it marked the halfway point between the Bali conference, which launched the Bali Roadmap, and the Copenhagen conference, the stated deadline for adoption of the post-2012 climate change regime. With the emission targets of the Kyoto Protocol's first commitment period due to expire in 2012, and owing to the time required for countries to ratify the new agreement, a successful outcome in 2009 was deemed essential to secure continued participation and avoid a gap in mitigation commitments from parties to the Kyoto Protocol. However, whereas in Bali the release of the IPCC's AR4 Report had catalysed strong ambition, the Poznań conference took place under the shadow of the global economic crisis. The prevailing instability caused many to argue in favour of prioritizing unemployment and bailing out the banking sector over continued mitigation. In a much quoted remark, Italy's Prime Minister Berlusconi noted:

> I think it is absurd to talk about emissions cuts in this crisis moment. It is as if someone suffering from pneumonia were to think of going to the hairdresser.
>
> (in Santarius *et al.* 2009, p. 76)

Others remained mindful of the Convention's purpose, cautioning against deflecting attention from climate change and emphasizing instead the potential for investments in low-carbon development to serve as an antidote to the global economic downturn (Depledge 2009d). The recent election of US President Obama, who had promised during his electoral campaign to implement a market-based cap-and-trade system and to reduce carbon emissions by 80 per cent below 1990 levels by 2050, also provided some room for optimism (Brewer 2012).

Unfortunately, fear of a pending economic recession prevented the Poznań COP from producing any notable breakthroughs. On the question of a shared vision for long-term action, most parties accepted the need for establishing a long-term emissions reduction goal, yet were unable to pin down a concrete target. On mitigation, the EU continued to encounter opposition when it came to defining the level of collective ambition for the next commitment period. In particular, its reiteration of the necessity for Annex I commitments to aggregate in the range of 25–40 per cent below 1990 levels by 2020 was strongly resisted by Umbrella Group parties, including Australia, Canada, Japan and Russia. Consequently, the AWG-KP's conclusions made little progress, essentially repeating the decisions reached the previous year in Bali, the only difference being a statement noting that further commitments for Annex I parties should 'principally' take the form of quantified emission limitation or reduction objectives. As Depledge (2009d, p. 25) notes, this formulation at least helped to sweep away fears at the time that developed countries might somehow try to 'seek looser forms of commitments … (e.g. intensity targets)'.

Quite similar was the situation with the EU's proposals on developing country actions. Up to that point, the EU had vaguely advocated for non-Annex I actions that would result in ambitious deviations of emissions from business as usual. In its UNFCCC submissions in the weeks leading up to Poznań, however, the EU became more specific, tabling a proposal for (advanced) developing countries to reduce their emissions by 15–30 per cent below business as usual (UNFCCC 2008b). The EU, along with other parties, also called for a registry that would list these adopted actions, as well as register their outcome. In rejecting such proposals, developing countries cited historical responsibility of Annex I parties. In addition, they dismissed suggestions by most Annex I parties for the work of the two AWGs to be better coordinated (Santarius *et al.* 2009). This came as a response to the EU's proposal for a 'package' and 'comprehensive agreement' in Copenhagen, given that both AWGs addressed common themes, such as mitigation. Developing countries, however, followed by the US, successfully withstood any attempts to link the Convention and Protocol tracks (ENB 2008a). While the former feared that that this could divert attention away from Annex I targets, the latter was eager to avoid being dragged into any debates relating to the Protocol.

The Adaptation Fund was another topic that was extensively deliberated upon in Poznań (Czarnecki and Guilanpour 2009). A first controversial issue concerned the demand of developing countries to be able to submit proposals directly to the Fund, instead of having to go via intermediary UN organizations. Direct access required granting legal status to the Adaptation Fund Board so as to be able to undertake contracts and fund projects. Although this had in principle been agreed upon in Bali (Depledge 2009d), various parties, including the EU, were sceptical of the disbursement capacity of the Board and thus called for a feasibility study into the legal implications before moving forward (ENB 2008a). The issue was eventually forwarded to the ministerial level, with developing countries succeeding in getting their preferences granted. A second sticking point related to how finance would be directed into the Adaptation Fund. With only $80 million in contributions up to that point, it was grossly ill-equipped to adequately address the pressing needs of poor developing countries to adapt to the impacts of climate change (Ingram and Irwin 2009). As noted earlier, the bulk of its proceeds originated from a 2 per cent levy on CERs issued for each CDM project. Coming up with innovative solutions for expanding the financial means available to the Adaptation Fund dominated the discussions held in the context of the second review of the Kyoto Protocol, taking place in Poznań. There, various parties argued in favour of extending this arrangement to JI and emissions trading, albeit in vain, as various developed country parties, including the EU, argued that doing so could discourage carbon trading and reduce cost-effectiveness (UNFCCC 2008e). The EU's proposal was less specific, simply noting the need for developing an 'improved understanding of the financial potentials of available and new mechanisms' (ENB 2008a, p. 10). A decision on this was only reached in 2012.[3]

Overall, the Poznań COP was rather uneventful, with very few decisions of any substance adopted. The full operationalization of the Adaptation Fund, plus some methodological improvements with respect to LULUCF and the CDM were basically all that delegates had to show for their efforts in Poznań. There was some progress in technology transfer, however (Lovett *et al.* 2009; Abayasekara 2009). Overall, decisions on most items were left for Copenhagen. Other highlights included a pledge by Mexico to reduce its emissions by 50 per cent of 2002 levels by the year 2050, an announcement by Brazil of its intention to cut deforestation rates by 70 per cent by 2017, plus the decision by the Environmental Integrity Group (EIG) countries – i.e. Switzerland, South Korea and Mexico – to join the club of countries officially supporting the 2°C target.[4]

As far as the EU is concerned, its effective participation in the Poznań talks was largely hampered by the protracted negotiations taking place simultaneously in Brussels on its climate and energy package. Back in January 2008, the Commission had launched a formal implementing proposal, which, as far as the emissions trading scheme was concerned, included recommendations for taking power away from Member States and capping total emissions, as well as allocating allowances centrally with a view to reaching full auctioning in 2020 (see European Commission 2008). For sectors outside the scheme (e.g. agriculture, waste and transport), the Commission's proposal was for a 10 per cent reduction in emissions from 2005 levels, with specific targets set for each Member State. Furthermore, the use of credits generated by the Kyoto Protocol's flexible mechanisms would be limited to 3 per cent. Additional measures were included for the promotion of energy-efficiency and renewable energy sources.

As these intra-EU negotiations were unfolding against the backdrop of the turmoil on global financial markets, various Member States pushed hard for concessions in order to shield their industrial sectors from the impact of the measures (Jankowska 2011; Massai 2009a). Quite pertinent were fears of 'carbon leakage' (Vogler 2016). This refers to the phenomenon whereby energy-intensive sectors of an economy relocate their manufacturing base from a developed country which may have introduced carbon price legislation, such as an emissions trading scheme, to a developing country that is currently subject to limited emissions controls. A series of compromises were thus negotiated by the French Presidency of the EU, which included *inter alia* for full auctioning to be pushed back to 2027 and for industrial sectors exposed to the risk of carbon leakage to be granted significantly more free allowances (Jordan and Rayner 2010). In addition to cohesion and Eastern European Member States, 'rich and green' countries, such as Sweden and Germany, were also instrumental in watering down the Commission proposals, causing many to wonder whether the EU's leadership on climate change was faltering just when it was needed the most (Burns and Carter 2011; Santarius *et al.* 2009; ENB 2008a). Yet, a point needs to be made here that adopting the 2008 climate and energy package was a far more complex process compared with that leading to the burden-sharing agreements back in the 1990s, as in the former case the package was subject to 'the rigours of co-decision' (Vogler 2011, p. 152).

Negotiations enter crucial phase

Following Poznań, five preparatory meetings took place, with the first three held in Bonn (dubbed Bonn I, II and III) and the last two in Bangkok and Barcelona.[5] These meetings were the first for the Obama administration, and were thus notable for the 'return' of a US delegation with a constructive negotiating mindset. At each session, however, optimism about a positive outcome progressively diminished, to the point that by the time of the November 2009 Barcelona talks it had become apparent that Copenhagen would not be able to meet its objective and agree on a post-2012 climate regime architecture.

In terms of EU positions, the most significant development during the first three 2009 sessions in Bonn concerned the further refinement of its proposals for developing country mitigation action and the manner in which they could achieve a deviation of emission growth rates in the order of 15–30 per cent below business as usual by 2020. In a nutshell, the EU proposed that all developing countries put in place by 2012 comprehensive low carbon development strategies and plans (LCDS), which would describe the nationally appropriate mitigation actions (NAMAs) undertaken for all key emitting sectors. Despite the G-77/China's adamant resistance to calls for differentiation among its members, the EU continued to insist that it expected advanced developing countries to lead via the adoption of LCDSs that were more ambitious and quantitative in nature. The NAMAs outlined in these LCDSs should contain a long-term strategy in line with the 2°C threshold, including emissions pathways.

They should also differentiate between those actions that could be undertaken autonomously and those that would need to be supported and enabled by technology, financing and capacity-building in a measurable, reportable and verifiable (MRV) manner by developed countries. All NAMAs and corresponding support were to be inscribed in a register, while LCDSs would be facilitated through a coordinating mechanism that would *inter alia* assess their mitigation potential. Finally, carbon market-based mechanisms, like the CDM or sectoral crediting and sectoral trading, were recommended as a means through which to incentivize the implementation of NAMAs by developing countries (see UNFCCC 2009b; UNFCCC 2009c).

The Bonn meetings halted progress because of various contentious topics which eroded trust between parties. A first issue concerned a legalistic disagreement over interpretation of the AWG-KP's mandate, namely the amendment of Annex B of the Kyoto Protocol listing the targets of developed country parties. Developing countries argued that AWG-KP deliberations should only be concerned with amending this list of targets, while Annex I parties, including the EU, posited that the mandate allowed for the tabling of all issues affecting their further commitments (e.g. developing country mitigation contributions), stating that it would be unwise to repeat the Kyoto experience and set targets without first establishing the rules (Massai 2009b; ENB 2009c).

A second dispute pertained to the legal form of the expected Copenhagen agreement. Developing countries, eager to maintain the 'firewall' between the two groups of states, insisted on retaining the Kyoto Protocol under the principle of common but differentiated responsibility. In contrast, developed countries framed the annex approach as outdated, arguing that it should be replaced by a new approach to the Convention which unified all country obligations under a single legal umbrella (Jinnah *et al.* 2009; ENB 2009f).

A third topic of contention related to finance modalities, with parties proving largely unable to move away from their entrenched positions over the role of the public sector vis-à-vis private investments, including the carbon markets.

A fourth controversial issue revolved around the aggregate scale of emissions to be achieved by developed countries. On their part, developing countries were in favour of a 'top–down' approach, applicable only to Annex I parties following the definition of an ambitious aggregate target in the range of 40 per cent and over. Most developed countries, however, advocated for a Kyoto-style approach, whereby the aggregate target would derive from the summation of their individual targets (Depledge 2009a). Furthermore, various Annex I parties, like Russia and Japan, argued that they were not prepared to engage in a debate on aggregates without a clear picture of the nature of commitments from the US or major developing economies (ENB 2009f). The EU, while spearheading calls for Annex I leadership, highlighted the usefulness of holding joint AWG-LCA and AWG-KP sessions in order to discuss aggregates for Annex I parties, noting the 'difficultly in discussing these numbers in the absence of some major emitting countries' (ENB 2009d, p. 4). With respect to the US, all eyes were on the trip of the Waxman-Markey Bill through Congress, which envisaged a 17 per cent cut by 2020 of 2005 levels.[6] Given that this target was more or less equivalent to a return to 1990 levels, the EU was quick to note that it failed to pass the 'comparability' test (ENDS 2009a). Consequently, whereas by the end of the Bonn III meeting almost all Annex I parties had proposed targets for themselves (see UNFCCC 2009d), their differing base years and target periods, as well as divergence over the inclusion or not of flexibility mechanisms and LULUCF activities, thwarted any attempted to assess their overall ambition (Depledge 2009a, 2009b).

The result of the three Bonn sessions was a voluminous negotiating text riddled with brackets and proposals that was supposed to serve as the basis of discussions for the remaining two preparatory meetings in Bangkok and Barcelona. Prior to Bangkok, the UN Secretary-General convened a climate change summit in New York in September, where world leaders reiterated their commitment to reach an agreement in Copenhagen and acknowledged the necessity of cutting global greenhouse gas emissions by at least 50 per cent below 1990 levels by 2050 if global warming was to be kept below 2°C. This conclusion had also been adopted a couple of months before, during the July 2009 G-8 summit in L'Aquila, Italy (G-8 2009). However, the enormous complexity of the task at hand and the failure of the UNFCCC negotiations to resolve key crunch issues in the previous sessions made it clear that any substantive decisions could only be made by world leaders themselves during the final days of the Copenhagen summit.

During the Bangkok and Barcelona meetings, the EU attracted considerable criticism from developing countries following (i) its failure to adopt an environmentally progressive line on the issue of financing, and (ii) its sudden diplomatic U-turn on the question of the future of the Kyoto Protocol. Starting with financing, the EU Member States had fruitlessly spent the preceding months seeking to establish a common position on financial assistance to developing countries. In particular, various Member States, particularly those of Eastern and Central Europe, had proved unwilling to scale up their financial support to developing countries, many of which, they claimed, were 'not much poorer than themselves' (Depledge 2009c, p. 278). Eventually, the Commission released a communication on climate finance that was widely perceived as inadequate because of its lack of concrete numbers on the actual amount the EU was willing to put on the table. While the EU estimated that approximately €100 billion by 2020 would be required for adaptation and mitigation purposes in developing countries, it then went on to vaguely break down this figure into percentages, according to which domestic finance (public and private) in developing countries would deliver between 20 and 40 per cent, while the carbon market and international public finance would contribute up to around 40 per cent each (European Commission 2009). When it came to the latter stream of money, the EU was again explicit in its insistence that apart from the LDCs, all other countries, including the most affluent developing ones, should contribute climate finance in accordance with their emission levels and GDP. In 2020, the report continued, international public finance should amount in the range of €22–50 billion per year, with the EU's ambitious and fair global contribution being €2–15 billion (European Commission 2009). With the exception of the latter figure, the European Council of October 2009 largely backed the Commission's proposal, provoking an angry backlash from developing countries, which highlighted that the Bali Action Plan said nothing about contributions from non-Annex I parties (ENB 2009b).

The EU remained in the spotlight for yet another reason, namely for its sudden U-turn regarding the future direction of the climate regime. Up to that point, the EU had largely stood behind the existing two-track approach of the climate regime, which inscribed binding targets for Annex I parties and obligations of non-Annex I parties in the Kyoto Protocol and the Framework Convention respectively. In Bangkok, however, the EU announced that instead of amending the Kyoto Protocol, its preferred outcome from Copenhagen would now be a single legal instrument integrating the obligations of both developing and developed countries (Rajamani 2009). Furthermore this new single legal instrument should also incorporate the Protocol's key elements, including binding targets, the flexibility mechanisms, as well as compliance, reporting and accounting modalities (ENB 2009a). This sudden volte-face was justified by the EU on the basis of the need for US participation in the post-2012 climate regime, given the latter's aversion to adopt Kyoto-style agreements (ENDS 2009b). While the EU insisted its intention had not been to 'kill' the Kyoto Protocol, trust had withered, as various developing countries accused the EU of 'attempted murder' (ENB 2009a, p. 20).

The Copenhagen COP/MOP-5

Bangkok and Barcelona had brought to the fore the uncertain future of the Kyoto Protocol. Ever since the Protocol's entry into force, attention had always focused on what to do post-2012. In Barcelona, however, parties publicly acknowledged that achieving a new legally binding agreement in Copenhagen was a relatively unrealistic goal. Instead, officials started referring to the need for a strong political decision at COP-15 that would contain a commitment for deliberations to continue towards a full-fledged legal instrument to be adopted at some time in the future (Massai 2009b). EU officials were quick to adopt this new narrative, with Stavros Dimas, the EU Environment Commissioner, stressing that the EU's objective for Copenhagen would now be to secure 'a substantial deal' that contained pledges on emission reduction targets from developed countries and finance for poor countries, as well as a timetable outlining the process for agreeing the legal text during 2010 (Rankin 2009). Danish Prime Minister Lars Løkke Rasmussen even resorted to using paradoxical language, calling for parties to reach a 'politically binding agreement in Copenhagen' (see Fogarty 2009).

A number of factors were to blame for this unfavourable turn of events. The global economic downturn was certainly one of the culprits, as many developed countries now perceived it to be in their national interest to prioritize economic growth at the expense of climate policy (Vogler 2016). Writing before the COP, Victor (2009, p. 342) foresaw the 'looming disaster' that short-term political thinking would perpetuate, arguing that while the financial crisis would certainly be one of the causes of the Copenhagen failure, the other was 'bad strategy'. Quite simply, the tight 2009 deadline agreed back in 2007 for responding to an over-packed agenda had never been realistic, especially given that half that schedule was lost because of the sluggish pace of the negotiations during 2008. This was also acknowledged by one interviewee, who noted that 'it was the process itself that put the process under pressure'.[7] As he further explained:

> The first meeting after Bali was a pure discussion about process. And the process was organized in a way that all the important things were put in the back end of the agenda. So the key question of who is doing what on mitigation was only to be discussed a year – more than a year – after Bali. There was just very little time.[8]

In any case, the Copenhagen COP took place in December 2009, marking the culmination of a two-year negotiating process to settle a successor treaty to the Kyoto Protocol. The literature on the Copenhagen saga is vast, with several scholars having offered comprehensive accounts of everything one needs to know about its various aspects (see e.g. Bodansky 2010; Dimitrov 2010a, 2010b). Thus, only the main negotiation events and key elements of the Copenhagen Accord will be highlighted here, leaving more room to focus on the EU's performance.

During the first week of the conference, negotiations continued in the AWG with minimal progress. From the outset, however, the Copenhagen COP was clouded by rumours that the Danish Presidency and a selected group of parties had already sidestepped the AWG to craft a compromise text behind closed doors which was meant to serve as the basis for negotiations. When this document was leaked by the *Guardian* newspaper (see Vidal 2009), it was greeted with cries of horror by a great number of developing countries which expressed their frustration over the lack of transparency. Concurrent efforts by the Danes to convene a 'Friends of the Chair' group to address the core issues were equally undermined, as developing countries questioned the legitimacy and democracy of such processes and insisted on the negotiations continuing entirely in open settings and on the basis of the heavily bracketed text forwarded by the AWG (Christoff 2010). Perceiving that the AWG text was unfit to proceed with, and eager to ensure that agreement could be reached, the COP Presidency convened an informal 'Friends of the Chair' group anyway upon the arrival of the Heads of State in the final days of the conference. Initially, a group of officials from 20–30 countries, including the EU's Swedish Presidency and various Member States, developed a succession of drafts, with the breakthrough finally coming in an even smaller meeting behind closed doors between the US and the BASIC countries (i.e. Brazil, South Africa, India and China). The climate leader, the EU, had surprisingly been sidelined (Dimitrov 2010a).

Expressing dismay at the turn of events, various EU delegates suggested in the heat of the moment that the EU should voice its disagreement and reject the Accord.[9] In the end, EU leaders decided otherwise. One interviewee explained why:

> Once the Heads of State are there, the cohorts around them will always try to make them look successful. They will try to protect them from the perception of political failure, even when the conference is failing.[10]

Another interviewee concurred, offering a similar explanation:

> Heads of State were very careful. They were arguing that there was nothing else that could be adopted during the last night. It is also about psychology, related to communication. Let's say that you, a single country or a group of countries, raise your plate and say: no, no consensus, I object. It may turn out that you will be blamed; that because of you there was nothing when otherwise there could have been some progress. This hesitation, late at night, when you are tired, is not an easy one. High-level politicians also think about reputation; how they will explain things back home.[11]

The Copenhagen Accord

The final agreement (the Copenhagen Accord) was publicly announced by US President Obama before it was even presented to the COP for approval, thus adding further fuel to the flames of resentment. What follows is a brief account of the main features of the Accord, which is a political rather than a legal document (see UNFCCC 2009a; de Berdt Romilly and Clark 2010). First, with respect to shared vision, the Accord only highlights the need for 'deep cuts' in emissions in order to keep the increase in global temperature below 2°C. References for developed countries to reduce their emissions by 80 per cent by 2050 were included in earlier drafts, but did not eventually make it into the final Accord – despite Germany's strong objections (Christoff 2010; Dimitrov 2010a). Efforts for the agreement to contain a long-term target for global emissions to be reduced by 50 per cent by 2050 were equally unsuccessful, as major developing countries were well aware of the fact that insertion of such a goal would imply that their emissions would need to peak and begin to decline prior to 2050 (Bodansky 2010).

Second, the Accord contains no mandatory mitigation targets. Annex I parties are merely required to adopt quantified economy-wide national emissions reduction targets for 2020. Importantly, the Accord endorses the bottom–up approach to emission targets, as the actual goals and baselines are to be self-determined by each party. In turn, non-Annex I parties are called upon to implement mitigation actions, with those funded internationally being subject to international measurement, reporting and verification (MRV). In Copenhagen, MRV became highly controversial, as the US and several other developed countries argued in favour of all developing country actions being subject to some form of international review – a position adamantly rejected by China. The aforementioned formulation eventually emerged as a torturous compromise on this issue.

Third, and with respect to finance, the Accord establishes the Copenhagen Green Climate Fund to serve as an operating entity of the Convention's financial mechanism, with developed countries pledging *inter alia* to mobilize US$100 billion per year by 2020 for adaptation, mitigation, forestry and technology transfer in developing countries. Funding was to be raised from a variety of bilateral and multilateral sources, including private and public finance. Finally, the Accord called for the setting-up of a mechanism aimed at reducing deforestation, forest degradation and promoting forest conservation.

Because of disagreements among parties, the COP was not able to adopt the Accord as an official decision, but only to take note of it. Its legal status in international law was thus left vague. The Accord also did not delve into the legal form of the post-2012 climate change regime. Even though drafts of the Accord contained a reference on the need for the 2010 Cancún COP to produce a legally binding instrument, this was eventually removed from the final version. In the aftermath of the Copenhagen COP, views and reactions as to its outcome were varied. On the one hand, critics argued that Copenhagen failed in its prime objective – that is, seal a legally binding agreement with robust mitigation goals and targets (Christoff 2010). On the other hand, others focused on the positive aspects, highlighting for example that via the acceptance of the 2°C temperature target parties had been able for the first time to quantitatively elaborate on what constituted dangerous climate change (Kjellén 2011; Gupta 2010). In addition, that all countries, developed and developing alike, offered mitigation targets (of different forms, but again for the first time ever), was also interpreted as a sign that the so-called firewall between the two groups of countries was apparently beginning to break (Brenton 2013). Finally, Depledge (2010) and Averchenkova (2010) argue that flaws aside, Copenhagen was eventually able to produce a coherent outcome that at least charted the way ahead for the next (bottom–up) stage of the climate regime.

The EU in Copenhagen

Apart from the 2°C goal, the EU achieved none of its other objectives in Copenhagen. There was no legally binding agreement, no ambitious targets and no mention of sectoral approaches in which the EU had, since Bali, invested so much time and effort. The contents of the final deal, which contained voluntary pledges with no concrete recommendations regarding the compliance regime, were determined by the US and the BASIC countries, with the EU and many other parties finding themselves marginalized. Estimates at the time highlighted that even if pledges were achieved in full, they would not suffice to meet the 2°C objective, locking the world instead into a 3°C warming future above pre-industrial levels (Rogelj *et al.* 2010). Adding together Annex I emissions pledges would only lead to reductions of 12–19 per cent, far below levels considered necessary by the IPCC (see Averchenkova 2010).

There are many reasons why EU expectations for Copenhagen were not fulfilled and this heavily criticized outcome arose. The next chapter applies Underdal's theory of 'negotiation failure' to unpack some of the main factors in detail. As noted in the Introduction, Copenhagen represented for all intents and purposes the practical end of the climate regime's top–down era. Hence, Copenhagen serves as the starting point for a longitudinal investigation into the EU's failure to accomplish its overarching climate change objective for the post-2012 regime.

This chapter therefore concludes by briefly mentioning a number of problems that confronted the EU, but were specific to Copenhagen. A first one relates to the EU bunker, which again made its appearance in the Danish capital. In a much-quoted remark during her hearing as Commissioner-designate for Climate Action in 2010, Connie Hedegaard, the Danish minister who chaired most of the Copenhagen summit, noted: 'Those last hours in Copenhagen, China, India, Japan, Russia, the US … each spoke with one voice, while Europe spoke with many different voices.' Later she added: 'I know very well that it is easier said than done … [but] in an international world Europe must stand more united if we are to be heard' (quoted in Rankin 2010).

A second issue relates to the Swedish Presidency of the EU and the Danish Presidency of the COP, which both came under fire, albeit for different reasons. The Swedish were deemed ineffective for their inability to take the lead in the negotiations with third parties, allowing instead the leaders of the UK, Germany and France to assume that role in informal meetings during the last days of the summit (Groen and Niemann 2013). Regarding the Danes, their Presidency was described as a 'complete catastrophe'.[12] To start with, interviewees flagged up the resignation a couple of months prior to the COP of Thomas Becker, Denmark's chief climate negotiator, as a big mistake and a serious blow to the Danish Presidency.[13] Allegedly brought down by minor financial irregularities, Becker was Denmark's most experienced and respected climate negotiator, with strong links to his developing country counterparts (Meilstrup 2010). He was a person that 'knew everybody and everybody knew'.[14]

The Danish COP Presidency was also criticized for poorly managing the talks. At the start of the high-level segment Connie Hedegaard, who had up to that point acted as COP/MOP President, abruptly handed over to Danish Prime Minister Lars Løkke Rasmussen. This move was justified on grounds of rank and seniority, given the presence of an unprecedented number of Heads of State at the summit. The task, however, proved much beyond his capacities, to the extent that he had to step down during the last night of the COP (Haug and Berkhout 2010). Depledge (2010, p. 19) is especially critical of Prime Minister Rasmussen's handling of duties, noting, among others:

> Inexperience, exhaustion, poor English, and a breathtaking misunderstanding of procedure meant that the final plenary, under his presidency,

descended into farce. [...] Aside from many other gaffes – such as interrupting the President of the Maldives in full flow to take another speaker – Rasmussen was completely unable to manoeuvre round the critical notion of consensus. In the end, he simply gave up, stating that, since there was no agreement, the Accord should be abandoned and confined to informal documentation. It was at this point, luckily, that UK Minister Ed Miliband stepped in to demand the adjournment of the meeting, allowing space and time to find a solution.

Finally, EU coherence and leadership were severely questioned, given that Member States had proven unable in the run-up to Copenhagen to agree on a range of pivotal issues. One such issue was that of the EU's financial contribution for mitigation and adaptation measures in developing countries, which was highlighted earlier. Another related to excess greenhouse gas emission permits ('hot air') allocated under the Kyoto Protocol to many countries that had in the meantime joined the EU. Even though carrying the excess permits over to the next commitment period would contradict the EU rhetoric on ambition, eliminating them was vehemently resisted by most EU Eastern European and Baltic members, such as Poland and Romania (Groen and Niemann 2013; see also Afionis *et al.* 2012). Finally, there was the issue of divergent Member States' opinions over the question of whether the EU should increase its commitment to 30 per cent for the post-2012 commitment period (see Skovgaard 2014). While doing so would strengthen the EU's credibility and leadership, plus reinvigorate the EU carbon market, various Member States, such as Poland and Italy, voiced their opposition, citing competitiveness concerns.

Notes

1 Examples included HFCs and PFCs.
2 Market-based options included national or international emissions trading, sectoral no-lose mechanisms and sectoral crediting mechanisms, while non-market ones where defined as 'cooperative approaches based on technology cooperation and/or domestic sectoral mitigation policies could contribute to removing barriers that are specific to certain sectors, increase technology deployment and enhance technology RD&D [research, development and demonstration] in key sectors in developing countries' (UNFCCC 2008c, p. 4).
3 "During the Doha 2012 COP/MOP, the decision was taken that the Adaptation Fund "shall be further augmented through a 2 per cent share of the proceeds levied on the first international transfers of AAUs and the issuance of ERUs for Article 6 projects immediately upon the conversion to ERUs of AAUs or RMUs previously held by Parties" (see FCCC/KP/CMP/2012/13/Add.1)."
4 The other were the EU, Chile, Norway, Iceland and the African States (Santarius *et al.* 2009).
5 Bonn I took place in March/April 2009, Bonn II in June and Bonn III in August, while the Bangkok and Barcelona meetings took place in October and November 2009 respectively.

6 In June 2009, the House of Representatives passed the Waxman–Markey Bill. In July 2010, however, the bill failed to pass the Senate.
7 Interview No. 9 (Commission official).
8 Interview No. 9 (Commission official).
9 Interview No. 1 (Member State official – Former Head of Delegation); Interview No. 7 (Member State official – Former Head of Delegation).
10 Interview No. 6 (Member State official).
11 Interview No. 7 (Member State official – Former Head of Delegation).
12 Interview No. 12 (Commission official).
13 Interview No. 1 (Member State official – Former Head of Delegation); Interview No. 2 (Member State official – Former Head of Delegation); Interview No. 8 (Member State official – Former Minister).
14 Interview No. 1 (Member State official – Former Head of Delegation).

References

Abayasekara, Sadhana (2009). The international climate negotiations in Bali and Poznań: steps forward and backward on the road to Copenhagen. *Asia Pacific Journal of Environmental Law* 12 (1): 227–35.

Afionis, Stavros, Adrian Fenton and Jouni Paavola (2012). EU climate leadership under test. *Nature Climate Change* 2: 837–8.

Averchenkova, Alina (2010). The outcomes of Copenhagen: the negotiations and the accord. UNDP Environment & Energy Group climate policy series, February 2010. Available at: www.cccep.ac.uk/publication/the-outcomes-of-copenhagen-the-negotiations-and-the-accord/.

Bodansky, Daniel (2010). The Copenhagen Climate Change Conference: a postmortem. *American Journal of International Law* 104 (2): 230–40.

Brenton, Anthony (2013). 'Great powers' in climate politics. *Climate Policy* 13 (5): 541–6.

Brewer, Paul R. (2012). Polarisation in the USA: climate change, party politics, and public opinion in the Obama era. *European Political Science* 11: 7–17.

Burns, Charlotte and Neil Carter (2011). The European Parliament and climate change: from symbolism to heroism and back again. In Wurzel, Rüdiger K.W. and James Connelly (eds) *The European Union as a leader in international climate change politics*. London: Routledge, 58–73.

Christoff, Peter (2010). Cold climate in Copenhagen: China and the United States at COP15. *Environmental Politics* 19 (4): 637–56.

Czarnecki, Ralph and Kaveh Guilanpour (2009). The Adaptation Fund after Poznań. *Carbon & Climate Law Review* 1: 79–87.

de Berdt Romilly, George and Lorne S. Clark (2010). Building block or a faltering step? *Environmental Policy and Law* 40 (1): 11–17.

Depledge, Joanna (2008). Spring 2008 climate meetings: Bangkok and Bonn. *Environmental Policy and Law* 38 (4): 194–200.

Depledge, Joanna (2009a). Bonn climate talks: the end of the beginning. *Environmental Policy and Law* 39 (3): 136–40.

Depledge, Joanna (2009b). Bonn III climate talks: treading water. *Environmental Policy and Law* 39 (4–5): 190–92.

Depledge, Joanna (2009c). On the eve of Copenhagen: insights into the negotiation. *Environmental Policy and Law* 39 (6): 277–81.

Depledge, Joanna (2009d). Poznan: midway to Copenhagen. *Environmental Policy and Law* 39 (1): 24–7.

Depledge, Joanna (2010). At the limits of global diplomacy? *Environmental Policy and Law* 40 (1): 17–22.

Dimitrov, Radoslav S. (2010a). Inside Copenhagen: the state of climate governance. *Global Environmental Politics* 10 (2): 18–24.

Dimitrov, Radoslav S. (2010b). Inside UN climate change negotiations: the Copenhagen Conference. *Review of Policy Research* 27 (6): 795–821.

ENB (2008a). Summary of the Fourteenth Conference of Parties to the UN Framework Convention on Climate Change and Fourth Meeting of Parties to the Kyoto Protocol: 1–12 December 2008. *Earth Negotiations Bulletin* 12 (395): 1–20.

ENB (2008b). Summary of the Third Session of the Ad hoc Working Group under the Convention and Sixth Session (Part One) of the Ad hoc Working Group under the Kyoto Protocol: 21–27 August 2008. *Earth Negotiations Bulletin* 12 (383): 1–11.

ENB (2008c). Twenty-eighth Sessions of the UNFCCC Subsidiary Bodies, Second Session of the Ad hoc Working Group under the Convention, and Fifth Session of the Ad hoc Working Group under the Kyoto Protocol: 2–13 June 2008. *Earth Negotiations Bulletin* 12 (375): 1–20.

ENB (2009a). Summary of the Bangkok Climate Change Talks: 28 September – 9 October 2009. *Earth Negotiations Bulletin* 12 (439): 1–21.

ENB (2009b). Summary of the Barcelona Climate Change Talks: 2–6 November 2009. *Earth Negotiations Bulletin* 12 (447): 1–17.

ENB (2009c). Summary of the Bonn Climate Change Talks: 1–12 June 2009. *Earth Negotiations Bulletin* 12 (241): 1–26.

ENB (2009d). Summary of the Bonn Climate Change Talks: 10–14 August 2009. *Earth Negotiations Bulletin* 12 (427): 1–18.

ENB (2009f). Summary of the Fifth Session of the Ad hoc Working Group on Long-term Cooperative Action under the UN Framework Convention on Climate Change (AWG-LCA 5) and Seventh Session of the Ad hoc Working Group on Further Commitments for Annex I Parties under the Kyoto Protocol (AWG-KP 7). *Earth Negotiations Bulletin* 12 (407): 1–15.

ENDS (2009a). Dimas upbeat about proposed US climate target, 2 April.

ENDS (2009b). EU joins US in pushing for Kyoto alternative, 7 October.

European Commission (2008). 20 20 by 2020: Europe's climate change opportunity. COM(2008) 30 final, Brussels, 23 January.

European Commission (2009). Stepping up international climate finance: a European blueprint for the Copenhagen deal. COM(2009) 475 final, Brussels, 10 September.

Fogarty, David (2009). Snap analysis: APEC nations back face-saving climate plan. *Reuters*, 15 November. Available at: www.reuters.com/article/us-apec-climate-snap-analysis-idUSTRE5AE0EQ20091115.

G-8 (2009). Chair's summary, L'Aquila, 10 July 2009. Available at: www.g8italia2009.it/static/G8_Allegato/Chair_Summary%2c1.pdf.

Groen, Lisanne and Arne Niemann (2013). The European Union at the Copenhagen climate negotiations: a case of contested EU actorness and effectiveness. *International Relations* 27 (3): 308–24.

Gupta, Joyeeta (2010). A history of international climate change policy. *WIREs Climate Change* 1: 636–53.

Haug, Constanze and Frans Berkhout (2010). Learning the hard way? European climate policy after Copenhagen. *Environment* 52 (3): 20–27.

Ingram, Kyle and Matt Irwin (2009). Poznań Climate Conference 2008. *Sustainable Development Law & Policy* 9 (2): 15.

Jankowska, Karolina (2011). Poland's climate change policy struggle: greening the East? In Wurzel, Rüdiger K.W. and James Connelly (eds) *The European Union as a leader in international climate change politics.* London: Routledge, 163–78.

Jinnah, Sikina, Douglas Bushey, Miquel Muñoz and Kati Kulovesi (2009). Tripping points: barriers and bargaining chips on the road to Copenhagen. *Environmental Research Letters* 4: 1–6.

Jordan, Andrew and Tim Rayner (2010). The evolution of climate policy in the European Union: a historical perspective. In Jordan, Andrew, Dave Huitema, Harro Van Asselt, Tim Rayner and Frans Berkhout (eds) *Climate change policy in the European Union: confronting the dilemmas of mitigation and adaptation?* Cambridge: Cambridge University Press, 52–80.

Kjellén, Bo (2011). Climate conundrum: could a transitional agreement offer a way out? *Global Policy* 2 (1): 112–14.

Kulovesi, Kati and María Gutiérrez (2009). Climate change negotiations update: process and prospects for a Copenhagen agreed outcome in December 2009. *Review of European Community and International Environmental Law* 18 (3): 229–43.

Lovett, Jon C., Peter S. Hofman, Karlijn Morsink, Arturo Balderas Torres, Joy S. Clancy and Koos Krabbendam (2009). Review of the 2008 UNFCCC meeting in Poznań. *Energy Policy* 37: 3701–5.

Massai, Leonardo (2009a). Current developments in carbon and climate law: European Union. *Carbon & Climate Law Review* 1: 117–20.

Massai, Leonardo (2009b). The long way to the Copenhagen Accord: climate change negotiations in 2009. *Review of European Community and International Environmental Law* 19 (1): 104–21.

Meilstrup, Per (2010). The runaway summit: the background story of the Danish Presidency of COP15, the UN Climate Change Conference. In Hvidt, Nanna and Hans Mouritzen (eds) *Danish foreign policy yearbook 2010.* Copenhagen: Danish Institute for International Studies, DIIS, 113–35.

Rajamani, Lavanya (2009). Cloud over climate negotiations: from Bangkok to Barcelona and beyond. *Economic and Political Weekly* 44 (43): 11–15.

Rankin, Jennifer (2009). EU tells China and US to improve climate pledges. *Politico.* Available at: www.politico.eu/article/eu-tells-china-and-us-to-improve-climate-pledges/.

Rankin, Jennifer (2010). Hedegaard wins plaudits. *Politico.* Available at: www.politico.eu/article/hedegaard-wins-plaudits/.

Rogelj, Joeri, Julia Nabel, Claudine Chen, William Hare, Kathleen Markmann, Malte Meinshausen, Michiel Schaeffer, Kirsten Macey and Niklas Höhne (2010). Copenhagen Accord pledges are paltry. *Nature* 464: 1126–8.

Santarius, Tilman, Christof Arens, Urda Eichhorst, Dagmar Kiyar, Florian Mersmann, Hermann E. Ott, Frederic Rudolph, Wolfgang Sterk and Rie Watanabe (2009). Pit stop Poznan: an analysis of negotiations on the Bali Action Plan at the stopover to Copenhagen. *Journal for European Environmental and Planning Law* 6 (1): 75–96.

Skovgaard, Jakob (2014). EU climate policy after the crisis. *Environmental Politics* 23 (1): 1–17.

UNFCCC (2008a). Ideas and proposals on the elements contained in paragraph 1 of the Bali Action Plan. FCCC/AWGLCA/2008/MISC.2.

UNFCCC (2008b). Ideas and proposals on the elements contained in paragraph 1 of the Bali Action Plan. FCCC/AWGLCA/2008/MISC.5/Add.1.

UNFCCC (2008c). Ideas and proposals on the subjects of the Ad hoc Working Group on Long-term Cooperative Action under the Convention workshops scheduled for 2008. FCCC/AWGLCA/2008/MISC.4.

UNFCCC (2008d). Views and information on the means to achieve mitigation objectives of Annex I parties. FCCC/KP/AWG/2008/MISC.1.

UNFCCC (2008e). Views from parties on extending the share of proceeds to assist in meeting the costs of adaptation to joint implementation and emissions trading. FCCC/KP/CMP/2008/MISC.1.

UNFCCC (2009a). Draft decision-/CP.15: Copenhagen Accord. FCCC/CP/2009/L.7.

UNFCCC (2009b). Ideas and proposals on the elements contained in paragraph 1 of the Bali Action Plan. FCCC/AWGLCA/2009/MISC.1/Add.4.

UNFCCC (2009c). Ideas and proposals on the elements contained in paragraph 1 of the Bali Action Plan. FCCC/AWGLCA/2009/MISC.4 (Part I).

UNFCCC (2009d). Information on possible quantified emission limitation and reduction objectives from Annex I parties. FCCC/KP/AWG/2009/MISC.15.

Victor, David G. (2009). Plan B for Copenhagen. *Nature* 461: 342–4.

Vidal, John (2009). Copenhagen climate summit in disarray after 'Danish text' leak. *Guardian*, 8 December. Available at: www.theguardian.com/environment/2009/dec/08/copenhagen-climate-summit-disarray-danish-text.

Vogler, John (2011). EU policy on global climate change: the negotiation of burden-sharing. In Thomas, Daniel C. (ed.) *Making EU foreign policy: national preferences, European norms and common policies.* Basingstoke: Palgrave Macmillan, 150–73.

Vogler, John (2016). *Climate change in world politics.* Basingstoke: Palgrave Macmillan.

10 The EU as a negotiator in the climate regime

It is often tempting to attribute the failure of negotiations to a single, over-arching cause. That is, negotiators disagree over the strategy for how to reduce greenhouse gas emissions, and by when; different parties dispute their responsibility and capacity to act on such a strategy; or concerns arise over whose interests are being advanced at the expense of others. Yet this misses the bigger picture.

Numerous factors work independently and collectively to prevent an agreement being reached. But some dominant factors do emerge (Underdal 1983). For example, politically inadequate solutions design models, inaccurate or unreliable information, process-generated stakes and uncertainty are all dominant factors. While the effect on negotiations from each obstacle may not be enough alone to derail the process, the combined effect could be that of 'disturbing and impeding the search for mutually advantageous solutions' (Underdal 1983, p. 192). Whereas the previous chapters charted the history of the EU's involvement in climate negotiations from the late 1980s to 2009, this chapter discusses the EU's role in the failure of the international community to adopt a Kyoto-style agreement for the post-2012 period. As we have previously seen, the top–down approach in climate change negotiations effectively met its demise in Copenhagen. Since the EU was its most staunch supporter, this failure consequently reflects badly on the EU. So why was the EU unable to get its climate change message across? The following sections go through each one of Underdal's factors to provide an answer.

Politically inadequate solution design models

To understand why negotiations failed in Copenhagen, it is necessary to look back over the last 20 years or so of international climate talks. Divisions among parties became more discernible as parties shifted to a 'bargaining mode' of negotiations following Bali. There were two main elements in the EU's position. The first was that the agreement should be top–down and the second that the promulgated targets should be ambitious and based on IPCC science. The main problem, however, with its negotiating approach was that it was proposing what Underdal (1983, 1991, 1998) refers to as a **politically inadequate solution**

design model'. Put simply, this refers to the distance between a scientifically 'appropriate' solution to a problem and a politically 'acceptable' or 'feasible' agreement. For a solution to a collective policy problem to qualify as 'good', it needs to meet three main criteria: efficiency, fairness and feasibility. Underdal (1983, 1991) notes that a regime qualifies as efficient primarily if it is ecologically sound. Yet, he then goes on to add that solutions that satisfy scientific standards will most often fall outside the actual settlement range. The EU's 'good' solution to the climate change challenge was one that relied on top–down targets and was underpinned by scientific evidence. This solution was dismissed by its major negotiating partners as being inattentive to issues of fairness and feasibility. Deep divisions were also created within the EU itself.

To start with, the appetite for the first part of the EU's solution, that is, a global top–down mitigation strategy, progressively diminished following Kyoto. Under the Bush administration, the US expressed hostility towards a second round of Kyoto-like differentiated commitments among parties, arguing that any top–down regulation should apply equally in all markets. Similar fairness concerns were also echoed by other major developed countries, such as Canada and Japan, with their ambivalence being demonstrated *inter alia* by their decision to join the AP6 in 2006 (Hovi and Skodvin 2008). Major developing countries for their part viewed fairness in a different light. They consistently invoked the historical responsibility concept and favoured binding top–down targets as a measure only applicable to others. The second element in the EU's solution (i.e. ambitiousness) was also problematic, this time on grounds of political feasibility. While the EU's position reflected the scientific consensus to a great extent, appetite for ambitious climate policy among most other major parties was relatively low, especially in the aftermath of the economic crisis. As Christoff 2010 (p. 638) notes, the economic recession 'sucked political attention, energy and momentum from the climate issue'.

Another point worth highlighting here relates to the EU's internal consensus-building processes. Interestingly, while the EU was trying to convince its external negotiating partners of the need to consider its preferred solution design model, it often struggled to sound convincing because of a lack of internal unity. Chapter 4 explained the post-Kyoto preference divergence among Member States with respect to the supplementarity of flexibility mechanisms. Despite agreement on the need for a 'concrete ceiling' on the use of these mechanisms, Member States struggled to agree on a figure or approach. EU institutions, like the Parliament, were also divided on this issue. Turning to the legal form of the post-2012 agreement, we saw in Chapter 7 the way in which a number of Member States, most prominently Italy, questioned the principle of legally binding targets and called for post-2012 targets to be voluntary in the hope of drawing the US back into the negotiating fold and securing the participation of major developing countries. This 'covert' intra-EU divide made its appearance again in the aftermath of Copenhagen, as Italy and the Central and Eastern European Member States went so far as to express their satisfaction with the COP's non-legally binding outcome (Groen *et al.* 2012).

Finally, EU actors were also split on the question of ambition. The two burden-sharing agreements of the 1990s highlight this to a great extent, as only a handful of Member States adopted targets that could be classified as ambitious, with many of the rest simply free-riding on others' contributions. Indicative of the lack of ambition in some Member States was the example of the Netherlands, which quickly moved to a significantly lower target in the burden-sharing agreement of 1998. Liefferink and Birkel (2011, p. 158) even suggested that the Netherlands was actually 'quite happy with the failure of the minus 15 per cent scenario in Kyoto'. Cracks in European unity also appeared during the period of waiting for Russia's ratification. Chapter 7 noted Spain and Italy's 2003 reference to Kyoto as a threat to business and the calls by the Commission and other EU actors for *inter alia* making future emission-cutting action conditional on Russia signing up to the Protocol. Divisions among Member States continued in the run-up period to Bali (see Chapters 8 and 9). During the March 2005 and March 2006 Councils, various Member States, such as Germany, Austria and Italy, appeared sceptical of supporting long-term ambitious targets. The December 2006 and February 2007 Environment Councils further highlighted the divides among Member States on target-setting. Various EU actors preferred a wait-and-see approach, whereas others opposed adopting a unilateral EU target, in contrast to those calling for reduction commitments in the range of 15–30 per cent. The prime example, however, relates to the intra-EU divide in the run-up to and aftermath of Copenhagen as to whether Member States should increase their common target beyond the existing 20 per cent. Various large Member States, such as Germany and France, appeared undecided at times, causing various external UNFCCC parties to question the EU's credibility as a whole (see Skovgaard 2014).

Zone of agreement

Difficulties in reaching an agreement amongst EU Member States should have been the first warning sign of problems to come. How could the EU convince the wide-ranging and varied group of parties involved in UNFCCC negotiations, when its own Member States struggled to agree? In the run-up to Copenhagen, the EU struggled to come to terms with the fact that there was simply no **zone of agreement** on either of the two elements it was championing (ambitiousness and legal form). As in The Hague, it insisted on a solution that fell outside the acceptance zone of its negotiating partners. A deadlock inevitably ensued. The problem was purely structural. The EU erroneously felt that putting down targets and timetables was the way to put pressure on others and shift their positions.[1]

The EU had come to Copenhagen with an agenda that was distinctly different from that of other major parties (Blühdorn 2012). Acting on the basis of scientific evidence, the EU advocated a top–down legally binding agreement. All the big emitters would be involved. Yet, as we have found before, other major negotiating counterparts remained committed to an antipodal model, where bottom–up voluntary pledges were emphasized instead. Invariably this mismatch embodied the highly politicized form climate change had now taken. The US and the BASIC countries were greatly constrained in their positions at Copenhagen. The former was held hostage to protracted domestic US infighting regarding the introduction of federal climate policy requiring mandatory emissions cuts. The latter countries for their part had prioritized a growing middle-class appetite for the luxuries economic growth brought and were hostile to the very idea of emission reductions (Groen and Niemann 2013; Haug and Berkhout 2010). Nevertheless, the EU did try to elevate 'its preferred policy solutions to the international level' (Van Schaik and Schunz 2012, p. 183). Yet little consideration was given to whether negotiating partners would be able to sell these cuts back home and achieve a compromise in Copenhagen that would take into account the EU's far-reaching demands. It came as no surprise then that its call for quantitative legally binding, scientifically based targets was ignored. Bäckstrand and Elgström (2013, p. 1379) go as far as to dismiss the EU's strategy as 'too normative and politically naïve', given its reformist ideas run counter to the preferences of the two big veto powers. It stood no chance whatsoever of influencing the final orientation of the agreement.

The EU gradually realized that it would be almost impossible to strike a deal in Copenhagen by late 2009.[2] As one interviewee explained, the EU had always hoped that at least seven years before the end of the first commitment period, parties would initiate negotiations on how to broaden participation in the post-2012 regime beyond developed countries. But 'what we were painfully experiencing was that nobody wanted to get into the Kyoto Protocol, starting of course with the US. And that did not allow any developing countries to come forward. Nobody wanted to stick out their neck from the developing countries'.[3] EU interviewees agreed that prior to Copenhagen it was increasingly recognized that China and the US were simply 'not mature enough to agree on a climate deal'.[4] This was greatly due, it was argued, to the fact that the 'international community in the run-up to Copenhagen had not properly identified what kind of deal it would be possible to strike there'.[5] A parallel can be drawn here with the Kyoto process as Copenhagen lacked its own Geneva COP. Poznań certainly did not serve such a purpose.

Conscious of the inevitable diplomatic dead-end, EU officials quickly turned their attention to how best to manage expectations. The worry was that a political failure might 'completely destroy faith in the process', prompting some to even consider alternative solutions outside of the UN system.[6] EU officialdom started intentionally downplaying prospects for a binding agreement in Copenhagen (see Chapter 9). As a senior EU Commission official reflected:

> At the time we were already thinking that if we get to ten pages or so that set out the principles, and then you probably need another round of discussions to go into detail, that would be the most we could get.[7]

Regrettably, as another senior EU Commission official admitted:

What we hadn't counted on – and which was the humiliation – was the apparent calculus by the US and the BASIC countries that we would essentially accept whatever it is they agreed amongst themselves. And that was the humiliation; that even though the EU had influenced many aspects of the Copenhagen outcome [e.g. the 2°C target or the $100 billion pledge[8]], we were not perceived as having contributed to it because the final deal itself was done without us.[9]

Plan B

Given its main negotiating partners' vehement opposition to its proposals, the EU is criticized for failing to come up with a comprehensive 'plan B' that would have allowed it to adjust its positions and exert some degree of influence when the time arrived for parties to strike the inevitable compromise (Groen and Niemann 2013). While correct in principle, what would plan B involve?

Following the Bali COP, the EU, as one interviewee put it, 'was kind of stuck between a rock and a hard place'.[10] On the one hand, it knew that continuing with the Kyoto Protocol was not the preferred option for a number of developed countries. On the flip side, it was also well aware that it would 'send out a very bad signal if it completely went against the idea of a second commitment period'.[11] Mapping out a pathway between the two was never going to be easy. For sure, there were various EU officials at the top echelons of EU governance that had realized – even before Copenhagen – that the international community was in the process of shifting away from legally binding commitments, to a pledge and review system with checks and balances. As an interviewee explained, 'we just could not play that card'.[12] The EU faced a conundrum. It was 'too hooked on the Kyoto target approach' or 'simply very much nailed on the Kyoto Protocol and its continuation', as interviewees remarked.[13] It was explained that, 'all the instructions that we had were very strict on this [...]; we wanted the continuation of the Kyoto Protocol approach.'[14]

The literature is certainly right to point out the absence of a plan B. In Copenhagen there was plan A and only plan A: a top–down, single legal instrument that would preserve the essential elements of the Kyoto Protocol and cover all major emitters. This is not to say that the EU was not discussing alternative courses of action or carefully weighing the costs and benefits of potential compromises. EU policymakers were not so 'naïve to think that [they] would get everything'.[15] After all, these were difficult negotiations in which the EU was 'the demandeur more than ever'.[16] Such signals of readiness for compromise were sent out *inter alia* by the October 2009 European Council. While EU leaders reiterated their preference for a single legal instrument, they nevertheless left open an 'escape route'.[17] They – rather vaguely – expressed their 'willingness to an open discussion with other Parties on different options to the same ends' (European Council 2009a). According to an EU Member State official who was closely involved in these deliberations, 'options to the same ends' was the part mandating flexibility. Among the alternatives that were discussed privately was a *legally binding* two-track regime –

that is, continuing with the Kyoto Protocol until 2020 and strengthening the Convention or having an additional protocol for parties not covered by Kyoto.[18] Intra-EU talks as to whether to demonstrate this requisite openness were even being held during the Copenhagen COP itself. Ultimately, the EU decided to stick to the single legal instrument option as the most reliable means of exerting pressure on other parties.

The Danish hosts also explored potential compromises. Mindful of the reputational impact, they worked feverishly publicly and behind the scenes to ensure a successful COP. Central to their efforts was the Greenland Dialogue. This platform enabled informal discussions to develop, aimed at facilitating a shared understanding on climate issues among high-ranking officials from key parties. For the Danes, this Dialogue was meant to help explore potential options for what they might perceive 'at the end of the day as an achievable and reasonably ambitious outcome, which was still a *legally binding agreement* that was heavily differentiated and had sufficient flexibility to bring the US on board' (emphasis added).[19] The 'firewall' between developed and developing countries was to be maintained, assuming that it would be the 'next generation [i.e. post-2020] that would significantly break it down'.[20]

As explained above, the EU was actively surveying fallback positions that might give way to a consensus. Yet, the common denominator in all of this was the notion of legal bindingness of the future agreement. This was the EU's red line; it would either get a legally binding agreement or there would be no agreement at all.[21] That said, the EU was open to identifying ways of downgrading the various levels of commitment, yet always within the confines of such a legally binding framework. In other words, on legal form the EU was determined to stand firm; on target ambitiousness it was prepared for compromises. In sum, the EU did not have a plan B; all it had were 50 shades of plan A, all within the same option.

Regrettably for the EU, its preferences were at odds with those of the US and major developing countries. Interviewees agreed that the latter parties in particular had come to Copenhagen unprepared 'for even minimum compromises'.[22] They were against taking on targets themselves and 'only wanted the same architecture and nothing else. It was not easy to overcome this resistance'.[23] Such a stance also rendered it impossible for the US to sign an agreement that had significant differences between what developed and developing countries were being asked to do. 'As we were afraid', a Commission official observed, the US compromised to the Chinese level, rather than raising them 'up to a higher, not a Kyoto Protocol level, but to a nonetheless higher level'.[24] So what happened in the end was that 'we went for pledge and review and everyone was equal in the relative weakness of the way in which the framework applied to them'.[25]

Coalition-building

In aiming to account for the EU's inability to acknowledge the lack of a zone of agreement and take remedial action, it is suggested that the EU failed to adjust to the newly emerging international order. In contrast to the 1990s, China in the run-up to Copenhagen had ascended from third place to CO_2 emissions leader, emitting 21 per cent of the global total in 2007 (up from 14 per cent in 2002 and 8 per cent in 1981) (Guan *et al.* 2009). The EU had now replaced China in third place with a 14 per cent share of global CO_2 emissions. It had been rendered a 'medium-sized power in climate politics' (Oberthür 2011a, p. 10). This had an unavoidable bearing on its negotiating power. The EU's contribution to global emissions was now relatively small compared with the combined total ($\approx$40 per cent) of the US and China. Still, the EU took the science-based, normative approach in Copenhagen, hoping to exert influence and shape the debate by arguing for ambitious emissions cuts (Van Schaik and Schunz 2012). This strategy foundered. There was practically no political support for such cuts, especially amongst the two 'carbon titans', whose consent was a precondition to successfully negotiating a global climate deal (Christoff 2010, p. 644).

There are two main strategies for buttressing an eroding power base: (i) issue-linkages and (ii) coalition-building. The first was discussed in EU circles during 2007. A French proposal was put forward to tax industrial goods imports from countries with less stringent climate mitigation regulation. However, imposing trade restrictions was rejected as technically unfeasible and politically unrealistic (Hovi and Skodvin 2008). Coalition-building appeared to offer a better way forward, especially since the EU had benefited immensely in the past whenever it had been proactive in seeking to forge alliances with other parties. Back in the 1990s, such alliances had proven pivotal on various occasions (e.g. Berlin and Kyoto), while in the early 2000s the EU had quickly adapted to the shock of the US exit and had acted as a bridge-builder to ensure the Kyoto Protocol survived.

The EU proved less successful when it came to putting together a coalition capable of boosting support for an ambitious post-2012 successor treaty, however. Researchers are highly critical of the EU in this respect. Bäckstrand and Elgström (2013, p. 1379), for instance, suggest that the EU tried in principle to 'go it alone'. Oberthür (2011b, p. 679) argues that the EU 'especially failed to make determined efforts' at coalition-building. Doing so with the US or China was a virtually non-existent option (Parker *et al.* 2012). The EU could, however, have turned to a group of progressive developing countries, which included AOSIS members and various Latin American and African states (Oberthür 2011b).

Again, such viewpoints require closer scrutiny. The EU did try to build alliances. Interviewees stressed that the EU officials in charge were experienced negotiators who knew that the EU would not achieve anything without getting others on board:

> Throughout the years we have always tried to build alliances because we know in terms of the mechanics of the negotiations that you need to have a large number of developing countries with you, otherwise it is not going to work and is not going to happen. And from that point of view we definitely tried to be as close as possible.[26]

As Copenhagen approached, there was indeed significant outreach to key players. This was facilitated by the great number of meetings around that time. Opportunities for the EU to speak to other parties included the G-8, the G-20, the Major Economies Forum (MEF),[27] plus the various back-to-back UNFCCC meetings or even the climate summit called in September 2009 by UN Secretary-General Ban Ki-moon. A great number of people from the Commission and the Member States 'were [also] travelling the world to meet their counterparts, both at political and technical levels'.[28] The Danes, in particular, were fairly active. They conducted a number of outreach visits to key countries in all continents. In addition to the Greenland Dialogue, various other informal meetings with heads of government groups were organized, including a pre-COP in November in Copenhagen. The Danes also sought to systematically engage with various world leaders via the Copenhagen Commitment Circle, an initiative launched with the aim of building agreement and shared understanding ahead of Copenhagen. Other Member States also stepped in to help, with the UK for example taking advantage of its 2009 chairmanship of the G-20 to engage finance ministers on issues relating to climate finance (Chirstensen 2011).

Going back to whether or not the EU invested in coalition-building, perhaps it was not so much a question of effort, as of potential to induce others into alliances in the first place. Claims of impracticability were regularly put forward in interviews. A Commission official, for instance, noted that negotiations in the nine to twelve months ahead of Copenhagen 'got so conflictual' that developing the necessary trust for alliances became rather tenuous.[29] 'The nuisance, or one of the points of division,' they went on to add, 'was always this issue of the Kyoto Protocol.' As we found in Chapter 9, following the three 2009 sessions in Bonn, the EU joined the consensus among Annex I parties for a one-track negotiation process towards a protocol including all developed and developing countries. But the outcry from the latter group of countries was such that the ties between the two were irreversibly severed. Even progressive developing countries that could have sided with the EU in pushing for a more ambitious result in the AWG-LCA track were alienated, including *inter alia* South Africa, Brazil and Mexico (Spencer *et al.* 2010).[30] AOSIS countries were also almost unanimously highly critical of the EU, vehemently accusing it of abandoning the Kyoto Protocol.

Van Schaik and Schunz (2012, p. 183) argue that 'in such a context, there is little, if any, negotiation space for persuading other actors of one's own position'. This assessment is arguably closer to the truth:

> The fact that we may not have been effective in building a consensus is another matter. Maybe political circumstances were not favourable, maybe our position was such that even if we tried others could not get on board because our position was too inflexible. You can find different justifications, but that there was not an effort to build alliances, no, that was not the case.[31]

Belated efforts during the first week of the Copenhagen COP to break the unity of G-77/China and lure away the LDCs and AOSIS by pledging to contribute fast-start funding of €2.4 billion annually for the years 2010 to 2012 failed entirely to convince (Parker *et al.* 2012; see also European Council 2009b). Overall, the EU's inability to build strategic alliances with other parties undermined its leadership potential and contributed to its isolation in the final stages of the Copenhagen talks.

Process-generated stakes

It was rather obvious during the early 2000s that the EU and US were at the opposite sides of the climate change divide and that this gulf was growing larger instead of smaller (Szarka 2011). But why had the EU not undertaken action to bridge this climate change divide? Much of the history of Kyoto Protocol negotiations understandably focuses on the duels between the US on the one hand and the EU on the other. The former is usually painted in negative colours, readily given the role of the 'laggard', while the latter is often portrayed as the champion or defender of the Protocol (see e.g. King 2008; Skodvin and Andresen 2006). The EU actively capitalized on the US's unpopularity in order to burnish its own credentials. As Vogler (2016) notes, the EU's climate activism is closely linked to its desire to construct its identity in the international arena.

According to Underdal (1983, 1991, 1998), one main cause for failure relates to **process-generated stakes** or, put differently, the manner in which pressure on a party to live up to its reputation could prevent it from capturing the bigger picture of the negotiation. The concept of process-generated stakes, Underdal (1991, p. 113) further explains, refers 'to potential gains and losses *pertaining to* or *generated by* negotiating behavior or process rather than explicit issues on the negotiation agenda' (original emphasis). When it comes to adversarial bargaining, process-generated stakes tend to 'impede rather than facilitate progress towards agreement' (Underdal 1991, p. 113).

The first sub-category of stakes pertains to the utility of making a certain move. In other words, by entering into negotiations a party enters 'a game that has certain bearings on its own image and reputation' (Underdal 1983, p. 190). He further clarifies this point by saying that 'negotiations [are] not only a decision-making process, [they are] also to some extent an unofficial game of performance and reputation'. Policymakers undertaking negotiations with third parties strive to appear politically strong, so as to maximize their profits from the process, both in terms of substantive outcome and prestige (Shapiro 2000). Moves that could have a positive effect upon the substantive outcome of the negotiating process may also have the reverse effect on a party's image and credibility. Equally important for parties therefore is how they are perceived to 'play the game', as their performance and recognition by domestic and global audiences will also be evaluated and awarded (respectively) on the basis of this criterion.

One could cite here various examples from the history of EU involvement in the UNFCCC regime. In the context of distributive bargaining, reputational concerns may result in parties being inclined to reject a solution simply because it originated from a foe rather than from an ally (Underdal 1983, p. 190). Emissions trading or the Marrakech Accords are prime examples. Regarding the former, the EU's critical stance towards the US on flexibility mechanisms during the 1990s meant it sided with developing countries. Yet, it quickly went from outright sceptic to eager enthusiast when emissions trading gained ground within EU circles from 1998 onwards (Wettestad 2005; Christiansen and Wettestad 2003). By the time this learning process had been completed, however, the US had already taken the decision to withdraw from the Kyoto regime. In the latter case, the EU rejected a 'take-it-or-leave-it' compromise proposal by the US in The Hague, only to subsequently accept a similar one in order to accommodate the interests of its newly found allies in the overall goal of saving the Kyoto Protocol.

Another quite interesting example would be about the EU's

> willingness to want to demonstrate leadership by continuing to commit to the Kyoto Protocol even in circumstances where it made less and less sense, either from a scientific perspective – given that it couldn't achieve its objectives if non-Annex I parties did not join – but also from a political and economic perspective.[32]

'And there,' an interviewee noted, 'it was – and still is – difficult for us to hold ourselves to that standard and keep all our stakeholders aligned if our competitors are not doing the same.'[33] One of the main components for this EU commitment to the Kyoto Protocol concerns the strong pressure from negotiating partners in the UNFCCC for the EU to act in a normative way.[34] What emerged rather interestingly from the interviews was the frequency in which this pressure was acknowledged.[35] 'We were too hooked on the Kyoto target approach,' one noted, 'also because developing countries wanted us to be hooked on that.'[36] Similarly, another interviewee said that 'pressure to maintain the Kyoto Protocol essentially came from the G-77/China'.[37] 'There was high expectancy in particular from the G-77/China that so should be the case,' a third interviewee concurred.[38]

The second sub-category of stakes concerns those that could emerge as a consequence of previous moves. In other words, having strongly opposed a certain proposal tends to make conceding to it much harder later on. Interestingly, this has applied to the EU only partially, as it has been relatively prone to compromises throughout the course of UNFCCC negotiations. An interviewee with close to 20 years of involvement in the negotiations noted that the history of EU participation in the climate change regime is one of constantly 'moving negotiation red lines'.[39] 'The EU,' they went on, 'never managed to say [to other parties], you know what? I do not want this, I do not accept it.' 'To be believable in the negotiations,' they concluded, 'you must say no from time to time.'

Yet this proneness to compromise is explained by the fact that the EU has always been the sole demandeur for this whole process:

> I think these are the dynamics of the climate change negotiations; that the EU is always the party that has to do most of the concessions. This is something we are prepared for; it has to be in this way because we are the demandeur. It is intrinsic I would say. It lies in the role.[40]

Of course, there have been exceptions where demands by other parties went beyond what the EU would be prepared to accept. There are times when moves by parties designed to put their opponents under pressure may in fact backfire and instead bolster their 'incentives to resist' (Underdal 1991, p. 113). The US's stance on forestry during The Hague COP led the majority of EU actors to harden their stance and reject further efforts to compromise on what appeared to them to be unreasonable US demands. This came at a cost, as the EU's sense of unity was put to the test as a result of the leadership aspirations of the French Presidency and the rigidity characterizing its negotiating strategy. Various EU officials at the time had referred to the French strategy as having been 'counterproductive' and as having 'inhibited a constructive evolution to a final agreement in the last night' (Egenhofer and Cornillie 2001, p. 10).

To conclude with process-generated stakes, another point to reflect on is that leadership ambitions and reputational concerns may prove problematic at the EU domestic level as well. The situation with the EU is inherently more complex compared with that of other parties as a result of its structural inflexibility. Internally, EU actors need to consider domestic EU specificities before establishing the leadership level of their negotiating strategies or proposals. Progressive stances, for example, may alienate some of their fellow EU partners and hinder a more ambitious EU climate policy. Tracing the EU's UNFCCC track record, we can observe what was also described earlier – that not all EU actors were on board with the various leadership-related elements that have underpinned EU positions over time. In the early stages of the UNFCCC process, the EU lacked the internal consistency that would have allowed it to successfully pursue its leadership ambitions. Chapter 2 discussed the internal friction that the proposal for a carbon/energy tax generated and the negative impact this had on the EU's leadership ambitions in the run-up to the 1992 Rio Summit. Similarly, in the run-up to Kyoto, leadership was all about pushing for ambitious targets. Again not all Member States were on board. This resulted in the emergence of a credibility gap (see below). Following Kyoto, what underpinned EU leadership activity was the issue of supplementarity, which again divided Member States and further inhibited EU leadership aspirations (e.g. COP-4 in Buenos Aires). In the aftermath of the 2001 US exit, leadership was all about establishing the alliances necessary for ensuring the entry into force of the Kyoto Protocol. Competitiveness concerns caused various EU actors to question the sensibility of going ahead with Kyoto in the absence of US involvement. Finally, during the period that lapsed between the 2005 Montreal and 2009 Copenhagen COPs, the topic of target ambitiousness resurfaced and polarized intra-EU debates once again.

Uncertainty

Parties in international negotiations may be **uncertain** of a host of political or other factors. What are the preferences, perceptions and beliefs of external and domestic actors? What will be the consequence of introducing new and unfamiliar solutions? And is the evidence available reliable and robust enough to act upon? With some exceptions (e.g. carbon/energy tax or aviation emissions trading), domestic EU actors have been largely supportive of climate change mitigation policy instruments (Grant 2013). But uncertainty still remains a concern. This is the case when it comes to intra-EU bargaining processes in the climate regime. As an EU veteran of the UNFCCC put it, 'even internal trust is a question within the EU'.[41] As they explained:

> As a Member State it is important to have contacts beyond the EU. I was close to friends in the US, AOSIS, Africa and Latin America. In the corridors you should also talk to them; you should not wait whether the troika will share with you all the information.

As Chapters 4 and 5 detailed, there were suspicions amongst some Member States about the relationship between the UK and US with regard to the UNFCCC, especially during the 1990s and early 2000s. Indeed,

> there had always been this suspicion back then that the two were making secret deals on how to deal with various climate issues. The UK in a sense was playing a double game; either by acting as a Trojan horse for the US in influencing the formulation of EU positions or by looking after its own national interests.[42]

Apart from domestic political contexts, uncertainty has also impeded the progress of international climate negotiations, as messages from opposing sides have often been received sceptically or treated with mistrust and disbelief. Hovi and Skodvin (2008, p. 135), for instance, quote a statement by one of US President Bush's advisers, who had argued that climate change was actually 'a European plot to undermine U.S. economic dominance'. Interviewees confirmed these stories. One remembered that India was highly distrustful of the EU in the period around the Bali COP, thinking that 'our exclusive agenda was about defending our industry and putting some commitment on them so that they would not be able to outcompete us on the basis of their comparative advantage'.[43] Another recalled having breakfast with an AOSIS high-ranking official during the 2011 Durban COP, who bluntly told him that he firmly believed the EU was 'pretending and lying' about wanting to help island nations with their climate predicament.[44]

Such perceptions influence how international negotiations progress. On reflection, a Commission official aptly summarized two decades of uncertainty and mistrust about the EU's standing as a climate change leader:

> Concerns were different over time. Were we serious about implementing what we had promised? When would we do the ratification? Wouldn't we like, after the US had walked away from the Kyoto Protocol, to do the same? Would we be able to bring the Russians on board? Did we want to maintain the Kyoto Protocol or move into something new?[45]

The latter question caused a lot of suspicion. It even prompted some developing countries to accuse the EU of playing the US's game – an allegation that was actually 'very, very wrong'.[46] Some parties, a Member State official argued,

> may have misinterpreted the EU when it tried to talk about the future. They might have thought that the EU wanted something else than the Kyoto Protocol; that it wanted to get out of it and that's why it was talking about the future.

Such misconceptions have caused concern among EU decision-makers: 'we have had various discussions internally as to why our message is not getting through; why it is being misperceived or misunderstood in the developing world.'[47] Finding an answer is critical because uncertainty, as Underdal (1983) suggests, slows down the negotiation process and disturbs the search for mutually advantageous solutions.

Effects of uncertainty

One consequence of uncertainty is a mistrustful, or hostile, response to unfamiliar solutions tabled by rivals (Underdal 1983, 1991). Such uncertainty is 'most likely in negotiations dealing [*inter alia*] with issues that are technically complex, and for solutions that are novel or pertain to a distant future...' (1983, p. 186). Fixed-pie bias regularly comes into play here. Parties assume (often erroneously) that 'what is good for them must be bad for us' (Odell and Tingley 2016, p. 239). Such biases slow down the negotiation process and disturb the search for common ground solutions (see Liu *et al.* 2016). When such uncertainties are brought to the fore, they introduce 'a bias in favour of the familiar, i.e. the status quo or solutions close to the status quo' (Underdal 1983, p. 187). During the INC negotiations in the early 1990s, the EC expressed reservations regarding the JI mechanism. Similarly, in the run-up to Kyoto, the EU's primary focus had been on traditional control and command regulation (i.e. PAMs), given its relative unfamiliarity at the time with the concept of emissions trading (Oberthür and Tänzler 2007). As was seen in Chapter 4, the EU was rather unsympathetic towards this flexibility mechanism and only accepted it as a trade-off for stronger mitigation targets. Interestingly, research has shown that such fixed-pie biases are rather resistant to change (Odell and Tingley 2016). The EU's position change on emissions trading serves as proof of its capacity to overcome such biases and adapt to changing circumstances.

Uncertainty can also encourage parties to adopt 'cautious behavior, characterized by low *specificity* and low *commitment*' (Underdal 1991, p. 1083, emphasis added). Again, this helps explain the EU's behaviour during the first two decades of the UNFCCC regime. While advocating for ambitious targets, the EU was cautious not to jump ahead too quickly. It always made its offers conditional on comparable action by its major industrial competitors. This was the case in the run-up period to Kyoto, as well as with the Kyoto COP itself. In the former case, the EU played safe and decided to work out its burden-sharing agreement only after the US had cleared the uncertainty by announcing its support for binding commitments (Yamin 2000). When it came to the real Kyoto negotiations, the EU followed suit and went down to a 8 per cent reduction target in order to make its burden comparable with that of the US and Japan. Prior to the 2007 Bali COP, the ambitious element of the EU target (i.e. 30 per cent) was again made conditional on other developed countries committing themselves to comparable reductions and developing countries contributing adequately.

This cautious nature has led other parties to accuse the EU – rightly or wrongly – of not following up on its rhetoric with strong action, effectively basing its leadership on the 'luxury of being greener than it is' (Gupta and van der Grijp 2000, p. 76). For negotiations to be conducted successfully, it's crucial that there is no bad faith over the motives of the leading state(s) (Underdal 1994). That is, if others are to follow the actions proposed by leading states, they must be viewed as sincere and selfless (see also Karlsson *et al.* 2012). Cheap talk and actions won't be enough, as 'the moral significance of a move will often depend [...] on the amount of sacrifice incurred by the leader' (Underdal 1994, p. 185).

The EU struggled to properly take this parameter into account, approaching climate change in the early 1990s more in strategic terms and less as an escalating environmental threat that needed to be urgently addressed. It approached it as representing a very suitable and low-cost candidate for leadership, offering a 'stepping stone [for the EU] to stand forth as a strong and unified block on the world scene' (Andresen and Agrawala 2002, p. 45). Skodvin and Andresen (2006, p. 22) note that EU climate policy to a large extent was 'based on self-interest and that it represented a mode of behavior it was likely to have pursued anyway'. They further argue that:

> In the 1990s it soon became clear that the basis for the EU's relatively ambitious climate policy was 'fortunate circumstances' unrelated to climate policies. Thus, the economic cost of an ambitious policy was [deemed to be] rather low while the potential political gain was quite high.
>
> (p. 22)

In addition to viewing the EU's stances as self-interested strategizing, the emergence of a credibility gap also led to increasing uncertainty among other parties as to whether the EU could match its words with actions and meet its own targets. Starting with the 1990s, we noted in Chapter 4 that combined commitments in the pre-Kyoto 1997 burden-sharing agreement only added up to a reduction of 9.2 per cent, with additional PAMs expected to cover the difference in the eventuality the final agreement went beyond a 10 per cent reduction (Environment Council 1997, para.16). Even though more progressive when compared with those of other parties, this cautious EU target was criticized for lacking both *specificity* and *commitment*.

Starting with *specificity*, the EU in Kyoto pursued the same problematic strategy as in Rio. In the latter case, the demise of the carbon/energy tax had effectively meant that the EU pushed others to adopt a stabilization target while itself lacking the requisite domestic policies to guide its mitigation planning and implementation efforts. Likewise in Kyoto, while European pressure was the main reason for the strict targets adopted in Kyoto, the EU 'had no idea how it would achieve the 15 percent target it proposed' (Victor 2001, p. 115). Jordan *et al.* (2012, p. 50) concur, noting that during the 1990s EU climate policy was essentially 'little more than an empty shell – some eye-catching common targets underpinned by a rough amalgam of national policies'. Even if one accepts the scenario that the 15 per cent reduction target was actually a negotiating ploy on the part of the Union (see Cass 2006, p. 144) aimed at getting other parties to accept an agreement in the vicinity of –8 per cent (the EU's actual preferred outcome), subsequent EU difficulties in meeting even that target revealed the ploy not to have been a very sound one. This picture rapidly changed during the early 2000s, once the EU initiated a range of policies to redress this specificity gap. The promulgation of emissions trading and the passing of the January 2008 climate and energy package proved instrumental in this regard, helping to reinforce the EU's leadership credentials.

As for *commitment*, establishing a link between leadership and a degree of sacrifice proved a more challenging task. Harrison and Sundstrom (2007, p. 4) argue that to get a more accurate picture of the magnitude of effort required to achieve compliance, one needs to look beyond formal Kyoto targets and take into account 'the anticipated cut below the business-as-usual projection'. The EU target looks much less onerous when compared this way with those of its major industrial counterparts (see Table 10.1). Jacoby and Reiner (2001) make a similar point when looking at the reductions required across different regions based on their forecast baselines.

Note here also that the EU was afforded in Kyoto both 'hot air' and geographical flexibility. The EU was able to benefit through the windfall emissions reductions created by Germany's post-reunification economic restructuring and the UK's transition from coal to gas energy production. As Aldy *et al.* (2003) argue, German and UK compliance with their internal EU-15 burden-sharing target would suffice on its own for the EU as a whole to meet its common target. The 'bubble' provision of the Kyoto Protocol allowed other Member States the freedom to increase their emissions by as much as 27 per cent.

Table 10.1 Comparison of Kyoto targets relative to business-as-usual trajectory

Party	Kyoto target (%)	Anticipated reduction relative to projected 'business as usual' emissions in 2010 (%)	Ratification
Russia	0	>0	Yes
EU-15	−8	−3 to −9	Yes
Japan	−6	−12	Yes
Australia	+8	−17	No*
Canada	−6	−29	Yes
USA	−7	−31	No

Source: Harrison and Sundstrom (2007, p. 5).

Note
* Australia ratified the Kyoto Protocol in December 2007.

Even so, the EU's journey towards meeting its first commitment emissions reduction target was far from easy. Between 1990 and 2000, the EU-15 reduced its emissions by 3.4 per cent, thereby meeting its UNFCCC stabilization target. Yet insufficient domestic action subsequently led to a 1.4 per cent increase, with overall emissions in 2005 having been reduced by only 2 per cent below baseline levels (Schatz 2009). Various Member States were far from compliant with their national targets. For example, Spanish emissions in 2006 hit new heights, being 53 per cent over 1990 levels (ENDS 2006). This underperformance had led analysts to doubt whether the EU-15 would be actually able to reach its shared target (Parker and Karlsson 2010). It also drew a lot of criticism from other parties:

> Developing countries, especially those that were very critical, knew exactly the numbers … and knew well what was expected, for example, of the cohesion countries, but especially of Spain and Portugal. I will not pinpoint Greece or Ireland, as they were especially critical of the two countries in the peninsula.[48]

Ultimately, the EU proved successful, aided *inter alia* by the economic recession and the consequent decrease in industrial activity and output (Oberthür and Dupont 2010). In 2014, it was reported that the EU-15 had reduced its emissions by 18.5 per cent during the first commitment period, if sinks from LULUCF and the intended use of the Kyoto mechanisms were taken into account (European Commission 2014).

Similarly to its Kyoto target, the EU's post-2012 one has also been labelled as inadequate in terms of a lack of commitment. Following the enlargement and the economic recession, expectations were that the now EU-27 would be in a position to meet its unilateral 20 per cent target relatively effortlessly and without much need for additional abatement, as it had already achieved more than half of that goal (Afionis 2011; Oberthür and Dupont 2010). In fact, its 20 per cent pledge was even considered weaker than those of some of its other industrialized counterparts, such as, for example, Japan (Spencer *et al.* 2010). Indeed, EU-27 collective emissions were 17.5 per cent below 1990 levels already in 2011, effectively meaning that the EU was well placed to reach its target well ahead of time (Jordan *et al.* 2012). The EU had consistently been vocal on the need to close the 'ambition gap' between emissions reduction commitments and the cuts considered necessary by science in order to avoid dangerous climate change. Consequently, the EU was severely criticized in the run-up to Copenhagen for not proceeding to a unilateral cut of 30 per cent, for not eliminating excess greenhouse-gas emission permits ('hot air'), as well as for taking steps backwards by watering down the provisions of the December 2008 climate package (see Afionis 2011; Kilian and Elgström 2010).

EU officials are well aware of this perceived misalignment between words and actions, or the manner in which 'it sees and describes itself as an ideal and the way in which it can actually deliver on that ideal'.[49] The justification here is that while the EU genuinely intends to position itself as a climate leader, it has to do so in the context where it has to negotiate amongst 29 different entities. It is often easier to reach 'agreement on generalities than it is to reach agreement on specifics'.[50] That said, the EU is often seen by its officials as more 'predictable and trustworthy' compared with its other negotiating partners, primarily because of its structure.[51] If the majority of the Member States really care about a policy, it is more probable that stronger action will be taken. Member States in the minority, such as the Visegrad Group, 'can slow us down a bit, but cannot significantly change the EU's overall policy orientation'.[52] When it comes to emissions reductions, the complaint was therefore expressed that:

> When the EU states that it will be ambitious it is presumed that it can be even more ambitious than what it is stating to be. And so therefore, with China or the US, any expression of ambition is taken as a great gift of that country to the international community or some international cause. When the EU states it, then it is always like well that's great but surely you can do more.[53]

EU officials may be justified in feeling this way, as even the 2014 EU energy and climate package that envisages greenhouse gas emissions being cut to 40 per cent below 1990 levels by 2030 has been criticized as not being adequate enough (see e.g. Schiermeier 2014). Yet, the EU has provided sceptics with ammunition for criticism, given for example its inability to ratify the 2012 Doha amendment to the Kyoto Protocol (see next chapter).

To conclude, this chapter has sought to explain the reasons for 'EU failure' in climate change talks over the years and its inability to successfully push other parties towards the adoption of a top–down climate regime. In this regard, the works of Underdal on negotiation theory are useful in exploring the whole idea of negotiating performance of the EU in the context of climate change. Understanding why the EU has failed historically is not only instructive, but also indispensable if the EU is to 'succeed in the future' (Archer *et al.* 2010: p. 7). In other words, knowing what went wrong is important, but knowing *why* is crucial.

A great part of the answer lies in adequately reflecting on issues relating to zones of agreement, uncertainty among other parties, mismatches between reputational concerns and substantive outcomes as well as elements of proposed solution designs. Obviously, the EU's complex structure means that several of the problems that were highlighted in this study are here more or less to stay. The EU needs to be aware of the factors that contribute to its occasional failures, accept them, and objectively study them. The literature on negotiation theory such as that formulated by Underdal has lots to offer in this respect by providing an additional lens through which a deeper understanding of the shortcomings of the EU as an international climate negotiator can be obtained. It represents an undertaking that needs to be taken into consideration by European officials if the EU is to continue having high aspirations on climate policy.

Notes

1 Interview No. 10 (Member State official – Head of Delegation).
2 Interview No. 12 (Commission official).
3 Interview No. 9 (Commission official).
4 Interview No. 2 (Member State official – Former Head of Delegation).
5 Interview No. 2 (Member State official – Former Head of Delegation).
6 Interview No. 12 (Commission official).
7 Interview No. 9 (Commission official).
8 The idea for the $100 billion pledge was initially tabled by former UK Prime Minister Gordon Brown.
9 Interview No. 11 (Commission official).
10 Interview No. 5 (Member State official).
11 Interview No. 5 (Member State official).
12 Interview No. 2 (Member State official – Former Head of Delegation).
13 Interview No. 2 (Member State official – Former Head of Delegation); Interview No. 12 (Commission official) respectively.
14 Interview No. 2 (Member State official – Former Head of Delegation).
15 Interview No. 12 (Commission official).
16 Interview No. 2 (Member State official – Former Head of Delegation).
17 Interview No. 12 (Commission official).
18 Interview No. 10 (Member State official – Head of Delegation).
19 Interview No. 11 (Commission official).
20 Interview No. 11 (Commission official).
21 Interview No. 12 (Commission official).
22 Interview No. 7 (Member State official – Former Head of Delegation).
23 Interview No. 7 (Member State official – Former Head of Delegation).
24 Interview No. 11 (Commission official).
25 Interview No. 11 (Commission official).
26 Interview No. 9 (Commission official).
27 The MEF was launched in March 2009 by US President Obama and is basically a continuation of President Bush's MEM.
28 Interview No. 12 (Commission official).
29 Interview No. 9 (Commission official).

30 Also interview No. 10 (Member State official – Head of Delegation).
31 Interview No. 12 (Commission official).
32 Interview No. 11 (Commission official).
33 Interview No. 11 (Commission official).
34 Another component is the view within the EU that as an international policy frame-work, the Kyoto Protocol is the most robust one can get in terms of objectives, trans-parency, compliance and accounting. It is, in other words, 'a good model of how you should organize international climate change processes' (Interview No. 10 (Member State official – Head of Delegation)). Another aspect relates to the stakes involved from the EU having acted as a front-runner in climate change mitigation policies. Hovi and Skodvin (2008, pp. 141–2) stress this point when they argue that substan-tial climate policy investment 'reduced the political feasibility of a policy reversal'. The promulgation of the emissions trading scheme in 2003 marked in their view the 'point of no return' (p. 142).
35 Such pressure is felt in other policy areas as well, such as in debates over the estab-lishment of the International Criminal Court or the abolition of the death penalty (see Vogler 2016).
36 Interview No. 12 (Commission official).
37 Interview No. 10 (Member State official – Head of Delegation).
38 Interview No. 2 (Member State official – Former Head of Delegation).
39 Interview No. 1 (Member State official – Former Head of Delegation).
40 Interview No. 2 (Member State official – Former Head of Delegation).
41 Interview No. 7 (Member State official – Former Head of Delegation).
42 Interview No. 1 (Member State official – Former Head of Delegation).
43 Interview No. 12 (Commission official).
44 Interview No. 6 (Member State official).
45 Interview No. 9 (Commission official).
46 Interview No. 2 (Member State official – Former Head of Delegation).
47 Interview No. 6 (Member State official).
48 Interview No. 7 (Member State official – Former Head of Delegation).
49 Interview No. 11 (Commission official).
50 Interview No. 11 (Commission official).
51 Interview No. 11 (Commission official).
52 Interview No. 11 (Commission official).
53 Interview No. 11 (Commission official).

References

Afionis, Stavros (2011). The European Union as a negotiator in the international climate change regime. *International Environmental Agreements: Politics, Law and Economics* 11: 341–60.

Aldy, Joseph E., Scott Barrett and Robert N. Stavins (2003). Thirteen plus one: a comparison of global climate policy architectures. *Climate Policy* 3 (4): 373–97.

Andresen, Steinar and Shardul Agrawala (2002). Leaders, pushers and laggards in the making of the climate regime. *Global Environmental Change* 12 (1): 41–51.

Archer, Toby, Timo Behr and Tuulia Nieminen (2010). Why the EU fails? Learning from past experiences to succeed better next time. *The Finnish Institute of International Affairs*. Report no. 23. Available at: www.fiia.fi/assets/publications/UPI_FIIA23_web.pdf.

Bäckstrand, Karin and Ole Elgström (2013). The EU's role in climate change negoti-ations: from leader to 'leadiator'. *Journal of European Public Policy* 20 (10): 1369–86.

Blühdorn, Ingolfur (2012). Introduction: international climate politics beyond the Copenhagen disaster. *European Political Science* 11: 1–6.

Cass, Loren R. (2006). *The failures of American and European climate policy: international norms, domestic politics, and unachievable commitments.* New York: State University of New York Press.

Chirstensen, Thomas M. (2011). Governments and climate change: the United Nations' negotiating process. In Bayne, Nicholas and Stephen Woolcock (eds) *The new economic diplomacy: decision making and negotiation in international economic relations.* Farnham: Ashgate, 303–22.

Christiansen, Atle C. and Jørgen Wettestad (2003). The EU as a frontrunner on greenhouse gas emissions trading: how did it happen and will the EU succeed? *Climate Policy* 3 (1): 3–18.

Christoff, Peter (2010). Cold climate in Copenhagen: China and the United States at COP15. *Environmental Politics* 19 (4): 637–56.

Egenhofer, Christian and Jan Cornillie (2001). Reinventing the climate negotiations: an analysis of COP6. CEPS Policy Brief No. 1, March. Available at: www.ceps.eu/system/files/book/102.pdf.

ENDS (2006). Spain's greenhouse emissions hit new high, 24 April.

Environment Council (1997). *Environment Council Press Release,* 60 No. 6309/97, Brussels, 3 March.

European Commission (2014). Progress towards achieving the Kyoto and EU 2020 objectives. COM(2014) 689 final, Brussels, 28 October.

European Council (2009a). Council conclusions on EU position for the Copenhagen Climate Conference (7–18 December 2009). Luxembourg, 21 October.

European Council (2009b). European Council 10/11 December 2009 – conclusions. Brussels, 11 December.

Grant, Wyn (2013). Business. In Jordan, Andrew and Camilla Adelle (eds) *Environmental policy in the EU: actors, institutions and processes.* London: Earthscan, 170–88.

Groen, Lisanne, Arne Niemann and Sebastian Oberthür (2012). The EU as a global leader? The Copenhagen and Cancun UN Climate Change Negotiations. *Journal of Contemporary European Research* 8 (2): 173–91.

Groen, Lisanne and Arne Niemann (2013). The European Union at the Copenhagen climate negotiations: a case of contested EU actorness and effectiveness. *International Relations* 27 (3): 308–24.

Guan, Dabo, Glen P. Peters, Christopher L. Weber and Klaus Hubacek (2009). Journey to world top emitter: an analysis of the driving forces of China's recent CO_2 emissions surge. *Geophysical Research Letters* 36 (4): 1–5.

Gupta, Joyeeta and Nicolien van der Grijp (2000). Perceptions of the EU's role: is the EU a leader? In Gupta, Joyeeta and Michael Grubb (eds) *Climate change and European leadership: a sustainable role for Europe?* Dordrecht: Kluwer, 67–82.

Harrison, Kathryn and Lisa McIntosh Sundstrom (2007). The comparative politics of climate change. *Global Environmental Politics* 7 (4): 1–18.

Haug, Constanze and Frans Berkhout (2010). Learning the hard way? European climate policy after Copenhagen. *Environment* 52 (3): 20–27.

Hovi, Jon and Tora Skodvin (2008). Which way to U.S. climate cooperation? Issue linkage versus a U.S.-based agreement. *Review of Policy Research,* 25 (2): 129–48.

Jacoby, Henry D. and David M. Reiner (2001). Getting climate policy on track after The Hague. *International Affairs* 77 (2): 297–312.

Jordan, Andrew, Harro van Asselt, Frans Berkhout, Dave Huitema, and Tim Rayner (2012). Understanding the paradoxes of multilevel governing: climate change policy in the European Union. *Global Environmental Politics* 12 (2): 43–66.

Karlsson, Christer, Mattias Hjerpe, Charles Parker and Björn-Ola Linnér (2012). The legitimacy of leadership in international climate change negotiations. *Ambio* 41: 46–55.

Kilian, Bertil and Ole Elgström (2010). Still a green leader? The European Union's role in international climate negotiations. *Cooperation and Conflict* 45 (3): 255–73.

King, Michael R. (2008). No carbon copy: while Canada and the US dithered, the European Union built a carbon emissions trading mechanism. *Alternatives Journal* 36 (4): 10–13.

Liefferink, Duncan and Kathrin Birkel (2011). The Netherlands: a case of 'cost-free leadership'. In Wurzel, Rüdiger K.W. and James Connelly (eds) *The European Union as a leader in international climate change politics*. London: Routledge, 163–78.

Liu, Wu, Leigh Anne Liu and Jian-Dong Zhang (2016). How to dissolve fixed-pie bias in negotiation? Social antecedents and the mediating effect of mental-model adjustment. *Journal of Organizational Behavior* 37 (1): 85–107.

Oberthür, Sebastian (2011a). Global climate governance after Cancun: options for EU leadership. *The International Spectator* 46 (1): 5–13.

Oberthür, Sebastian (2011b). The European Union's performance in the international climate change regime. *Journal of European Integration* 33 (6): 667–82.

Oberthür, Sebastian and Claire Dupont (2010). The Council, the European Council and international climate policy. In Wurzel, Rüdiger K.W. and James Connelly (eds) *The European Union as a leader in international climate change politics*. London: Routledge, 74–91.

Oberthür, Sebastian and Dennis Tänzler (2007). Climate policy in the EU: international regimes and policy diffusion. In Harris, Paul G. (ed.) *Europe and global climate change: politics, foreign policy and regional cooperation*. Cheltenham: Edward Elgar, 255–77.

Odell, John S. and Dustin Tingley (2016). Negotiating agreements in international relations. In Mansbridge, Jane and Cathie Jo Martin (eds) *Political negotiation: a handbook*. Washington D.C: Brookings Institution Press, 231–85.

Parker, Charles F. and Christer Karlsson (2010). Climate change and the European Union's leadership moment: an inconvenient truth? *Journal of Common Market Studies* 48 (4): 923–43.

Parker, Charles F., Christer Karlsson, Mattias Hjerpe and Björn-Ola Linnér (2012). Fragmented climate change leadership: making sense of the ambiguous outcome of COP-15. *Environmental Politics* 21 (2): 268–86.

Schatz, Andrew (2009). A tale of three signatories: learning from the European Union, Japanese, and Canadian Kyoto experiences in crafting a superior United States climate change regime. *University of Pittsburgh Law Review* 70: 593–645.

Schiermeier, Quirin (2014). EU climate targets under fire. *Nature* 505 (7485): 597.

Shapiro, Daniel L. (2000). Supplemental joint brainstorming: navigating past the perils of traditional bargaining. *Negotiation Journal* 16 (4): 409–19.

Skodvin, Tora and Steinar Andresen (2006). Leadership revisited. *Global Environmental Politics* 6 (3): 13–27.

Skovgaard, Jakob (2014). EU climate policy after the crisis. *Environmental Politics* 23 (1): 1–17.

Spencer, Thomas, Kristinan Tangen and Anna Korppoo (2010). The EU and the global climate regime: getting back in the game. *The Finnish Institute of International Affairs*. Briefing Paper 55, 25 February. Available at: www.fiia.fi/en/publication/106/the_eu_and_the_global_climate_regime/.

Szarka, Joseph (2011). France's troubled bids to climate leadership. In Wurzel, Rüdiger

K.W. and James Connelly (eds) *The European Union as a leader in international climate change politics*. London: Routledge, 112–28.

Underdal, Arild (1983). Causes of negotiation 'failure'. *European Journal of Political Research*, 11 (2): 183–95.

Underdal, Arild (1991). International cooperation and political engineering. In Nagel, Stuart (ed.) *Global policy studies: international interaction toward improving public policy*. Basingstoke: Palgrave Macmillan, 98–120.

Underdal, Arild (1998). Leadership in international environmental negotiations: designing feasible solutions. In Underdal, Arild (ed.) *The politics of international environmental management*. Dordrecht: Kluwer, 101–27.

Underdal, Arild (1994). Leadership theory: rediscovering the arts of management. In Zartman, William I. (ed.) *International multilateral negotiation: approaches to the management of complexity*. San Francisco, CA: Jossey-Bass Publishers, 178–97.

Van Schaik, Louise and Simon Schunz (2012). Explaining EU activism and impact in global climate politics: is the Union a norm- or interest-driven actor? *Journal of Common Market Studies* 50 (1): 169–86.

Victor, David G. (2001). *The collapse of the Kyoto Protocol and the struggle to slow global warming*. Princeton: Princeton University Press.

Vogler, John (2016). *Climate change in world politics*. Basingstoke: Palgrave Macmillan.

Wettestad, Jørgen (2005). The making of the 2003 EU Emissions Trading Directive: an ultra-quick process due to entrepreneurial proficiency? *Global Environmental Politics* 5 (1): 1–23.

Yamin, Farhana (2000). The role of the EU in climate negotiations. In Gupta, Joyeeta and Michael Grubb (eds) *Climate change and European leadership: a sustainable role for Europe?* Dordrecht: Kluwer, 47–66.

Conclusion

Success ... right? That was the question on the lips of observers as the ink dried on the first-ever universal climate change treaty to be signed into international law in Paris in December 2015. Years of failed negotiations suddenly gave way as 195 countries agreed to limit rising global temperatures to below 2°C this century. Each country submitted voluntary pledges that set out the actions they would take. These are still inadequate to meeting the objectives enshrined in the agreement and are as 'different as the countries they are coming from' (Clémençon 2016, p. 4). Consequently, growing unease exists over what exactly each country plans to do, and by when. Naming and shaming laggards through a new monitoring system intent on transparency and accountability, although welcome, is not the same as legal sanctions.

Even so, the international community had adopted a single legal instrument. Whereas the EU had pushed for a legally binding single legal instrument back in Copenhagen, it failed to win support from other parties. An EU official reflected:

> Probably we were a little bit ahead of time. Because climate policy in the EU had gone so much further at that time. It was much more advanced than the US's, which has recently done some catching up. But even in developing countries climate policy has since developed. China for example is putting in place an emissions trading scheme. [In Copenhagen] that was still a very remote possibility. So because we were so much ahead, we felt that we could pull others in our direction more quickly than realistically could have happened.[1]

Over the course of this book we have seen the wide range of factors that help to explain why international climate negotiations have failed – political disagreements, divisive solutions, uncertainties – and the role the EU has played in them. Despite the EU's official rhetoric highlighting success and leadership, this book emphasized its relative failures up until Copenhagen. First, we have seen how the EU's negotiating approach was underpinned by what Underdal (1983, 1991) calls a **'politically inadequate solution design model'**. The EU consistently adopted a scientific logic. It pushed other countries to accept its assessment of the climate change problem, and in turn, how it should be solved. During the 1990s, this took the form of a 'top–down' legally binding climate change regime with strong enforcement and compliance mechanisms. After Kyoto, the EU again adopted a strong scientific position towards supplementarity and forests. This approach contributed to the failure of the climate negotiations in The Hague in 2000. The EU positions came under fire, as the US attacked them on feasibility and fairness grounds. Eager to reduce the economic burden of the Kyoto Protocol on its economy, the US pushed for maximum flexibility in how Kyoto's mechanisms were designed. The EU remained unconvinced. In response, the US accused the EU of hypocrisy. It highlighted how the EU had benefited from both internal 'hot air' and the EU-wide burden-sharing arrangement (the 'EU bubble'). It had thus no right to object to others who sought similarly favourable treatment.

During the 2000s, and following its successful attempts to save the Kyoto Protocol, the EU pushed for a post-2012 regime relying on top–down targets and underpinned by scientific evidence. The EU advocated this approach because it believed it represented the 'best' solution to the challenge posed by climate change. To that end, the EU pushed for legally binding actions from major developing countries and legally binding economy-wide reduction commitments by developed countries. Such calls were largely dismissed by both groups of countries on fairness (e.g. historical responsibility concept) and feasibility grounds (e.g. recession).

Second, reputational concerns or **process-generated stakes** affected the EU's negotiating positions. In The Hague, for example, the strong Green contingent within the EU negotiating delegation, and its unwillingness to accept any compromise, contributed to the failed negotiations. In the run-up to Copenhagen, the EU felt pressured to gain recognition from developing countries by displaying its leadership in relation to the future of the Kyoto Protocol. That said, and in contrast to Underdal, who argues that initial opposition to proposals make it harder to accept them later on, the EU has always been willing to compromise in climate negotiations. Interviewees suggest that this willingness to compromise is closely linked to the EU being the sole demandeur for a climate regime.

Third, **uncertainty** can contribute to failure. Intra-EU trust is a particular issue here. This is tested when Member States negotiate deals without informing or including their EU counterparts (e.g. The Hague and the UK–US special relationship). This can create resentment of being cut out of the loop. For the EU to negotiate successfully, all Member States must play by the rules of the game to ensure an internally equitable and inclusive process develops. If Members do not observe these tacit rules, solutions can be viewed with suspicion or dismissed irrespective of their merits.

Uncertainty can also encourage parties to become more cautious, breeding vagueness and poor commitment. Competitiveness concerns have always been centre-stage, prompting the EU to make its mitigation offers conditional on comparable action by its major industrial competitors. Indeed, the EU's cautious behaviour led other parties to criticize the ambitiousness of the EU's targets, flagging up their lack of specificity and commitment. While the EU has since the 2000s taken steps to put in place the necessary policy instruments to allow it to meet its climate objectives, it still faces problems in convincing critics of the ambitiousness of its mitigation goals. In 2014, the EU adopted an energy and climate package that envisages greenhouse gas emissions being cut to 40 per cent below 1990 levels by 2030. Critics still argue that this target is achievable with a modest economic cost and is inconsistent with what science says is needed to prevent dangerous anthropogenic climate change (see Schiermeier 2014; Meinschausen *et al.* 2015). Studies have also highlighted that the 40 per cent target might not be in line with the EU's longer-term ambition of cutting emissions by 80 per cent by 2050 (Knopf *et al.* 2013).

Finally, according to Underdal's framework, a last reason for failure is inaccurate information, that is, a defective assessment of the existence of a '**zone of agreement**'. For parties to be able to identify acceptable outcomes, they must be able to understand the preference structure of their opponent(s). Negotiations may end in deadlock when (a) a party overestimates or underestimates this preference structure, or (b) a party believes the opponent to misperceive its preference structure (Underdal 1983).

As noted in the introductory chapter, from the early 1990s to 2009, there have been four main deadlines set by the international community relating to climate change cooperation. The first was to negotiate a framework convention for signature at the UNCED in Rio de Janeiro in June 1992. The second was to produce a protocol in time for COP-3 in Kyoto. The third was to complete discussions concerning the operationalization of the Kyoto Protocol at COP-6 in November 2000 (The Hague). The fourth was to adopt an agreement on the post-2012 architecture at COP-15 in 2009 (Copenhagen). The first two deadlines were successfully met, while the COPs on the latter two ended in failure. In addition, there were three main issues that dominated deliberations during the period under examination: legal form of agreements, regime ambitiousness and flexibility.

Starting with Rio, as shown in Chapters 1 and 3, while common objectives during the early 1990s were adopted in advance by the Council, both the EC and its Member States also submitted proposals at negotiating fora (Oberthür 2011b). Only as the Kyoto negotiations approached did the Member States progressively provide the EU with 'one voice' via the Council Presidency. During the 1991/92 INC preparatory talks, the EC was unable to push for a legally binding agreement, with efforts focusing instead on producing a compromise text that would bring the US on board. Various large EC Member States had circulated ambitious proposals calling for the establishment of short-term and long-term targets, including stabilization of emissions by 2000 or reduction by 50 per cent by 2030. With the US unwilling to subscribe to any binding agreements, a zone of agreement (that stopped developed countries splitting off) was only achieved through the UK's efforts. The compromise stated that the UNFCCC's stabilization target would be aspirational only and non-binding, void of any specific measures or quantified objectives.

Moving on to the run-up process to Kyoto, the EU misperceived the US preference structure on a number of fronts. It overestimated the willingness of the Clinton administration to engage in a debate on PAMs. Underdal (1983) notes that in such instances a party may be tempted to adopt an open, cooperative approach (instead of a bargaining one), which its opponent may subsequently exploit. Under the impression that the US was inclined to discuss PAMs instead of targets and timetables, the EU tabled long lists of PAMs only to find itself outflanked when the US suddenly expressed its willingness to consider targets following the release of the IPCC's SAR in 1996. Compared with Rio, however, the EU fared much better at Kyoto, at least in terms of ensuring the insertion of top–down, legally binding targets and timetables in the final agreement. To do so, the EU had to greatly compromise its positions on all other fronts to reach a negotiated settlement. The final Kyoto pact reflects the US's preferences and priorities, especially with respect to target ambitiousness and implementation flexibility. An important point to be made here is that while the two major transatlantic players had demarcated an acceptable zone of agreement, this zone had only been established between the EU and the Clinton administration, not with the US as a whole. The 1997 Byrd-Hagel Senate resolution effectively dampened any sense of success, as it severely undermined the treaty's longevity and rendered it in actual fact a 'dead letter' from the very moment it was signed. While this inconvenient truth was masked for several years by the withdrawal of the US, it resurfaced in full force in the run-up to Copenhagen.

With respect to the 2000 COP-6 in The Hague, the main topics under negotiation there were flexibility (supplementarity) and sinks. It undoubtedly represents the greatest failure (up until Copenhagen) of parties to reach agreement in a climate conference. As Chapter 5 explained, the EU was under the impression that the US misperceived the EU's preferences. Both at Rio and Kyoto, the EU went to considerable lengths to accommodate US demands, making many compromises in the process. Past experience had led the US to believe that under pressure the EU would eventually capitulate and accept a deal closer to the US's vision – a scenario that did not come to pass at The Hague.

The Hague failure effectively gave the newly elected Bush administration another excuse for the US to withdraw from the Kyoto regime. If the EU was looking for a compromise in The Hague, it should have been obvious to its delegation that it could not have its way on both supplementarity and the flexibility mechanisms. A positive zone of agreement was either lacking or the EU had not given enough effort to establish one.

The compromises the EU refused to make in The Hague were subsequently made a few months later to the 'Gang of Four' (Australia, Canada, Japan and Russia), albeit following the exit of the US from the Kyoto process. To save the Kyoto Protocol, the EU was forced to accept a weakening of the Protocol's environmental integrity. Bolstered by the 2004 success of securing Russia's vital ratification, the EU opted again for a cooperative approach on the issue of developing the post-2012 climate architecture, spearheaded initially by the UK's concurrent 2005 Presidencies of the EU and the G-8. Two tracks on future action on climate change were launched as a consequence, the first in 2005 (Montreal) and the second in 2007 (Bali). Pilloried by the media and civil society, this approach allowed the Bush administration to ease pressure by re-engaging with the climate regime process, but only on the basis that it would not be part of discussions relating to the Kyoto Protocol.

As it turned out in Copenhagen, two years were simply not enough for parties to hammer out the compromises needed for a consensus. The lack of a zone of agreement was a major factor in why the EU failed in Copenhagen. Chapter 10 focused on the lack of a plan B and the inability of the EU to build the alliances necessary to ensure a positive outcome in Copenhagen. The aforementioned chapter also touched upon the EU's difficulty to adapt to external changes; Faure (2012, p. 380) argues that 'analysing the situation adequately, selecting the right negotiation paradigm, and being able to shift if the context changes' are all important ingredients for negotiation success. In prolonged negotiations, the context often evolves, with new coalitions or technologies making their appearance, or with elections in one party shifting the balance of political power within the government and altering its preferences. Failing to take into account such changes can be a major cause of failure. Over the last two or so decades the EU has shown its capacity to adapt to changing circumstances, as evidenced by its position change on the use of greenhouse gas emissions trading (Christiansen and Wettestad 2003). On other occasions, the EU has appeared less able to adapt. The 2000 Hague COP highlighted that the EU had not been adequately prepared to deal with the transition from the Clinton to Bush administrations. In the run-up to Copenhagen, its preference for ambitious post-2012 targets led to the EU's marginalization. Most developed country parties had already massively overshot their Kyoto targets, and as a result there was little appetite to consider such demands at a time of global economic crisis (Afionis 2011).

The road to Paris and lessons learned

EU ambitiousness has always been motivated by the scientific urgency embodied in the IPCC's reports. In the run-up to Copenhagen, there was another reason behind the EU's calls for parties to conclude an agreement in the Danish capital: the economic crisis. As an EU official reflected:

> We were at the beginning of the economic crisis, which had started in the US and had already spread to the EU, but not at the levels seen much later. So somehow there was also a sense that if we did not close the deal in Copenhagen, it would become much more difficult to do so later on. The crisis would hit countries the hardest and we would lose some of the political support, or the economic support that you need to implement the policy.[2]

This EU official was right. It would take the international community another six years to conclude a meaningful agreement. The EU was quick though to adjust to the new realities and was able to play a constructive role during this period.

Starting with Cancun in 2010, the EU played an instrumental role in the adoption of the Cancun Agreements which revitalized the UNFCCC multilateral process. Following Copenhagen, expectations had been downplayed. Legally binding options were off the table, as parties focused on how to 'anchor' the pledges made in Copenhagen in the UNFCCC process (Sterk *et al.* 2010, p. 7). Interviewees agreed that what helped depolarize the debate was the announcement by Japan and Russia in Cancun that the Kyoto Protocol was not an option for them any longer. The realization by developing countries that the Kyoto Protocol 'had an expiry date' allowed parties to come to a general agreement as to the dimensions of a zone of agreement.[3] As Oberthür (2011a, p. 10) posits, the EU following Copenhagen learned the lesson that as a medium-sized power in climate politics it was not in a position any longer to determine 'the agenda or the outcome'. There was an 'acknowledgement following Copenhagen that the EU can be as ambitious as it wants, but if it is not something realistic then it will simply not be very helpful and will not fly with other parties'.[4] Consequently, the EU decided to perform as a bridge-builder between the major emitters to bring the other groups closer to its positions (Bäckstrand and Elgström 2013).

Instrumental to its success was its willingness to consider a second commitment period under the Kyoto Protocol as part of a wider outcome including all major economies. This move paved the way for coalition-building in the run-up to Cancun, with the establishment of the so-called 'Cartagena Dialogue for Progressive Action' allowing 30 like-minded progressive parties from different blocks to come together and identify areas of common ground (Audet 2013). Through this alliance, the EU was able to successfully push for a more ambitious final outcome, including *inter alia* the insertion in the Cancun Agreements of a call to developed country parties 'to increase the ambition of their economy-wide emission reduction targets' (UNFCCC 2010, p. 8).

In Durban, the EU was pivotal in getting other parties to agree to the Durban Platform and a second Kyoto Protocol commitment. The EU's strategy in Durban was to accept a renewed Kyoto Protocol under the condition that other parties would sign up to a roadmap for a new agreement that included all major emitters. The EU exploited resentment for the Copenhagen 'stitch-up' and mobilized a wide coalition of developed and developing parties in support of its roadmap. Thorough this alliance, the EU was able to push for an outcome which stated that a new multilateral treaty would be agreed by 2015 and in force by 2020, as well as for a second Kyoto Protocol commitment period, albeit with only the EU itself and a handful of other parties still on board. This alliance comprised the EU, AOSIS, LDCs and various middle-income countries, with Brazil and South Africa in particular showing a substantial degree of openness to the EU's approach.[5]

The Durban Platform for Enhanced Action required parties to 'launch a process to develop a protocol, another legal instrument or an agreed outcome with legal force under the Convention applicable to all Parties' (UNFCCC 2011, p. 2). While falling short of the EU's vision for a multilateral legally binding climate treaty, the Durban Platform signalled a return to multilateralism. After Durban, the EU relied massively on this alliance. As an EU Official noted:

[Durban] was critical in terms of trying to rescue multilateralism, rescue the top–down dimension. I think it was more about the fear that Copenhagen and Cancun would map out the future of what we could expect from this regime. So the Durban alliance tried to claw back into that more top–down elements, while recognizing the reality following Copenhagen.[6]

The Doha 2012 COP was a transitional COP. It nevertheless turned into a very negative experience for the EU. The main issue there was internal differences among EU Member States on how to deal with the surplus units from the first Kyoto commitment period. Carrying the excess permits over to the next commitment period would go against the EU rhetoric on ambition and drew heated criticism from developing countries and environmental watchdog groups. The elimination of excess permits was resisted by various EU Eastern European and Baltic members (Afionis *et al.* 2012). While an intra-EU compromise was reached at the last minute (see Korppoo 2013), EU officials in Doha spent 'many long hours arguing internally instead of focusing externally'.[7] 'We lost a lot of experts that way,' they went on to say, 'as they were tied up looking at internal issues.'[8] EU officials following Doha felt:

> We cannot go to COPs when things are not better prepared internally. We cannot spend all of our time in rooms arguing amongst ourselves, because we lose our international positions then.[9]

The 2013 Warsaw COP reached an important compromise which effectively marked the departure from the principles of the Kyoto Protocol. The Paris agreement would be bottom–up, with national pledges submitted by parties in the form of intended nationally determined contributions (INDCs). The discussion related to INDCs had started back in Doha and the feeling among EU officials had been that they 'were not going to be so voluntary in the end'.[10] The EU argued in favour of replacing 'contributions' with 'commitments', but to no avail (Vogler 2016). At least the EU was able to successfully push for these pledges to come onto the table well in advance of the Paris COP. One of the main lessons from Copenhagen, as an EU official noted, was that Paris had to avoid parties' mitigation positions 'coming in so late; and that it cannot just be the industrialized countries that have their pledges on the table and there is nothing else [i.e. from developing countries]'.[11] 'And this,' it was argued, 'was a key factor for the success of Paris; that you had in the month of September/ October [2015] this shower of pledges that was coming in, reaching 178 or 179 when we arrived there.'[12]

In Lima in 2014, the expectation was for the COP to clarify the scope of INDCs, specify the kind of information that should be provided alongside them to facilitate their assessment, as well as to decide whether an international review of the INDCs would take place prior to Paris (Ott *et al.* 2014). While the EU was able to influence a number of decisions relating to the information that parties should provide, it was not as successful in its demand for 'a strong review that would assess the aggregate effect of INDCs against the latest climate science' (ENB 2014, p. 44). While the EU would have liked to see meaningful text on this, 'there was significant push back against it'.[13]

In Paris, the EU 'operated at its fullest and best'.[14] It had ensured beforehand there would be a zone of agreement by making démarches globally and reaching out to its allies in the Durban Alliance.[15] It invested in building trust and reducing uncertainty by committing to a second Kyoto Protocol commitment period. This helped garner developing countries' support by alleviating their concerns that the EU was trying to 'kill' the Protocol (Oberthür 2011a). Also helpful were the pledges by EU leaders following Lima and in the run-up to Paris regarding the provision of substantial financial aid to assist developing countries defray the cost of mitigating their emissions and adapt to the consequences of climate change.[16]

Above all, it adopted a realistic stance and adjusted its expectations. The Paris Agreement became a hybrid model between the top–down elements of Kyoto and the bottom–up approach of the Copenhagen Accord. The EU strategy following Copenhagen and Cancun had been to try and 'rescue something out of a top–down approach'.[17] It linked its reputation to this end, and succeeded. The Paris COP put in place a timetable for parties to ratchet up their efforts. In 2018, an informal assessment of progress will take place, while there is an expectation for parties to submit new, more ambitious INDCs every five years, beginning in 2020. None of these would have been possible had it not been for the EU. Keeping its 'high ambition coalition' alive will therefore be key for the EU. As Obergassel *et al.* (2016, p. 4) note, this coalition is well placed to 'push for the agreement's early entry into force and for the quick strengthening of national contributions'. As an EU official reflected:

> If anything else, we must all be accountable for what we commit to, even if we are designing our own commitments. And we must all be willing to regularly strengthen them over time in light of the latest science.[18]

In the meantime, there is another, equally pressing need. Parties in Durban decided to establish the Kyoto Protocol's second commitment period (from 2013 until 2020). To this end, the Doha Amendment to the Kyoto Protocol was adopted in 2012. As of June 2016, Poland has refused to ratify. This has understandably led to 'disappointment amongst the EU's partners' and provides a blatant example of how a trust deficit can be created.[19] If the EU is to be the leader on climate change, that it believes itself to be, then it must first speak and act as one. Whether this alone will be enough to turn the tide of an adaptation and mitigation implementation deficit in the face of wider international shocks remains to be seen. Indeed, the newly elected US President, Donald Trump, has already vowed to 'cancel' the Paris Agreement as it's 'bad for US business' (Boccagno 2016); whilst the destabilizing effect of Brexit – Britain leaving the EU – represents similar concerns. Only time will tell whether the Paris Agreement will be consigned to history as yet another failure or whether meaningfully change still happens.

Notes

1 Interview No. 12 (Commission official).
2 Interview No. 12 (Commission official).
3 Interview No. 9 (Commission official); Interview No. 12 (Commission official).
4 Interview No. 4 (Member State official – Deputy Head of Delegation).
5 Interview No. 9 (Commission official).
6 Interview No. 11 (Commission official).
7 Interview No. 4 (Member State official – Deputy Head of Delegation).
8 Interview No. 5 (Member State official).
9 Interview No. 4 (Member State official – Deputy Head of Delegation).
10 Interview No. 1 (Member State official – Former Head of Delegation).
11 Interview No. 9 (Commission official).
12 Interview No. 9 (Commission official).
13 Interview No. 4 (Member State official – Deputy Head of Delegation).
14 Interview No. 4 (Member State official – Deputy Head of Delegation).
15 Interview No. 10 (Member State official – Head of Delegation).
16 Interview No. 10 (Member State official – Head of Delegation).
17 Interview No. 11 (Commission official).
18 Interview No. 11 (Commission official).
19 Interview No. 11 (Commission official).

References

Afionis, Stavros (2011). The European Union as a negotiator in the international climate change regime. *International Environmental Agreements: Politics, Law and Economics* 11: 341–60.
Afionis, Stavros, Adrian Fenton and Jouni Paavola (2012). EU climate leadership under test. *Nature Climate Change* 2: 837–8.
Audet, René (2013). Climate justice and bargaining coalitions: a discourse analysis. *International Environmental Agreements: Politics, Law and Economics* 13: 369–86.
Bäckstrand, Karin and Ole Elgström (2013). The EU's role in climate change negotiations: from leader to 'leadiator'. *Journal of European Public Policy* 20 (10): 1369–86.
Boccagno, Julia (2016). Climate change denier is leading Trump's EPA transition team. CBS News. November 11. Available at: www.cbsnews.com/news/leading-climate-change-denier-among-those-on-trumps-environmental-team.
Christiansen, Atle C. and Jørgen Wettestad (2003). The EU as a frontrunner on greenhouse gas emissions trading: how did it happen and will the EU succeed? *Climate Policy* 3 (1): 3–18.
Clémençon, Raymond (2016). The two sides of the Paris Climate Agreement: dismal failure or historic breakthrough? *Journal of Environment & Development* 25 (1): 3–24.
ENB (2014). Summary of the Lima Climate Change Conference: 1–14 December 2014. *Earth Negotiations Bulletin* 12 (619): 1–46.
Faure, Guy Olivier (2012). Failures: lessons from theory. In Faure, Guy Olivier (ed.) *Unfinished business: why international negotiations fail.* Athens, GA: University of Georgia Press, 357–82.
Knopf, Brigitte, Yen-Heng Henry Chen, Enrica De Cian, Hannah Förster, Amit Kanudia, Ioanna Karkatsouli, Ilkka Keppo, Tiina Koljonen, Katja Schumacher and Detlef P. Van Vuuren (2013). Beyond 2020 – strategies and costs for transforming the European energy system. *Climate Change Economics* 4 (Suppl. 1): 1–38.

Korppoo, Anna (2013). Does Doha's decision treat transition economies unequally? *Climate Policy* 13 (3): 403–7.

Meinshausen, Malte, Louise Jeffery, Johannes Guetschow, Yann Robiou du Pont, Joeri Rogelj, Michiel Schaeffer, Niklas Höhne, Michel den Elzen, Sebastian Oberthür and Nicolai Meinshausen (2015). National post-2020 greenhouse gas targets and diversity-aware leadership. *Nature Climate Change* 5: 1098–1106.

Obergassel (né Sterk), Wolfgang, Christof Arens, Lukas Hermwille, Nico Kreibich, Florian Mersmann, Hermann E. Ott, and Hanna Wang-Helmreich (2016). Phoenix from the ashes – an analysis of the Paris Agreement to the United Nations Framework Convention on Climate Change. *Wuppertal Institute for Climate, Environment and Energy*, March. Available at: http://wupperinst.org/fa/redaktion/downloads/publications/Paris_Results.pdf.

Oberthür, Sebastian (2011a). Global climate governance after Cancun: options for EU leadership. *International Spectator* 46 (1): 5–13.

Oberthür, Sebastian (2011b). The European Union's performance in the international climate change regime. *Journal of European Integration* 33 (6): 667–82.

Ott, Hermann, Wolfgang Obergassel, Christof Arens, Lukas Hermwille, Florian Mersmann and Hanna Wang-Helmreich (2014). Climate policy: road works and new horizons – an assessment of the UNFCCC process from Lima to Paris and beyond. *Environmental Liability – Law, Policy and Practice* 6: 223–38.

Schiermeier, Quirin (2014) EU climate targets under fire. *Nature* 505: 597.

Sterk, Wolfgang, Christof Arens, Urda Eichhorst, Florian Mersmann, Hanna Wang-Helmreich (2010). Processed, refried – little substance added: Cancún Climate Conference keeps United Nations process alive but raises more questions than it answers. *Wuppertal Institute for Climate, Environment and Energy*, March. Available at: http://wupperinst.org/uploads/tx_wupperinst/COP16-report.pdf.

Underdal, Arild (1983). Causes of negotiation 'failure'. *European Journal of Political Research* 11 (2): 183–95.

Underdal, Arild (1991). International cooperation and political engineering. In Nagel, Stuart (ed.) *Global policy studies: international interaction toward improving public policy*. Basingstoke: Palgrave Macmillan, 98–120.

UNFCCC (2010). The Cancun Agreements: Outcome of the work of the Ad hoc Working Group on Long-term Cooperative Action under the Convention. FCCC/CP/2010/7/Add.1.

UNFCCC (2011). Establishment of an Ad hoc Working Group on the Durban Platform for Enhanced Action. FCCC/CP/2011/9/Add.1.

Vogler, John (2016). *Climate change in world politics*. Basingstoke: Palgrave Macmillan.

Index

Page numbers in *italics* denote tables.

For Product Safety Concerns and Information please contact our EU
representative GPSR@taylorandfrancis.com
Taylor & Francis Verlag GmbH, Kaufingerstraße 24, 80331 München, Germany